LEADERSHIP
LESSONS
from the
CHEROKEE
NATION
Learn from All I Observe

CHAD "CORNTASSEL" SMITH

Mc
Graw
Hill
Education

NEW YORK CHICAGO SAN FRANCISCO
LISBON LONDON MADRID MEXICO CITY MILAN
NEW DELHI SAN JUAN SEOUL SINGAPORE
SYDNEY TORONTO

1 2 3 4 5 6 7 8 9 0   QFR/QFR   1 9 8 7 6 5 4 3

ISBN   978-0-07-180883-5
MHID   0-07-180883-3

e-ISBN   978-0-07-180884-2
e-MHID   0-07-180884-1

McGraw-Hill Education books are available at special quantity discounts to use as premiums and sales promotions or for use in corporate training programs. To contact a representative, please e-mail us at bulksales@mcgraw-hill.com.

This book is printed on acid-free paper.

Contents

PART 2

LESSONS APPLIED

DSGᏞᎥᎠᏪT TEWhᏔᎤᎠ

CONTENTS

Acknowledgments

I am thankful to the Cherokee people for allowing me to serve as their principal chief of the Cherokee Nation from 1999 to 2011. I am thankful and indebted to the following people for the lessons they taught me as reflected in this book and for their support, friendship, and community. Each and every one of them is a patriot of the Cherokee Nation.

Family: Bobbie Gail Smith, my Cherokee bilingual wife, who has been strong and contributed much from her native worldview. My children Kiah, Chris, Anaweg, Kyle, Cameron, and Caitlin for teaching me life lessons. My parents Nelson and Pauline Smith, who are no longer with us, were great teachers even though I did not listen as I should have. My brothers Shane, Kyle, and Dwight Smith, who have with their very different talents, shared lessons with me since childhood.

Tribal leaders: Ross Swimmer and the late Wilma Mankiller, two outstanding Cherokee Nation principal chiefs who each steered the Cherokee Nation through rough and uncharted waters as statesman and stateswoman. Bill Anoatubby, the governor of the Chickasaw Nation, a gentleman and leader with a great vision.

Business leaders: B.J. Dumond, Jay Hannah, Adolph Lechtenberger, David Steward, and David Tippenconic, who exhibited outstanding talent and the highest integrity.

Community and government leaders: Jack Baker, Orville Baldridge, Callie Catcher, Julia Coates, Congressman Tom Cole, Todd Enlow, the late Julian Fite, Melanie Fourkiller, Meredith Frailey, Melissa Gower, Congressman John Lewis, Norma Merriman, Mike Miller, Felicia Olaya, Pat and Paula Ragsdale, Sammye Rusco, Charlie Soap, Tommy Tucker, and Linda Turnbull-Lewis whose leadership and advice matured the Cherokee Nation.

Traditional leaders: the late David Blackbird, the late Jimmie McCoy, David Scott, Benny Smith, and the late William Smith, who taught the lessons of the Cherokee worldview.

Wado,

Your Humble Servant
Chad Smith

PART 1

ᎠᏎᏅᏛᎠ ᎠᎢᏎᏟᎢᎢ

LESSONS
LEARNED

CHEROKEE NATION SOVEREIGNTY

1721 The Cherokee Nation signs its first treaty with Great Britain for session of land in South Carolina. This was the first of 10 treaties with Great Britain and 13 more with the United States involving 81 million acres of land, and rights.

1830 The Indian Removal Act allowed the U.S. president to exchange lands of the Indians of the Southeast for U.S. lands in Indian Territory (Oklahoma).

1832 The U.S. Supreme Court, in *Cherokee Nation* v. *Georgia*, held that tribes were "dependent domestic nations" not subject to the laws of Georgia.

1835 The Treaty of New Echota was signed, forcibly removing Cherokees from their homes and creating the Cherokee Trail of Tears in which 4,000 of 16,000 Cherokees died in 1838–1839.

1866 The federal government extracted a retribution treaty in which the Cherokee Nation gave up rights for railway easements, land, and citizenship for non-Cherokees.

1898 The United States set out to forcibly assimilate the Cherokee people via the "Allotment Policy." The government liquidated the assets of the Cherokee Nation, stripping away inherent powers and creating a state around the Nation's territory. This came at a time when the Cherokee Nation was flourishing, with a 90 percent literacy rate, model governmental institutions, and a sustainable economy.

1906 The federal Five Civilized Tribes Act provided that "the tribal existence and present tribal governments of the Choctaw, Chickasaw, Cherokee, Creek, and Seminole tribes or nations are hereby continued in full force and effect for all purposes authorized by law, until otherwise provided by law" (Five Civilized Tribes Act of 1906, Section 28).

1906 The federal Oklahoma Enabling Act, which allowed Oklahoma to form as a state, provided that "the inhabitants of all that part of the area of the United States now constituting the Territory of Oklahoma and the Indian Territory, as at present described, may adopt a constitution and become the state of Oklahoma, as hereinafter provided: Provided, that nothing contained in the said constitution shall be construed to limit or impair the rights of the persons or property pertaining to the Indians of said territories." However, the Bureau of Indian Affairs completely took over the affairs of the Cherokee Nation in what one federal judge in a 1975 case described as "bureaucratic imperialism."

1917 The U.S. president began appointing the principal chief of the Cherokee Nation in order to execute allotment deeds.

1928 The Meriam Report revealed that the Allotment Policy was a failure and had resulted in vast amounts of tribal lands lost and that Indians were poorer than ever. By 1920, the Cherokees had lost 90 percent of their trust and restricted land and were driven into a cash economy.

1936 Fifty percent of Cherokees left Oklahoma during the Depression looking for work. *The Grapes of Wrath* was populated by Cherokees; U.S. Highway 66 became an economic "Trail of Tears." Many died of starvation even though Oklahoma was one of the richest states in the Union due to oil production.

1941 American Indians, including Cherokees, had the highest enlistment and wartime decoration rate of any ethnic group in American history. Participating in the war increased assimilation, and fewer Cherokee families taught their children the Cherokee language.

1949 W. W. Keeler, president and CEO of Phillips Petroleum, was appointed principal chief by President Truman. The predominantly Cherokee Adair County, Oklahoma, was the second poorest county in the United States.

1968 The Cherokee Nation government restarted after 70 years with three employees and a $10,000 budget.

1975 The Self-Determination Act was enacted, recognizing the sovereignty of the Cherokee Nation government. Ross Swimmer was appointed principal chief and focused on economic development.

1985 Wilma P. Mankiller became the first female elected principal chief of the Cherokee Nation. A national women's rights advocate, she focused on community and social development and received the Presidential Medal of Freedom from President Clinton in 1998.

1992 The Cherokee Nation executed the Self-Governance Compact with the U.S. Department of Interior.

1997 A constitutional crisis arose in Cherokee Nation when Principal Chief Joe Byrd fired the entire marshal service, the newspaper editor, and the court clerks, and led the impeachment of the entire Supreme Court after a search warrant incident.

1999 Chad Smith was inaugurated as principal chief of the Cherokee Nation. The Cherokee Nation had 2,500 employees, businesses generated $5 million gross profit, and the Nation provided $18 million in healthcare services.

2000–2011 The Cherokee Nation enacted the Independent Press Act, which provides the *Cherokee Phoenix* newspaper editorial independence and its editor protection from termination. It was the first such act by any Indian nation.

The Nation enacted the Freedom of Information Act and Open Records Act, providing transparency in government.

The Nation opened an office in Washington, D.C., to serve as a liaison between the Cherokee people and the U.S. Congress.

The Nation rebuilt broken financial systems and earned awards and recognition for "excellence in financial reporting" 11 years in a row from the Government Finance Officers Association.

The Nation employed 8,500 people, had a governmental budget of $600 million, provided $320 million in healthcare services, and became the largest Indian-run healthcare system in the United States.

The Nation awarded more than 23,000 higher education scholarships to Cherokee students.

The Nation developed the Cherokee Nation Immersion School, where more than 100 students speak and write in Cherokee every day.

The Nation restored the Cherokee Nation Supreme Court building, Ross School, the Springhouse at the Saline Courthouse, and the Cherokee National Prison.

The Nation offered a 40-hour Cherokee Nation history course providing a formal review of the Nation's history with over 10,000 people graduating, including Cherokee Nation employees.

The Nation worked with Apple, Inc. to include the Cherokee syllabary on the iPhone, MacPro, and iPad, the Nation increased assets from $150 million to $1.2 billion. Cherokee businesses generated $100 million in net profits.

2011 Chad Smith completed his third term as principal chief.

CHAPTER 1

ᎬᎻᎢᏒ ᎢᎬᏁᏀᏏ

Introduction

There is nothing as easy as denouncing. It don't take much to see that something is wrong, but it does take some eyesight to see what will put it right again.

WILL ROGERS
July 28, 1935

WHERE DO YOU START?

This book shares the lessons I learned over my twelve years, from 1999 to 2011, as principal chief, a time when the Cherokee Nation was transformed from chaos, confusion, and dysfunction to stability, prosperity, and a sense of accomplishment. The lessons to rebuild the Nation came from a number of sources: traditional Cherokee wisdom, common sense, corporate governance, marketing, biblical history, legal history, and "hard knocks"—we understood the language of many disciplines. The leadership lessons and language were not the stuff of stereotypes manufactured by Hollywood. Our work was nation building, similar to that of other governments of the world. As we all know, lessons are not learned linearly and sequentially, but rather organically and often without any apparent rhyme or reason. The concepts herein are not unusual. A fundamental premise is that we must frame and remember our lessons so that we don't have to relearn the same lessons over and

5

over with different words and from new circumstances. The vocabulary I choose, I remember and I use. Lessons accumulate into knowledge and integrate into wisdom.

As a result of these lessons, by 2011 the Cherokee Nation had developed, grown, and matured exponentially:

- Jobs created by the Cherokee Nation increased from 2,800 to 8,500.

- The healthcare system grew from $18 million of services to $310 million.

- Assets increased from $150 million to $1.2 billion.

- $600 million of construction was completed.

- 100 children were enrolled in a Cherokee language immersion school.

- The Cherokee Nation became a national model for accountability, transparency, and self-governance.

- The regional economic impact of the Cherokee Nation in 2010 was $1 billion.

This book is based on a very simple leadership model, where leadership is defined as going from Point A (where you are) to Point B (where you want to be). During my time as principal chief, it became clear to me that the more we focus on the final product, goal, objective, purpose, end, or destiny—i.e., Point B—things get accomplished and leaders learn what is necessary to succeed along the way. In other words, we ought to look at the end rather than get caught up in tanglefoot.

The lessons learned apply not only to the building of tribal nations but to business, government, nonprofit organizations, and, most importantly, to individuals, families, and communities.

The Cherokee Nation is the second-largest American Indian tribe or nation in the United States. It has a great legacy of facing adversity and adapting, prospering, and excelling. Many do not understand that the Cherokee Nation is a government designated by the U.S. Supreme

Court in 1830 as a "dependent domestic nation" and has been recognized in the world community of nations since 1721, with its first treaty with Great Britain. That international recognition occurred 55 years before there was a United States of America.

The Cherokee Nation faces external and internal adversity. The external adversity comprises hostile public sentiment and unfavorable federal and state policy. It is like the pendulum on a grandfather clock swinging from one extreme to the other. In the Nation's history with the United States, the full swing of the pendulum occurs every 20 to 40 years. At one extreme of the pendulum, the Indian tribes and nations prosper. After a time in this prosperous period, mainstream society begins to want the tribe's assets, such as logistics, sovereignty, hunting and fishing rights, or natural resources such as land, water, or oil and gas rights. At times, mainstream society has even coveted tribal children, artwork, and identity. When public sentiment grows strong enough, the federal government through treaty and law takes or permits the taking of those assets by whatever means necessary. Thus the pendulum swings the other way. At the opposite end of the swing, the Indian tribes and nations are poor, destitute, and desperate. During this desolate period, public sentiment once again begins to shift toward indifference or support of tribes, and the absence of hostile federal policy allows the tribes and nations to get back on their feet. As the tribes and nation begin to rebuild assets and to prosper, the pendulum begins to swing the other way, repeating the cycle.

The greater adversity involves the internal challenges of leadership, community cohesion, protecting family, and holding on to time-tested cultural values. Today, Indian tribes and nations face the same onslaught of mindless television, addictive social media, poverty culture, consumer convenience, political pandering, and crass marketing that weakens the informed resolve of all Americans.

CHEROKEE NATION SOVEREIGNTY AND HISTORY

A brief legal history shows how the foundation of social, political, and economic relationships between the people and governments of the

United States, the state of Oklahoma, and the Cherokee Nation developed through the years. On occasion, I hear anti-Indian business interests complain that the "playing field" is not level because Indian nations have "unfair advantages." Usually this assertion comes from certain businesspeople in industries that have enjoyed tremendous tax breaks and subsidies from both the federal and state governments. Part I began with a legal chronology of the Cherokee Nation. What this chronology shows is that the "playing field" was set at Oklahoma statehood in 1907, when the Indian nations, including the Cherokee Nation, again reserved their rights. The state of Oklahoma became a state subject to the rights of Indian nations. In fact, the Enabling Act of 1906 and the Constitution of Oklahoma in 1907 specifically disclaim the state from asserting any authority over tribal rights.

The rights the Cherokee Nation now hold were not given by the federal or state government; they are rights the Nation has always inherently possessed and retained since time immemorial.

The Decline of the Cherokee Nation

As a result of the federal intrusion into Cherokee government and society in 1898, the Cherokee Nation lost its lands, assets, and institutions, and the Cherokee people suffered greatly. Although federal law and the Oklahoma Constitution preserved Indian treaty and federal rights, the federal policy of allotment was devastating. White people flooded into Indian Territory, soon outnumbering the Indians, and began to devise ways of taking Indian land parcel by parcel. One federal case in 1912 cited 16,000 fraudulent land transactions in Indian Territory resulting from whites trying to take advantage of the forced allotment statutes.

By 1920, Cherokees had lost 90 percent of their lands and were forced into a cash economy. As a result, half the Cherokee population left Oklahoma during the Depression on the "Grapes of Wrath" exodus down U.S. Highway 66 to Bakersfield, California, and to other states including Texas, Washington, and Oregon. It was an economic "Trail of Tears." An iconic Depression-era photograph by Dorothea Lange captured a Cherokee woman showing her despair in a tent with her seven children outside of Bakersfield, California; the photograph is often referred to as the "Madonna of the Grapes of Wrath" or the "Destitute Pea Picker." For the next three generations, the Cherokees who remained in northeastern Oklahoma became a poverty class.

These federal treaties guaranteed the Cherokee Nation that it would never have to become part of a state. When that promise was broken, Cherokees were repeatedly assured by the United States that their government would continue in full force and effect, but in reality, because of federal bureaucracies, the Cherokee Nation government was nearly eliminated. The state of Oklahoma denied in its constitution any interest in Cherokee lands, but then it enabled and encouraged non-Indians to take Cherokee lands through a host of means.

The challenges facing the Cherokee Nation were not only external; the internal challenges were even more debilitating.

My father grew up in the heart of the Cherokee Nation during the Depression in Oklahoma and had 10 half-siblings. He helped raise the family by hunting, farming, and working. He was a full-blood Cherokee and graduated from Sequoyah High School, a Bureau of Indian Affairs boarding school. There he learned discipline and mechanics as a trade. He was handsome, athletic, and spoke Cherokee as a first language. After World War II, he married my mom, who lived 10 miles away from where he grew up. She was non-Indian and had 10 siblings also. He was a tail gunner in the Army Air Corps, and she was a "Rosie the Riveter" during the war. They were married in 1947, and I was born in 1950. Because of the desperate economy in eastern Oklahoma, they went looking for work. They ended up in Denver, Colorado, and my dad started a 33-year career with Gates Rubber Company, beginning as a tool crib helper and working his way up to an industrial plant maintenance manager. He was transferred to Nashville, Tennessee, in 1959 and supervised 130 employees. They moved back to Oklahoma in 1973, and I came back to Oklahoma in 1975 after graduate school. That year I began working at the Cherokee Nation as a planner for Principal Chief Ross Swimmer. That job lasted several years, and I went to law school.

Growing up, we would visit Rachael Quinton, my Cherokee grandmother, in Oklahoma, attend her one-room church, go to stomp grounds, and swim in the creek. I have three brothers and two half-siblings. I remember when I was 12 years old, I was determined to teach myself to speak Cherokee after visiting my grandmother. I found a bible in the Cherokee language and a Cherokee dictionary, and I put them in my briefcase because I was going to teach myself to speak Cherokee. My dad did not teach us because, like others in his generation, he accepted the myth that speaking Cherokee was less important than speaking English.

I married Bobbie Gail Smith, a full-blood Cherokee, in 1978, and our oldest son was born in 1980. When he was 12 years old, I watched him do something I had never discussed with him. He got a bible in the Cherokee language and a Cherokee dictionary, and he put them in a briefcase because he was going to teach himself to speak Cherokee just like I did 30 years prior.

My great-grandfather, Redbird Smith, was a Cherokee Nation senator in the 1890s and was jailed by the United States for protesting its forcible assimilation policy of land allotment. My grandmother was a grassroots advocate for the Cherokee people. Working for the "tribe" was something I wanted to do since college. I was an ironworker during high school and college, putting up the structural steel for buildings and bridges. I enjoyed at the end of a day seeing what I had accomplished. In the early 1990s I returned to work at the Cherokee Nation for Principal Chief Wilma Mankiller, who had a nurturing strength and believed in building communities.

Those were influences that encouraged me to run for principal chief in 1995 when Wilma Mankiller retired; I lost to Joe Byrd. His tenure between 1995 and 1999 was disastrous. He stated he could decide for himself what orders of the Cherokee Nation Supreme Court were constitutional, and then he fired the entire marshal service for serving a search warrant in order to get copies of attorney fee records that he would not release. He then fired the newspaper editor and the court clerks. His friends on the tribal council impeached the entire Supreme Court for issuing the search warrant. It was called the Constitutional Crisis. As a result, the Cherokee Nation's reputation was shot, Cherokees were embarrassed by the resulting press, 600 employees were furloughed, and another 200 were laid off. The Bureau of Indian Affairs put the

Cherokee Nation on a monthly allowance because of mismanagement of cash flow and books that could not be audited.

In 1997, I protested my predecessor forcibly taking over the Cherokee Nation courthouse with his security force where the Cherokee Nation marshals were stationed as ordered by the Cherokee Nation Supreme Court. In 1999, I ran again and won, but the Cherokee Nation was in shambles. These were the circumstances when I was inaugurated as principal chief on August 14, 1999 (see Figure 1.1). That is when my learning began with great intensity.

FIGURE 1.1 *The author, Chad "Corntassel" Smith, is sworn in as principal chief of the Cherokee Nation on August 14, 1999, as his wife, Bobbie Gail Smith, looks on.*
Photo by Tulsa World.

The Cherokee Nation had enjoyed outstanding leadership in the past, namely principal chiefs W. W. Keeler, Ross Swimmer, and Wilma Mankiller. W. W. Keeler was the president and CEO of Phillips Petroleum and presidentially appointed principal chief between 1950 and 1970 who strove to pull the Cherokees out of an economic and political abyss. Ross Swimmer, principal chief between 1975 and 1985, established a sound financial and business foundation for the Cherokee Nation. Wilma Mankiller was the first woman elected principal chief and was a champion of community self-help, women's rights, and Indian rights during her tenure between 1985 and 1995.

My favorite saying is, "Adversity creates opportunity." For the Cherokee Nation and most organizations and governments, the greatest adversity is lack of leadership, and the greatest opportunity is to develop leadership. The adversity of the Constitutional Crisis of 1999 created an opportunity for the people of the Cherokee Nation to develop leadership and gain perspective. They knew what they didn't want and that they needed to seek leadership, solutions, and resources to make things better.

How do you rebuild a nation after decades of "bureaucratic imperialism" by the federal government, erosion of traditional culture by the mainstream poverty culture, and the patronizing belief of the American citizenry that American Indians are cartoon characters or casino rich?

Green Roof: Who Should Take Care of My Mama?

A poverty culture based on being a victim, blaming others, expecting something for nothing, and transferring responsibility to others encroached on the traditional Cherokee values and attributes of self-reliance, cooperation, and confidence. The result: a number of Cherokees felt helpless and like victims. It was a feeling imported from and shared with the general population. Some people call this an "entitlement" mentality. Like a disease, an undeserved sense of entitlement seemed to have spread across America, infecting many poor and even well-to-do Cherokees.

I remember very little from my sophomore English composition class at the University of Georgia in 1970 except for a personal story told by the professor. He was a small man with a mustache; he was complaining about the small Social Security check his mother got and how it was not enough money for her to get by. He said she had raised four boys, and the U.S. government should provide her enough money to live with dignity. He was Canadian! I was afraid to ask the question on my mind: "If the government is not taking care of your mother, why don't you and your three brothers do it?"

Contrast his story to that of Lizzie Whitekiller, a 96-year-old full-blood bilingual Cherokee woman. She is the type of person who lives life fully. Forty years ago, she and her husband, "Gete," built a U.S. Department of Housing Mutual Help "Indian house." The house had wood siding and was designed to last only 30 years. It is immaculate today because her 11 children take care of her and the house. At age 62, she went back to school and got her GED. Every year, 100 children, grandchildren, great-grandchildren, and great-great-grandchildren come home to her house for a family reunion. She handmade a quilt including each one's picture. Their family is truly a family because of her. She showed that we did not have to feel helpless and like victims.

As principal chief, the first column I wrote for the *Cherokee Phoenix* in 1999 was called "Green Roof." I wrote it at the beginning of my administration, when we were searching for the ideas, words, and ways to lead our people and ourselves to be stronger and more positive. This column foreshadowed many of the lessons I would learn in greater detail and articulate better in the coming years.

"Green Roof"
By Chad Smith, Principal Chief

Almost a decade ago, my father passed away. Left behind was my mother, who lives alone in the home my family built. Several years ago, the home developed a roof leak.

Whose duty was it to fix the leak? Whose obligation to replace the roof? Who had the obligation to see that my mother was warm, dry, and comfortable? Was it the federal government's responsibility through some federal program? Was it the state government? Was it Cherokee Nation?

The answer is a simple one that is found in the lessons my father taught each of us as a part of his legacy; it stems from the culture of the Cherokee Nation. He was a special man.

I have three brothers. It was our duty and responsibility to fix the roof. To us belonged the honor of taking care of our mother. That honor is a great one, which was accepted with pride and joy. My brothers and I replaced the shingles with a green metal roof. It was our privilege.

I have heard many stories about families since I took office as principal chief. One of the saddest was from a grandmother who came into my office in a wheelchair. She deeded her comfortable home to a son in return for her care for the rest of her life. The son mortgaged the house for $30,000. He took the money and wasted it in Las Vegas and other places. Then he vanished, leaving his mother defenseless and with a mortgage that she could not pay. The elderly woman had five other adult children. She came to my office asking for help because the county sheriff was going to foreclose on her home. None of her children offered to take her in. None of her children offered to make the payments on the modest house. None of the adult children provided alternative housing for her.

This woman came to the Cherokee Nation for help because her family would not assist her. We found her housing.

Today, we have many Cherokees who desperately need help but have no family to help them, and the Cherokee Nation should and does help them. Then there are Cherokees, like the woman in the wheelchair, who have family, but the family believes it is the duty of some government program to provide for their elderly parent.

Taking care of one's own family and helping neighbors is a core Cherokee value. Why have so many of our people drifted away from that value?

We need every community leader in public office, in churches, and at the stomp grounds to remind our people of this most important Cherokee value.

Without question, the Cherokee Nation should help those who need it. However, the tribe has very limited funding. It will not stretch to care for all of those who need and deserve help.

We have set out on a mission to redesign our programs at the tribe to help people help themselves, their families, and their neighbors. When we all work together, the funds will stretch to meet the needs of more of our elderly, our children, and our victims of disaster.

The bottom line, however, is that it is the duty and honor of each Cherokee citizen to care for his or her family. We will be neither a strong people, nor a strong nation, if we do not accept the honor of taking loving responsibility for our own family.

The traditional Cherokee thought about responsibility was expressed by Redbird Smith (see Figure 1.2), my great-grandfather, a member of

FIGURE 1.2   *Painting of Redbird Smith, a member of the Cherokee Nation senate in the 1890s and the author's great-grandfather. Redbird Smith is seated, and Dick Scott is standing.*
Photo courtesy of Oklahoma Historical Society.

the Cherokee Nation senate in the 1890s, when he said, "A kindly man cannot help his neighbor in need unless he has a surplus, and he cannot have a surplus unless he works." Somehow, over time, many of our people moved further away from our cultural values of self-responsibility and became more like the mainstream society. But on the other hand, there were many Cherokees carrying on a rich tradition of developing their talent, exercising leadership, and maintaining a resolve to pass on their historical legacy.

THE RESOLVE TO REBUILD THE CHEROKEE NATION

A history of political betrayal by the federal government, failed elected leadership in the Cherokee Nation, and an encroaching poverty culture characterized in part the legal, political, and economic landscape I faced when I was elected principal chief in 1999. I had the duty, obligation, opportunity, honor, and desire to lead and rebuild my nation.

The questions were: Where do you start? Where do you go? What is the Cherokee Nation? What should the Nation become? What is best for the Cherokee Nation?

CHAPTER 2

ᏂᏏ ᎠᏣᎦᏫᏩᎥ ᎠᏍᎦᏬᎠᏓ

Learn from All I Observe

You are already coming out, rising fast, I will follow you all day, I will "learn from all that I observe" in the world. Late in the evening as you disappear, I shall be that much wiser.

BENNY SMITH
Full-blood bilingual Cherokee traditionalist

WHAT IS THE FIRST LESSON?

For me, the first lesson began appropriately enough at my inauguration as principal chief in 1999. We chose to conduct the ceremonies at the Cherokee Nation capitol building in Tahlequah, Oklahoma. Tahlequah became the capital of the Cherokee Nation after the infamous removal of Cherokees from our homelands in the southeastern United States in 1838. This removal was called the "Trail of Tears" because, in violation of a number of treaties and a U.S. Supreme Court decision, the United States forcibly removed 16,000 Cherokees from our homeland, and 4,000 died as a result. The red brick, two-story capitol, built in 1867, sits in the middle of the town square. It is a grand symbol and monument of the historical insistence of the Cherokee people to self-govern. On the front steps, with an audience sitting under the oak trees, Benny Smith, a full-blood bilingual Cherokee traditionalist, cautioned me as principal chief to be a student of the Cherokee people and Cherokee Nation, to be flexible, and to be point-blank honest. Of course, in Oklahoma, August days are hot even under the trees, and a lot can and will be forgotten, but his instruction as a respected community leader I remembered. His words became a constant daily reminder: "Be a student of the Cherokee people and Nation." And I did. Every day from morning to evening, I watched, observed, learned, listened, and digested the words and actions of all connected with the Cherokee Nation. Being a student requires no response or reaction. Even the venting or frustration expressed by some people led to other questions of why they had this emotional response and what the issue really was. How could we improve, resolve the conflict, or explain the situation? The study of our people taught me to want to learn more.

FIGURE 2.1 *Benny Smith giving the author, Chad Smith, a fan of white eagle feathers as a symbol of the office of Principal Chief.*

Photo by Will Chavez/Cherokee Phoenix.

Going to Water: Learn from All I Observe

There is a Cherokee historical custom called "going to the water." The simple practice involved going to moving water such as a creek or river early in the morning, washing your face, and saying certain prayers in Cherokee. One prayer is to "learn from all you observe." The idea is simple and profound. As the sun rises, it illuminates the world, lighting certain fragments because of the angle of the early morning light and the shadows it casts upon the Earth. The world looks a particular way, and the sunlight creates a unique contrast and focus. The colors of sunrise are different than those of the rest of the day.

The prayer is to learn from all you observe and not just what you see. Observing is the study of things around you. To observe is to examine both the sunlit and the shaded sides of the objects and to learn from the objects an intelligence that you may have missed before. As the sun rises in the sky, the color, angle, and perspective of those sunlit objects changes. As the sun approaches noon, the colors seem less vivid, the angles of shadows are less dramatic, and there is a new way to see the same objects. The process continues past noon, to afternoon, and on to the evening sunset. The same objects can be seen differently at each position of the sun in the sky and can offer impressions, information, and teaching. By sunset, we now have seen the same objects in a number of different angles, perspectives, colors, and contexts. Our intelligence and understanding by the end of the day is greater because we learn from all we observe.

The meaning of the metaphor is obvious. When we get up in the morning, we should be alert and attentive to all around us so we can observe and learn throughout the day, every day. There is also a greater meaning, which is that we observe and learn throughout our lives, from childhood through old age. As our lives continue, we have greater and more complete perspectives; we observe an object, person, or situation differently over the course of time. The admonition is still stern. We should observe and learn our entire lives; we should be lifelong learners. We come to realize that our first youthful impressions may change; with more information and different perspectives, we may obtain a more complete picture. Among Cherokee people, we respect and honor our elders in part because they carry our oral history and traditional culture. We incorporate this core value into everyday work. As principal chief, it was my custom to go to groups of Cherokee speakers, often elders, and ask them how they would interpret a certain situation or concept. One time I asked, "How would you describe a young person in his or her late twenties or early thirties who has a meaningful job, has started a loving family, takes care of his or her parents, is a good neighbor, takes personal responsibility, and is a patriot to the Cherokee Nation?" After several weeks, they concluded that in the Cherokee language, you would describe such a person as "mature."

It seems so simple that when we learn from all we observe, we mature, but is it a powerful way to shape your life and organization. In Cherokee thought, we mature.

Solar Envelope: Forced to Look

In 1982, alternative energy was an important issue, and I researched a number of solar and alternative energy home-design technologies including active, passive, geothermal, and earth berm construction. The solar envelope home concept is to create at least a one-foot envelope around the living space of the home so air can move by convection loop: up a solarium facing south, over the attic space, down a double north wall, and back to the solarium under a raised floor. The inside and outside walls of the south facing solarium are predominantly glass and force the occupant to look outside of the house. So those rooms adjacent to the solarium, such as the master bedroom, the living room, and dining room/kitchen, cannot avoid offering views of the environment. The design truly embraces the environment rather than trying to shelter you from it.

So my family and I designed and built a solar envelope home. The house is a good example of how to learn from all you observe. Thermally, it worked great. It saved on utilities, minimized draftiness, and increased humidity in the winter. However, the greatest attribute was that it forced us during the course of the day and the days over a season to watch the sun move across the sky and to watch shadows move not only through the house but across the environment outside. We could not avoid watching time go by when the shadows in the house and outside slowly but surely changed minute by minute. From day to day, we were forced to see the change in the trees, grass, and flowers. We got to watch the rain, lightning, and snow from inside the cozy house proper. It was tranquil and profound. We noticed things we had missed so many times about how we fit into the grand scheme of things because now we were visually connected with nature. Simple. Generally, the public lives in housing designed to hide us from nature and its elements, focusing our attention instead on a television or dining room table. We work in buildings with few precious windows, and the view outside is usually concrete and industrial. The solar envelope design connected my family with the outdoors.

The solar envelope house demonstrated the literal lesson of Benny Smith to learn from all you observe during the course of a day. The poignant lesson is to learn, not only from the physical environment but from the people and circumstances around you. They too change over the course of seasons. Of course, observing also includes reading, listening to music, watching performances, and participating in life.

Doofus: What I Don't Know that I Need to Know

The lesson to "learn from all you observe" is reinforced by the discussion distinguishing a genius from a doofus. A doofus is someone who thinks he knows everything but in fact knows very little. We know lots of doofuses, ranging from *Mad* magazine's Alfred E. Neuman to a host of politicians during a campaign. Popular politicians have an answer for every problem and for situations that are not problems. A doofus is a "know it all" who must bluff to disguise his ignorance. The opposite of a doofus is a genius. A genius is someone who knows so much he realizes he does not know everything. He knows that there is a universe of knowledge out there that he does not understand but that he needs to know in order to make sound decisions. A genius knows how to go about finding out these things that he does not know in order to make a good decision. A genius learns from all he observes. A doofus is arrogant. A genius is humble.

There are a number of sayings people use that signal the difference between genius and doofus. During political campaigns, lots of politicians are doofuses when responding to questions that they don't understand, much less have an answer for.

One such statement used by political doofuses in the Cherokee Nation is, "I just think." I have heard politicians use this phrase when they have run out of substantive things to say. They seem to believe that if they "just think" something, it has some moral or logical merit when, in fact, they are confessing that they don't know what they're talking about. I remember an incident when an elderly woman reported that she had roaches in her house. The tribal politician told her, "I just think we send an exterminator out there and spray for roaches." His "just thinking" was a signal he was not thinking, had no command of the facts, and refused to consider unintended consequences. In reality, the elderly woman was on oxygen, and spraying an insecticide might have been detrimental to her health. Perhaps the tribal politician should have provided her with education about what attracts roaches and about non-insecticide extermination techniques that would keep her house free from roaches in the future. Another doofus statement is, "I would have done it different." This saying is typically invoked after the fact, often when the speaker had ample opportunity to provide input from the beginning but didn't. I have heard this phrase used after a construction project is completed and there is nothing that can be done economically to address an issue or concern. Why did the person not say or do something when he had the chance? Why not voice concerns or offer constructive input before it's too late? To say "I would have done it different" is to confess that you did not know what you wanted or what the project could become when you had the chance to contribute. It's the sort of statement you hear from a Monday morning quarterback who *knows it all*. Another doofus saying is, "I just don't understand why." This saying is quite ironic, because it is used after the fact to belittle someone for his actions or decisions rather than to find out the facts about an issue. To say "I just don't understand why he did such and such" is to insinuate that the other person did not know what he was doing. It is often a snide comment.

At the other end of the intelligence spectrum is sincere learning. It is so pleasant to watch people learn, even if it is learning the hard way or by accident. Epiphany is a wonderful concept and word.

As a public defender for a year, I found that most of my clients were quite familiar with their "Miranda rights," the right against self-incrimination as guaranteed by the Fifth Amendment of the U.S. Constitution. The U.S. Supreme Court in the *Miranda* case created a requirement that law enforcement officers advise detained suspects of this right. We have all have heard the result on television: "You have the right to remain silent. Anything you say may be used against you in a court of law. You have a right to an attorney, and if you can't afford one, one may be appointed for you." I remind students that these rights are situational, and the most precious right everyone has is the right to ask a reasonable question of anyone and to receive a reasonable answer. No one should feel timid about asking questions. It is a fundamental right, opportunity, and often an obligation. It is a wonderful right to learn from all you observe, including asking questions. It is what a genius does.

Drawing Outside the Lines: They Are Not My Lines

One of my favorite stories about learning was told by a friend who visited his daughter's day-care class. The children were coloring on an outline of a duck that the teacher had given them. He was concerned because his daughter was drawing outside the lines, and he wondered if her actions were a sign of some disability. He said to her, "Honey, you are not drawing within the lines." Then he saw she was drawing a sailing ship over the duck. She responded matter of factly, "Daddy, they are not my lines." This child was unrestrained in her desire to learn and express herself. Of course, we learn by observing, reading, listening, and asking.

Learn from All I Observe: One Democratic Universal Right

Learning from all we observe, being forced to learn by following the shadows of the sun, having the humility to recognize we don't know everything, and knowing we have the freedom to explore outside the lines underscore our one democratic universal right: the right to learn. We learn even more when we face adversity.

There is tremendous learning to be had by running out of gas. Unfortunately, I do so periodically. I either think I have the number of miles calculated so I can make it to the next gas station, or I forget to look at the gas gauge, or I am in such a hurry I don't have time to get gas. And then it happens: the gas gauge reads empty, and the car stops. Regardless of the reason, the laws of physics deliver a consequence: if you don't put gas in the tank, the car will eventually stop. First, I feel disbelief that I ran out of gas—again. Then I coast, looking for a place to safely park the car. I survey the horizon and try to remember where the closest gas station is. I get out of the car irritated with myself, knowing I should have known better, but apparently I did not learn the lesson well enough the last time I ran out of gas. Then the real lesson starts. I tend to run out of gas when the weather is bad, very cold or very hot. The weather can't be 70 degrees and sunny; it has to be 30 degrees with sleet or 106 degrees with no wind. Then I walk. And walk. And walk. Every time I run out of gas, I think, "You know, this is how people got around 100 years ago. But for smart people inventing cars, I would still be walking around today. There are lots of people who walk because they don't have a dependable car." Finally, I think, "It is time to slow down and look around, at the people and the environment. Don't get ahead of yourself." I get my gas somehow and go back to the car. I feel a small sense of accomplishment and great relief when I pour the can of gas into the tank and the car starts. Running out of gas teaches me that we all have the democratic right to get up each morning, make the best of the day, have something to show at the end of the day, and learn from the day's experiences. Those experiences can be as seemingly insignificant as making a meeting on time or running out of gas. Learning from adversity can be a rewarding and humbling experience.

We have the choice and the right to learn. Following is my January 2009 letter to employees of the Cherokee Nation regarding learning.

"I Learn from All I Observe"
By Chad Smith, Principal Chief

I would like to remind our citizens and neighbors that each day we have choices and opportunities. We have but one democratic universal right: to daily choose what we want to become.

From a Cherokee morning prayer, we acknowledge that we can observe the world in the light of the sun from sunrise to sunset and learn from all we see, hear, touch, feel, smell, and sense. At the end of the day, we understand more and have helped ourselves.

We each have a responsibility that cannot be shifted to anyone else to help ourselves by learning during the course of each day, month, year, and lifetime. This year's theme and focus at Cherokee Nation is our responsibility to help ourselves by learning all we can. When we help ourselves, we can help our families, communities, nation, and country. From the development of our own written language and building the first institutions of education west of the Mississippi to our immersion school today, our history is rich with learning achievements.

In the past years we have focused on community and family: ᏍᏚᎩ (gadugi), coming together to work for the benefit of the community; ᏂᏓᏘ ᎤᎾᎵᏎᎳᏙᏗ ᎠᎴ ᏂᏓᏘ ᏧᎾᎳᏏᏙᏗ, (nigadiyu unaliselvdodi ale nigadiyu tsunalasidodi), common values and common grounds; ᏧᏂᎸᏫᏍᏓᏁᏗ, ᎦᏬᏂᎯᏍᏗ ᎠᎴ ᏍᎦᏚᎩ (tsunilvwisdanedi, gawonihisdi ale sgadugi), jobs, language, and community; and ᏗᏂᏲᏟ ᎤᎾᎵᏍᏕᎸᏙᏗ (diniyotli unalistelvdodi), do this so our children can help themselves. Now we focus on the individual: I learn from all I observe.

Education, wisdom, and knowledge are all achieved by learning. That is how we help ourselves and provide an example of leadership to those around us. I encourage us to carry this message all year, to learn from everything around us, and to remember that our youth are watching us and learning as well.

The first lesson is to study and to learn from all you observe. The question is, "What have you missed?"

CHAPTER 3

ᏍᎦᏒᎭᏖᎢ

Leadership
The Ability to Go from Point A to Point B

If you don't know where you are going, any road will take you there.

LEWIS CARROLL
Alice in Wonderland

There are hundreds of books, theories, seminars, videos, and audio tapes on the topic of leadership. It is a word so often used for different things that its meaning becomes vague. Debates and discussions about whether leadership is inherent or learned and about the difference between management and leadership fill volumes. There are books from the perspective of leaders in business, government, sports, religion, the military, and all other walks of life and corners of the planet. Great authors, storytellers, analysts, and teachers have added to the body of leadership knowledge. I have read many of these books, and each is helpful in learning from all we observe. Having traveled a lot as principal chief, I had a stack of management, leadership, and organization books by my desk and would take one for airplane reading.

In 2000, with the help of Kyle Smith, Mark Rhodes, Paul Gustafson, and others, we studied organizational design processes and undertook a reorganization of the Cherokee Nation that established a sound structure for the Cherokee Nation administration. Kyle Smith, an MBA and my brother, had done a major organization reengineering project with a large oil and gas company, and he was funded by the Ford Foundation to facilitate a group of consultants, employees, and community people to review the operations of the Cherokee Nation.

The complexity of the Cherokee Nation made it difficult to identify a suitable leadership model. The Cherokee Nation is a government; it also operates businesses, provides social services, and functions as a cultural entity. Within the tribal government community, it is called the work of "Nation building."

Our program's staff engaged consultants from different disciplines such as health, education, social science, and business who brought different models, languages, concepts, metrics, and twists to leadership theory and practice as they tried to build on the foundation that Kyle Smith helped establish in 2000. When all was said and done, our staff would try to digest the models and language of one particular theory or discipline and apply it with limited success. It was hard to integrate them. This difficulty was foreseeable. Our staff got confused about which models and languages they should use. With such confusion, consistency became a problem. We delivered goods and services in areas where the trade and occupation language, management models, and ultimate products were vastly different. The Nation produces or provides more than 100 goods and services including law enforcement, schools, daycare, healthcare, aerospace assembly, gaming, food and beverage, tourism, housing, social services, and cultural enrichment. Each had its own management, organizational history, and perspective.

As a government, the Cherokee Nation defends and exercises its sovereignty, develops relationships with other governments, and provides its citizens with services for order, safety, and security, such as law enforcement, a judiciary, taxation, and regulation. The government is a constitutional form with three branches—executive, legislative, and judicial—similar to the United States and most states. It is a political model with elected officials who serve and represent constituents. Elected officials serve at the pleasure of voters. Unfortunately, voters can be shortsighted, selfish, and exploited by unscrupulous politicians.

The three branches of the federal government offer checks and balances on one another as outlined by the 1803 U.S. Supreme Court case of *Marbury v. Madison*. In *Marbury*, the Supreme Court defined the roles of the fledgling United States' branches of government as follows: the role of the legislature is to enact law, the executive is to carry out the law, and the court is to tell what the law is. The roles of the executive and the legislature are in constant tension and properly so. The executive wants greater policy authority to execute the business of the government, and the legislature wants to exert governmental controls in response to the interests of its local constituencies and sometimes attempts to micromanage the executive staff. Cherokee Nation governmental branches have the same roles as outlined in the Cherokee Nation Constitution enacted in 1839. Political decisions are very different than business decisions. Political decisions are self-regulating and have no uniform or enforceable principles that apply. The interest or driver for an elected official is his own conscience. He can espouse and adhere to a set of principles that are beneficial, foresighted, sustaining, and honorable, or he can pander to a majority of his constituents, deceive them, and use the position for self-aggrandizement. In the political model, the elected official can be a statesmen, public servant, or classic narcissistic sociopath.

Within the executive branch, there are a number of functions including police power, regulation, taxation, business development, and social service delivery. The government hierarchical management system is generally referred to as a bureaucracy. Complicating matters for the Cherokee Nation is the fact that within that bureaucracy, there are different traditional management norms or models for different disciplines or services. To execute police power with the marshal service, the normal management model requires a paramilitary structure with corporals, lieutenants, captains, and so forth. The expectation is that officers will carry out orders with little consultation with lower level staff. The normal management model for health is a dual administration with parallel lines of authority between the clinic or hospital administrator and the medical chief of staff. The clinic administrator makes all operational, budget, personnel, and support decisions, but the final arbiter of medical decisions and policy is the medical chief of staff. There may be a conflict between the two on whether the financial ability of the clinic and the medical needs of the patients coincide. Clearly, a paramilitary model would be foreign and objectionable to health care administrators. Education professionals expect to be managed with a participatory model that includes teachers and administrators developing a policy consensus. Social service and housing programs are counseling-based, with case managers having some autonomy for their respective clients. Other disciplines, goods, and services feature different management expectations or models.

The Cherokee Nation followed a well-established model separating "for profit" business from government operations by creating a tribal corporation to run businesses. By statute, the principal chief appoints a board of directors confirmed by the legislative branch, and the board has autonomy to run the business. The representative of the Cherokee Nation is the principal chief. The value of such a structure is that the corporation can make decisions based on business principles, not political considerations. However, even within the corporate side of the Cherokee Nation, tribal businesses have different management styles and norms. Construction, assembly line businesses, hospitality (hotel and gaming), government contracting, computer technology, and staff placement businesses each have unique management styles, norms, and models.

Further, within the executive branch of the government, there should be checks and balances to ensure faithful execution of the laws of the Nation. For example, a gaming commission requires compliance with gaming laws by the gaming company, whose primary interest is to be profitable; a newspaper editorial board ensures the tribal newspaper does not become an in-house organ for elected officials; and an environmental protection commission ensures that tribal operations do not take shortcuts that are detrimental to the environment. The regulatory commissions and agencies themselves represent another management style, norm, and model.

With all of these various management models, disciplines, products, and services, how do you develop an effective overarching management system to deal with the complexity of the Cherokee Nation? Furthermore, how do you use these assets, programs, and businesses to help the citizens of the Cherokee Nation to mature in their own lives? The matrix of all these considerations combined seemed overwhelming.

We needed something simple to bring organization to the operations delivering these 100+ goods and services. The employees needed order to be engaged in their work, our citizenry wanted to understand what was going on, and we needed an answer to the elementary questions of "What is the Cherokee Nation?" and "Where should it go?"

GO BACK TO FUNDAMENTALS

Francisco, one of Ayn Rand's characters in *Atlas Shrugged*, stated, "Contradictions do not exist. Whenever you think that you are facing a contradiction, check your premises." So we went to the intellectual basics: the dictionary. What is the definition of *lead*? The *Random House College Dictionary* defines *lead* as "to take or conduct on the way." Therefore, leadership is the ability to take or conduct on the way. To conduct on the way means you must start somewhere and go somewhere. Using mathematical language, Point A is where you start, and Point B is where you want to go. Leadership is the ability to go from Point A to Point B.

Figure 3.1 offers an applied example of the Cherokee leadership model: Point A to Point B.

We know going from Point A to Point B seems simple enough, but between those two points are challenges, lessons, adversities, joys, and heartbreaks. What lies between Points A and B, between now and the future, is unknown and uncertain. Leadership is what drives and motivates us to begin and complete the journey. We can prepare ourselves for the journey of leadership by learning skills to navigate the way, understanding the challenges, and overcoming the adversity.

Defining leadership as the ability to go from Point A to Point B simplified the leadership and management philosophy at the Cherokee Nation and made it easier for us to communicate. By definition, everyone is a leader. There would be only one exception. If you had everyone in the

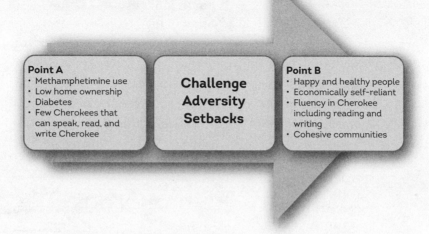

Point A
• Methamphetimine use
• Low home ownership
• Diabetes
• Few Cherokees that can speak, read, and write Cherokee

Challenge Adversity Setbacks

Point B
• Happy and healthy people
• Economically self-reliant
• Fluency in Cherokee including reading and writing
• Cohesive communities

FIGURE 3.1 *An example of the application of the leadership model.*

world line up, only one person would be at the end of the line; everyone but that last person in line would be leading someone. People follow us whether we notice it or not. Some people will follow our example whether the behavior and words we exhibit are good, bad, or indifferent. The silent influence we have on those around us is a powerful aspect of leadership.

The most important leadership is personal leadership, each of us making decisions for ourselves. We are responsible for those decisions, which take us from where we are to where we want to go. Often people find themselves in awkward or destructive situations such as addiction to drugs or alcohol, obesity, domestic abuse, and others. No one chooses those situations. No one goes to college to learn to become a methamphetamine addict. The decisions that lead to these destructive behaviors are often made by others, and the person chooses to follow. The value of understanding leadership as the ability to go from Point A to Point B is that it not only applies to personal behavior, but it also provides a very understandable view of personal responsibility. This model applies equally in building and maturing the family, community, and Nation.

After a few years as principal chief and after a number of organizational analyses and leadership development efforts, I realized that my most important work was developing and recruiting leaders. A leader will design an organization to get from Point A to Point B. Also, an organization will take on the characteristics and style of its leader. If the leader is trusting and dynamic, the organization will become the same. If the leader is petty and short-sighted, the organization will become the same. The saying "One bad apple spoils the whole barrel" applies to organizations, especially if the bad apple is at the top.

My job was to recruit and develop "horses and fishes."

Leadership: Get You Some Horses and Fishes

Several years into my tenure as principal chief, I learned a lesson from a story I heard 40 years ago as a college sophomore. I was attending the University of Tennessee and was walking down Neyland Stadium Drive with a fellow student I really did not know. We passed a new building and he said, "There is our new swimming natatorium." I said, "That is nice." He said, "And we have only had a swimming team four years." I said, "Good." Then he said, "They are nationally ranked." I said, "Wow, that is something!" And then he said, "And the coach had never coached swimming before." Now he had my attention. I asked, "How did he do that?" The guy said, "He had a simple philosophy: if you want a football team, you get some horses; if you want a swim team, you get some fishes." It dawned on me that the coach must have been outstanding in recruiting student athletes with talent and excellent assistant coaches who knew how to teach techniques. That was one of my most important jobs, to recruit and develop horses and fishes.

Leaders have different styles and methods. Some can be very combative and commanding, some can be gentle and supportive, some can be progressive and stimulating, and some can be measured and cautious. The style and method of leadership may depend on the situation, the industry, the culture of the group, or one's personality and worldview. The style and method of leadership will depend on where you want to go, where you are, who is going with you, and at what cost. People have different leadership attributes and styles, but the measure of them all is whether they take us where we want to go.

Attributes: What Does Your Leadership Look Like?

If it looks like a duck, walks like a duck, and quacks like a duck, then it's not George Clooney.

REN RIESS

Attributes are cultural values, qualities, or characteristics. A group's leadership influences the behavior of its members and establishes desired outcomes. To determine what a leader was in Cherokee thought, custom, and tradition, we set out to identify a set of leadership attributes. Attributes are cultural values, qualities or characteristics and describe our understanding of leadership. Our leadership influences and shapes the behaviors of those around us and determines the outcomes we choose. We asked Cherokee community leaders and Cherokee speakers, "How would you describe a Cherokee leader? How would he or she look or act?" For the Cherokee Nation, encouraging these Cherokee leadership attributes (see "Cherokee Way of Life: What We Were Taught Growing Up") became part and parcel of developing individuals and the government to achieve our Designed Purpose.

TGᎎᎠᎯ ᎡᏆᏌᏬ ᏚᏍᏬᎡᎿ
(iyusdi egeyonv degatvsvi)
Cherokee Way of Life:
What We Were Taught Growing Up

- ᎫᏢᏂᎪᎫ (tsudadanilvtsati)–Respectful/acknowledgment: Hold one another sacred, or be "stingy" with another person and yourself.

- ᏂᎣᎵᏛᏬᎠᎬᎾ (nidvdayosgvna)–Determined/persistent: Never give up.

- ᎤᏢᏬᎯ (kaliwohi)–Integrity: Full (to the greatest extent possible). Act in the same manner regardless of the situation. Do what is right and complete, even when no one is watching.

- ᎠᏓᏂᎬᏍ (hadatinuga)–Leader: Lead by example. Show the way by acting the way we want others to treat us. Our actions influence the behavior of others.

- ᏗᏓᎫᎪᏗᏗ (didadvgododi)–Communicative: Be sure to let the other(s) know.

- ᎤᏓᏙᎯᏳᎯ (udadohiyuhi)–Confident: Have confidence in yourself, and do not doubt your abilities, but temper all with humility.

- ᏗᏟᏍᏕᎸᏗ (dilisdelvdi)–Cooperative: Help one another.

- ᎠᏚᎸᏗ (adudalvdi)–Responsible: Commit yourself to your task or assignment.

- ᏗᏗᏲᎲᏍᎩ (dideyohvsgi)–Teacher: Share your knowledge and wisdom with others to improve that individual, family, or group.

- ᎠᏅᏂᏗᏳ (anvnidiyu)–Patient: Be patient, no matter what you are going through.

- ᎡᎳᏗ ᏯᏓᏛᏁᏗ (eladi yadadvnedi)–Humble: Never boast; never think you are better or higher than anyone else.

- ᎤᏔᏂᎩᏓ (utlanigida)–Strong: Be strong in whatever you do. Take comfort in the strength of the Creator and your ancestors.

We believed we should strive to live these Cherokee attributes and values. They are characteristics that belong to a happy and healthy people. However, different cultures and organizations value different attributes. For example, some would argue courage is an attribute for success, but courage was not one of the attributes identified by Cherokee traditionalists. The *Random House College Dictionary* defines courage as the "quality of mind or spirit which enables a person to face difficulty, danger, pain." To many, courage may suggest welling up an emotion in order to face an adversary. By contrast, the list of Cherokee attributes includes confidence, which was translated from the Cherokee word udadohiyuhi: "Have confidence in yourself and do not doubt your abilities, but temper all with humility." Stephen Covey, author of *The Seven Habits of Highly Effective People*, discusses "win-win" as the "balancing act between courage and consideration," which includes consideration of others, empathy, and confidence. The contrast between Covey's conception of courage and the Cherokee speaker's conception of confidence can be seen in a basketball game where there is no time left on the clock, the team is one point down, and the star player has two free throws. If the player relies on courage as an emotion, she must collect her resolve and feelings to face adversity. However, if she relies on confidence, she does not have to gather emotion and can reframe the situation not as adversity but as an opportunity to do what she had done a hundred times: go to the free-throw line and sink two free throws. The result is that she wins the game.

Cherokee attributes are based on a history, tradition, and culture; attributes can also be based on economic, political, ideological, religious, or designed cultures. Religions promote certain attributes; many organizations develop their own culture and produce particular attributes. Identifying and inventorying an organization's leadership attributes provides insight into whether the existing attributes are consistent with taking the organization from Point A to Point B.

LEADERSHIP BY EXAMPLE

I admire any man that can rise above his surroundings.
WILL ROGERS
May 18, 1930

Leaders are identified not by title but by example, through the attributes they exhibit. Following are letters to Cherokee Nation employees and columns from the *Cherokee Phoenix* newspaper that speak of leadership by example and attributes. By studying those who lead by example, we can learn to improve our own leadership, know what traits are desirable in recruiting staff, and understand the leadership development needs of an organization. First is a February 12, 2009, letter to employees ("Touching Lives: Nelson Smith") that reflects the attribute of ᏗᏟᏍᏕᎸᏗ (dilisdelvdi), to be cooperative: help one another.

"Touching Lives: Nelson Smith"
By Chad Smith, Principal Chief

As I sit in the stands at Sequoyah High School watching my 15-year-old practice basketball, I begin to reflect upon this gym and the school. I begin to wonder what Sequoyah will be like in the future. Will the building still be here, and what will have changed? What will the students of the future remember about the school, and what will we remember of those students who walked the halls of Sequoyah?

My dad, Nelson Smith, who passed at 71, went to Sequoyah in the late 1930s. He walked the halls of Sequoyah six decades ago, and what do we remember about his time? As I sit here watching my daughter, it dawns on me that she too will pause six decades from now when she is in her seventies and reflect on Sequoyah. Will the gym be here, or will it just be a faded memory? Will she have great stories about Sequoyah, just as my dad did? Will her life be better because of her experience at Sequoyah, just like my dad?

Each of us has the opportunity to touch the lives of others. Each of us can leave an impression so that six decades from now, people will remember us and be thankful. People's great experiences from Sequoyah, from Cherokee Nation, are not because of the institutions but because of the people who touched their lives.

Underlying all discussions of leadership is the fundamental idea that leadership is leading people. My dad was a quiet leader, but he was remembered by the many whose lives he touched.

Goodwill Trailer: Work Done Well

The story in the next letter is another inspired by my father who, for me, was one of the great leaders by example. He was a remarkable man. He faced the hardships of the Depression and, being a full-blood Cherokee, faced racism. His hardships were never stories that framed his success or allowed him to blame others. His was a bootstrap success story, having worked his way up from being a laborer in the tool bin at a tire manufacturing company to a maintenance manager with a department of 130 employees. He was respected by his peers and subordinates. He was loved by his family. In an April 20, 2001, letter to employees ("Goodwill Store Employees: Value of Work"), I discussed leadership by example by doing honorable work. It reflects the attribute of being DSƚᎯᎠ (adudalvdi) responsible: commit yourself to your task or assignment.

"Goodwill Store Employee: Value of Work"
By Chad Smith, Principal Chief

Dear Employees,

Our work at the Cherokee Nation is perhaps the most important work that can be done. We are about the business of rebuilding a nation. That is one reason our history course is rewarding. From our history, we can readily see where we can go by knowing where we have been and where we are.

When we feel "down" or when we ask ourselves if our work is valuable or appreciated, we should remember the inspiration from the trials and tribulations memorialized in our history.

In addition to historical inspiration from our ancestors, I remember once, about a decade ago, dropping items off at a Goodwill store. An old man sat in a lumpy, beaten-up sofa situated in a semi-trailer. He looked through the discarded items, sorted them, and gave receipts. At first glance, I thought, "What a boring job," but then immediately it hit me that I would give my arm if my deceased father could be there doing that work. It would have been work enjoyed and work done well. It would have been work that ultimately helped poor people by making furniture and clothing available. I immediately felt bad for thinking the job was undeserving or without value.

Everyone at the Cherokee Nation has a valuable job. Eighty percent of our staff's work directly contributes back to our people. The other 20 percent provides the support that enables us to provide services to our people. But each contributes directly to the work of the Cherokee Nation, which is to help our people, our communities, and our nation become stronger. From the child welfare workers, to those remodeling homes, to nurses, to accountants, we each play an integral part.

We each should feel proud at having the opportunity to do so. Many of our people could go work elsewhere and make more money. Many of our people have no work experience outside the Cherokee Nation and may not appreciate the value of our work. However, is there any question that working for a private corporation would be as fulfilling as rebuilding a nation?

We are a proud people and deserve to be proud of our work.

The old adage "If it is worth doing, it is worth doing right" is very true, and when we do work right, we bring dignity to the work and to ourselves. In traditional Cherokee thought, doing work right involves commitment. I admire people who know what they are doing and do it right, whether they are laying carpet, filling cavities, or trying a legal case.

However, we can get discouraged, frustrated, tired, and disheartened when we are not validated or appreciated. In those times, we question the value of our work and wonder whether it is worth the effort. I once heard Congressman Abercrombie from Hawaii say there are three rules of politics. Rule number one: "Never, never, never, never expect gratitude for your work." Rule number two: "Never, never, never, never ever forget rule number one. If you expect gratitude, you are doing it for the wrong reason." You should be working because it is the right thing to do, not because you seek gratitude. The third rule: "Never be right, because the guy on the other side will hold a grudge until he can get you back. The best thing to do is apologize, say you're sorry, and wait for the next time to try your initiative." I disagree with his last rule, but his first two rules are very true. Here is a story about those who lead by example and the value of not expecting gratitude.

Redbird Smith: Protect His People

Redbird Smith was my great-grandfather, a senator in the Cherokee Nation legislature in the 1890s and a traditional leader. In the 1890s, he resisted the federal allotment policy and was jailed for civil disobedience. He helped revitalize the Keetoowah Society as a traditional religious association and served as its chairman or chief until he died in 1918. There were 5,789 Cherokees enrolled in the Keetoowah Society, which sought to live and worship by traditional thought and ways. His humble style of leadership is a traditional one well accepted by the Cherokee community. He never expected gratitude for his public and community service. In a graduation speech I gave at Sequoyah High School in 2005 ("Redbird Smith: Servant Citizen"), I described his leadership style. He reflected the attribute of ᏧᏔᏂᎥᏗᎢ (tsudadanilvtsati) respectful/acknowledgment: hold one another sacred, or be "stingy" with another person and yourself.

"Redbird Smith: Servant Citizen"
By Chad Smith, Principal Chief

Sequoyah High School originated in 1871 when the Cherokee National Council passed an act setting up an orphan asylum to take care of many orphans who lost their parents in the American Civil War. In 1914, the Cherokee National Council authorized Chief Rogers to sell and convey the property of the Cherokee Orphan Training School, including 40 acres of land and all the buildings, to the United States Department of Interior for $5,000. In 1925, the name of the institution was changed to Sequoyah Orphan Training School in honor of Sequoyah, a Cherokee who developed the Cherokee syllabary.

After being known as Sequoyah Vocational School for a time, it was eventually named Sequoyah High School. In November 1985, the Cherokee Nation resumed operation of SHS from the Bureau of Indian Affairs. Sequoyah High School was born of a time of suffering and pain. Adversity creates opportunity. Now Sequoyah has become the leadership academy for the Cherokee Nation and Indian Country.

Tonight is special. In 1940, my father, Nelson Smith, graduated from Sequoyah. His class picture is located outside Superintendent Stanley's office. He was my best friend; he died in 1991. He was a tie-cutter and became an industrial engineer at Gates Rubber Company. He grew up in Adair and Sequoyah counties in the 1920s and 1930s. A tie-cutter cuts down trees and shapes them square with a broad axe into railroad ties. He sold them for 25 cents a tie. He lived during the Depression, when people actually died of starvation. He had many fond and mischievous stories about his time here at Sequoyah. He too would be proud of the progress this school and each of you have made. I was proud of him.

My wife, Bobbie Gail, and I have additional reasons to be proud this evening. Our son, Chris, will graduate, making complete a cycle of family members graduating from Sequoyah.

People naturally look up to good leaders. Take a leap of faith in yourself and take the lead. Who knows? You may turn around someday to see others following you.

If I had to recommend one leader for you to emulate in your life, it would be our own Cherokee leader Redbird Smith.

When Redbird Smith died in 1918, the local newspaper wrote that he "was distinguished by his plain mannerisms, his rugged character, and his constant desire to promote the welfare of his tribe. While not an educated man, he possessed a keen and penetrating intellect, thought profoundly, and was a rare interpreter of philosophy. People of his time probably saw Redbird Smith as a Renaissance man—a philosophical man with many talents and interests."

To Cherokees, this translates as being a traditional person. He cared for his tribe and community as though they were his family. The newspaper continued:

> Redbird Smith was also smart in business, was frugal in his lifestyle, and made a comfortable living for his large family during a trying period in history. But just as strong as his intellect was his keen commitment to his Cherokee community. This was evident by his many political actions to protect his people. His great concern for the welfare of others was evident up to his last few days. With children sick with influenza, Redbird Smith kept vigil around-the-clock over his children, until he too succumbed to the illness.
>
> Redbird Smith was a great man who dedicated his life to his people and family.

Many Eastern tribes historically memorialized principles with wampum belts. These belts were made using seashell beads woven into images. The Keetoowah Society, as a religious society, had a wampum belt call the "White Path." It was a belt with two darker stripes of seashells separated by a white stripe that portrayed the white path. Its meaning was to think right and do right by staying on the white path and not get off on the dark shoulders.

History has recorded Redbird Smith as a patriot and traditional leader of the Cherokee Nation, but he too had his challenges. He said toward the end of his life:

> After my selection as a chief, I awakened to the grave and great responsibilities of a leader of men. I looked about and saw I had led my people down a long and steep mountainside; now it was my duty to turn and lead them back upward and save them. The unfortunate thing in the mistakes and errors of leaders or of governments is the penalty the innocent and loyal followers have to pay. My greatest ambition has always been to think right and do right. It is my belief that this is the fulfilling of the law of the Great Creator.

In the up-building of my people, it is my purpose that we shall be spiritually right and industrially strong.

Redbird Smith led by example, held the existence of others sacred, understood he was leading, and did not expect gratitude.

The Cherokee Gift: Our Turn to Step Up

When we lose those who lead by example, we begin to understand more clearly that we have a duty to lead. "The Cherokee Gift," originally published in the *Cherokee Phoenix* on December 8, 2005, tells the story of Oosqualug. Unfortunately, human nature is such that we don't appreciate what we have until it is gone. That is especially true when we lose those who lead by example. Often we don't recognize that leadership in our midst because those who lead by example don't self-promote and show off. Oosqualug is one of the best examples of quiet community leadership that I found as principal chief. He was a ᏉᏝᎢᏋᏍ (hadatinuga) leader: lead by example; show the way by acting the way we want others to treat us. His actions influenced the behavior of others in the community of Evening Shade.

"The Cherokee Gift"
By Chad Smith, Principal Chief

In this season of thankfulness and giving, I want to share with you a story about one of our Cherokee elders and how grateful I am to have known him.

A couple of days after Veterans Day, I arrived at a modest house in Sequoyah County. There were a number of cars parked outside, and a host of people lined the sidewalk. Down the handicap ramp came the body of Oosqualug, to be taken by hearse. He had passed.

He was 89 years old and quite a remarkable and rare man, unassuming and humble, who lived in the same house his entire life. He drove a school bus in the Vian area for 30 years. He served the country well in World War II and Korea. He spoke Cherokee as his first language, Creek as his second, and English his third. When you came around Oosqualug, although he was a small man, his smile and demeanor filled the room. Those in Evening Shade knew him as the anchor of that community, and an event was not complete unless Oosqualug was there. When he arrived, everything was proper and balanced and good.

The community used his property for turkey shoots to raise money. At Thanksgiving meals and other events, his arrival changed the whole perspective of those gathered there. Oosqualug was one of the last who knew the Cherokee ways of healing and counseling.

He was one of those who really lived Cherokee values. It was only within the last couple of years, over his resistance, that he would accept anything from the Cherokee Nation. He finally accepted help to remodel his bathroom and install a handi-cap ramp. He wouldn't file for federal programs like Medicaid or Social Security; he said they asked too many questions, it was none of their business, and he had all that he needed. He never wanted anything from the Cherokee Nation, no subsidies for utilities, commodities, or other things. He was right; he had everything that he needed.

Although his wife had passed away decades ago, he still resided in the house where they raised their five children, sev-eral nephews, nieces, and grandchildren. Every day until the recent illness that took his life, he was outside working, and even though it was a rocky hillside, his lawn was manicured better than most golf courses. And when he finished there, he would go down to the Evening Shade cemetery and clear brush and mow. He was always busy, always working, always happy, and always had his door open for anyone who needed help or guidance.

This was Oosqualug: a man who exemplified the Cherokee attributes we respect. He valued independence and self-reliance and believed in contributing to ᎦᏚᎩ (gadugi). It was a blessing to know him. His family and friends all understand how great a blessing he was. He was a gift to the entire community.

As principal chief, it gives me great sorrow to see him go. He was not only a friend but an example of true Cherokee values and culture. There are very few like him left. My greatest fear is that the generations that follow him will never know someone like Oosqualug, or see and practice Cherokee values and attributes, or hear the Cherokee language spoken as he did spontaneously.

Fifteen years ago, my dad, Nelson Smith, passed away. He was one of those who lived the Cherokee way of life. William Smith, leader of the Keetoowah Nighthawks, was another one. With Oosqualug's passing, I am struck by how fragile a culture is and how quickly it can change. Now it is our turn to step up and practice the Cherokee ways, to learn and speak the Cherokee language, to work hard and be happy with what the Creator has blessed us with, and to carry on traditional Cherokee values.

For those of you who did not know Oosqualug by his Cherokee name, his English name was Jimmy McCoy. A grateful Cherokee Nation will miss him.

It was a sad day when Oosqualug passed. The void he leaves is a reminder of the importance of passing on our great Cherokee legacy, stories, and wisdom. It is our honor to do so. During the holiday season of thankfulness, giving, and renewal, there is no better time to dedicate ourselves to preserving our culture and no better gift to give our children.

Most people did not know Jimmie McCoy's Cherokee name. They did know that he was the glue that kept his community together and heading down the right path.

David Blackbird was another traditional leader; he worked all his life as a construction worker and lived at Rocky Ford Community, north of Tahlequah, Oklahoma. The Cherokee Nation had a self-help community building program. The Nation would provide the materials, and the community would construct the building with volunteer labor. A church is not the building; it is the congregation. The hands-on volunteer construction of a community building became a vehicle for people to come together as a community. At Rocky Ford, a building was started but not finished because the initial enthusiasm of the community waned. No one stepped up until David, at 76 years old, politely called on the community to finish what they started. His quiet leadership brought families and workers back to not only finish the building but to use it as a center for a flourishing community. Weddings, funerals, anniversaries, parties, revivals, fund raisers and other get-togethers happened there weekly. Then David's health started to fail. One day, he came to my office and presented me with a beautiful hand-carved walking cane with my Cherokee name carved into it. He said he thought for a long time about what to give me. He said the cane was to help me stand upright when the weight of the Cherokee Nation was on my shoulders. He too was the glue of his community.

Jimmie McCoy and David Blackbird, quietly thoughtful, led by example and were characteristic of the older traditional Cherokee gentlemen and ladies.

Fern Holland: Honor the Wisdom of Our Women

The Cherokee Nation had 10 treaties with Great Britain before there was a United States. As the story goes, when the Cherokees and British gathered at the treaty table, the Cherokees would ask the British, "Where are your women?" questioning how the British could make good decisions without their women present. The British accused the Cherokees of having a petticoat government. In the 1820s, the Cherokees memorialized their law that women could dispose of their separate property without their husband's permission. American women didn't get that right until after World War II, when states changed their laws to recognize women's separate property rights. The women's rights movement seems strange to traditional Cherokees because there was not a status difference between sexes among Cherokees. Each gender had a family and community role, and the roles were neither higher nor lower. Fern Holland was a contemporary Cherokee woman. We saw by her story that leadership and legacy were not bound by sex, position, or location. "Cherokee and American

Hero: Fern Holland" appeared in the *Cherokee Phoenix* in 2004. The column reflects Fern Holland as ᏂᏛᏓᏲᏍᎬᎾ (nidvdayosgvna) determined/persistent: never give up.

"Cherokee and American Hero: Fern Holland"

By Chad Smith, Principal Chief

Throughout history, Cherokee citizens have been known for our bravery in battle, our intellect in legal matters, and for the place of honor women hold in our society. No Cherokee citizen in recent memory typifies those traditional characteristics better than the late Fern Holland, who was assassinated in Iraq on March 9.

Fern Holland was in Iraq to help women there emerge from an oppressive culture and to make sure they had equal rights under the new Iraqi constitution. This was not a popular stance among some militant Iraqis, who threatened and intimidated Holland and her coworkers.

In the face of this opposition, Holland held dear to the principles that have shaped Cherokee society for centuries.

She carried on the tradition of legal excellence among Cherokees. The Cherokee Nation set the fundamental principles of Indian law, which still apply today and preserve our sovereignty as a nation, the same Nation that has existed since time immemorial. She used her skills as an accomplished attorney to fight for women's rights.

In our matrilineal society, we have always honored the wisdom of our women. We take our mother's clan. Our grandmothers name us. Fern Holland was killed because she thought that Iraqi mothers and grandmothers deserved the same basic rights Cherokee women have had for centuries and American women have had for decades: the right to vote, the right to an education, the right to be free.

Finally, Fern Holland exhibited courage in the face of danger, as so many Cherokees have through history. Knowing that her life was in danger, Fern Holland did not run. She did not turn her back on the Iraqi women who were counting on her. She honored her Cherokee ancestry by using her legal expertise to preserve the honor of women, even at the risk of her own safety. Fern Holland was a great Cherokee woman, and she will be missed.

At the age of 33, in the middle of a successful legal career, Fern Holland joined the Coalition Provision Authority of Iraq to provide women of the Middle East education on women's activities and rights. On March 9, 2004, she was gunned down in her car near Hilla, Iraq. Her name appears in a place of special prominence at the Cherokee Patriots Memorial in Tahlequah, Oklahoma, even though she was not in the military, because she gave her all for her country; she never gave up.

Konrad Holmes: Pursuing a Worthy Goal

Another very powerful story of leadership involves Konrad Holmes, who as a sophomore was a cross-country runner at Sequoyah High School. He had a battle with cancer, which he drove into submission several times, but finally it claimed him as his senior class graduated. He had an early graduation anticipating his death. His story is moving not only for his courage in fighting a deadly disease but for the grace and wisdom in his youthful leadership. On October 31, 2003, I wrote a letter to employees about Konrad's inspiring presence before he passed. Konrad reflects the attributes of ᏗᏎᎰᎥᎩ (dideyohvsgi) teach: share your knowledge and wisdom with others to improve that individual, family, or group and ᏄᏪᎵᎯᏍᎬᎾ (nuwelihisgvna) patient: be patient, no matter what you are going through.

"Konrad Holmes"
By Chad Smith, Principal Chief

Dear Cherokee Citizens:
I want to share with you the bright story of Konrad Holmes, who recently graduated early from Sequoyah High School. Konrad ran cross-country until he was diagnosed with cancer in his sophomore year. Since then he has been in a battle for his life.

Since his diagnosis, he has worked hard to complete his high school coursework early, and he graduated earlier this month. His goal has always been to graduate from Sequoyah, and he has overcome every obstacle that has been put in his way. He has reached his goal.

I had the opportunity to speak at Konrad's graduation ceremony. At that ceremony, it became apparent that Konrad's hard work and determination have served as an example to the students and staff at Sequoyah. Sequoyah is a training ground for the future leaders of the Cherokee Nation, and Konrad has shown the power of leadership and the strength that comes from pursuing a worthy goal.

Many of you know about the unprecedented success the cross-country team has achieved this year. While much of their success is because of their hard work, their talent, and the quality of their coaches, some of their success can also be attributed to the example set by their teammate, Konrad Holmes.

That is why we have named the new walking trail around Sequoyah the "Konrad Holmes Walking Trail." The new sign on the trail quotes 2 Timothy 4:6—"I have fought the good fight, I have finished the race, I have kept the faith." Konrad continues to fight the good fight and achieve his goals. We can all learn a lot from this young Cherokee leader.

Konrad's talk at his graduation was emotional and inspiring for all in attendance. It was truly a moment in which he was the teacher and we were the students. It is moments like his graduation that begin to move people and organizations. I believe his early graduation was the defining moment at which Sequoyah School began to be a leadership academy and a "school of choice." He clearly set the standard and established the path by his example of leadership.

Sequoyah Basketball Teams: Very Little Excuse

In addition to the lessons learned from those who have passed on, there are also great lessons to be learned in the vibrancy of our daily lives, lessons we should not take for granted. Sports are popular in part because of the vicarious leadership we feel in each game. We as spectators can see the effort, drive, training, determination, teamwork, and leadership of players. In this way, sports can offer an inspiration for us in our daily lives as we face adversity and succeed. Leading by example is seen at every practice, game, and post-game event. This is my *Cherokee Phoenix* column for April 8, 2005, "Sequoyah Basketball Teams Are Role Models for All," which reflects RWᎫ ᏆᏞᏈᎥᏞᎫ (eladi yadadvnedi) humble: never boast; never think you are better or higher than anyone else.

"Sequoyah Basketball Teams Are Role Models for All"
By Chad Smith, Principal Chief

Much has been written about the athletic achievement of Sequoyah's boys and girls basketball teams, which advanced to the state finals. The girls brought home the gold ball as state champions, and the boys brought home the silver ball as state runner-up. These achievements are even more remarkable when you consider how each and every player conducted himself or herself throughout the playoffs.

Each player showed class, dignity, sportsmanship, and leadership. In winning, they were magnanimous; in losing, they were gracious. As I followed both teams to gyms across the state this winter, I was always impressed with their talent and sportsmanship.

Young adults can sometimes be the best teachers, and the student athletes at Sequoyah certainly are. One thing they help teach us is the joy of strong families and communities.

Sequoyah's fans are extremely supportive and come out in record numbers. A reporter asked me why so many fans supported the team. I told him that it is because aunts and uncles, cousins, grandparents, and parents come to support their children, children their children know, and other children simply because they are Cherokee or Indian. The Cherokee people have a great sense of community, and the fans come because they want to show their support for the Sequoyah students. When you see players on the court, you can look in the stands and see their extended families. I've heard story after story about how these families supported these children when they started in basketball very young, at school tournament after school tournament, game after game. Many families used their yearly vacation time just to come to the state tournament. The Sequoyah coaches, staff, administration, and fans are there, game after game, because they care about the students.

Another lesson we can learn from Sequoyah's success is that we can achieve greatness with discipline, teamwork, and dedication. These athletes got the most from their abilities and overcame many obstacles to reach their goals. The work started early, before the season, in anticipation of the job ahead. Their expectations were high. The coaches and athletes put in long hours, more than was required of them because they wanted to achieve excellence. Along the way there were moments of frustration, hurt feelings, and even anger. But the teams remained focused on the goal and didn't let small stuff get in the way of achieving greatness. All of these things were lessons—a part of learning, a part of training, and a part of the effort to excel.

On the basketball court, it's easy to see what we refer to as the Cherokee spirit or Indian spirit, but it's really in a broader sense the human spirit. The greatest part of that human spirit is the effort to achieve. You can see that same spirit in other places, in academics, in other extracurricular activities, in family. You see it with those who have health challenges, continuing through pain, frustration, and dire illness.

I submit as part of our great legacy that we are people who face adversity, survive, adapt, prosper, and excel. I sincerely thank the coaches and staff and especially the players of the Sequoyah boys and girls teams this basketball season for showing us the excellence in human spirit.

There is a final lesson to be learned from all of this. When we see the excellence, determination, and perseverance happening on the courts and the sports fields, we know we have very little excuse not to pursue the same kind of spirit in our own work and daily lives. It is my blessing to be able to see these inspirations as principal chief, and I'm very thankful for that opportunity.

The girls won the state championship game that year before 10,000 people, most of whom were Indians, at the Fairgrounds Pavilion in Oklahoma City. As the two teams walked in lines after the game to congratulate each other, I witnessed something I had never seen in sports. I am not sure who on the Sequoyah team orchestrated it, but the players from both sides formed a circle holding hands at midcourt, dropped their heads for a moment of prayer, and then dispersed. No one knows what was said in that circle. The coaches from both teams looked on befuddled; the entire body of spectators fell silent and, after the closing of the prayer, applauded louder than they had at any time during the exciting game. Everyone in the pavilion seemed to understand what a unique and rare example of sportsmanship and genuine humility they had just seen; the moment was very special, and regardless of the team, every girl was a winner and leader.

That is why sports should be a laboratory for leadership. Sports should teach sportsmanship: never boast; never think you are better than anyone else.

Special Olympics: Indomitable Spirit

If there is one organization that serves as an inspiration for leadership, a vivid expression of the best in the human spirit, and provides a humbling experience for spectators, it is the Special Olympics. Not only are the participants victorious over their own adversities, but so are the families and people around them who by their love make the lives of Special Olympians better. I helped raise money for the Special Olympics by rappelling off a 19-story hotel and doing winter polar plunges in the Illinois River, but these were small contributions for the inspiration I got in return. The example shown by Special Olympics is one all leaders should learn from. The following column, "Special Olympics Are an Inspiration," appeared in the *Cherokee Phoenix* on April 20, 2004. It reflects ᎤᏓᏙᎯᏳᎯ (udadohiyuhi) confident: have confidence in yourself and do not doubt your abilities, but temper all with humility.

"Special Olympics Are an Inspiration"
By Chad Smith, Principal Chief

The Special Olympics provide an opportunity for mentally or physically challenged children and adults to perform in Olympic track and field events. I enjoy going to the Special Olympics because of the inspiration the special athletes provide. Nowhere else will you see a purer or more intense display of the human spirit, courage, and fortitude. It is truly moving to watch a young person who has difficulty walking complete a 40-yard dash. To watch one of those Special Olympians, you see someone trying his or her hardest under adverse conditions. It is a lesson that each of us should remember on a daily basis.

The other side of that coin is that we see people with great talent and limitless opportunities fail to live up to that talent and opportunity. We as citizens of the Cherokee Nation have a great opportunity before us to improve the quality of life for our children, our communities, and ourselves. Whenever we get discouraged, disheartened, or challenged, we ought to reflect back or, even better, attend a Special Olympics event. Seeing others striving to do their best under adverse conditions will certainly inspire us to do our best.

The Special Olympics show us a sustainable spirit based on confidence to make it down the sometimes tough road between points A and B.

Message: Everyone Is a Leader

Congressman John Lewis of Georgia is well-known as the "Dean of Civil Rights" in the U.S. Congress. His presence is comforting, demanding, and charismatic. He was beaten by the Alabama State Police with scores of others including Martin Luther King Jr. and Jesse Jackson in 1965 when they, in peaceful protest, crossed the Edmund Pettis Bridge in Selma, Alabama. He invited several of us to the commemoration of the forty-fifth anniversary of Bloody Sunday in 2010. We attended a church service at the Brown's Chapel A.M.E. Church and then walked over the Edmund Pettis Bridge. It was moving to see the place and people who advanced the cause of civil rights through peaceful protest.

Previously, Congressman Lewis accepted our invitation to attend the Cherokee National Holiday in September 2009, and we saw the depth of his leadership. The Cherokee Nation Holiday commemorates the signing of the Cherokee Nation Constitution on September 4, 1839, one of the first political acts of the Cherokee Nation in Indian Territory after the horrible Trail of Tears. The Cherokee National Holiday is the Cherokees' Fourth of July and has grown into a three-day celebration in Tahlequah, Oklahoma, with scores of events and tens of thousands of attendees. On Saturday, there is a long parade with 150 entries of bands, floats, civil groups, businesses, and horses. After the parade, the state of the nation address is delivered by the principal chief on the capitol square in front of the capitol building. Congressman John Lewis walked the three-mile parade route and shook the hand of every person he could. His attentiveness to the crowd delayed by 20 minutes the parade participants behind him. His presence filled the streets. He was invited to speak at the state of the nation, and in his booming deep voice that reverberated off the capitol building behind him, he spoke of the kindness of the Cherokee people and the things he learned about our history. He concluded by saying, "To my last day in Congress, I will be a friend of the Cherokee people."

A delightful moment showing that everyone is a leader occurred the night before at the powwow. A powwow is not a traditional Cherokee event; it is a gathering of singers and dancers performing Kiowa and other plains tribes' songs and dances. It is offered at the Cherokee National Holiday as an invitation and a welcome to other tribes. The first dance or event at a powwow is the grand entry when the dancers come into the arena single file by class of dancing (e.g., fancy, straight, grass, buckskin, jingle, cloth, and others). Honored guests lead the procession behind the American flag and flags of tribes to the beat and song of the lead drum. It is a colorful event, and it is impressive to see 200 dancers and several singers with drums in the open arena. Congressman John Lewis and I led the grand entry.

After several hours of various dances and protocol, the announcer called for a two step, a woman's choice dance where the woman and her partner holding both hands follow the head man and head lady dancer in a processional two-step dance around the arena. There were hundreds of husbands and wives, boyfriends and girlfriends, and "just friends" dancing. The two step had begun, and all the women and girls were taking their choice out in the arena. Congressman Lewis was standing in the crowd watching and admiring the dancers. A little Indian girl about eight years old came up to Congressman Lewis and said, "Let's dance." Congressman Lewis bent over and replied with his kind and deep voice, "No, young lady, I don't know how to dance." She then grabbed his hand, taking him into the arena, and said with insistence, "All you have to do is move your feet." Congressman Lewis did the two step at the Cherokee National Holiday powwow with a beautiful little girl.

Both were leaders.

She reflected the attribute of ᎤᏟᏂᎩᏛ (ultanigida) strong: be strong in whatever you do; take comfort in the strength of the Creator and your ancestors.

Each of these stories demonstrates leadership by example, a Cherokee cultural attribute. Defining leadership as the process of taking yourself from Point A to Point B means everyone—regardless of role, position, station in life, or job title—is a leader and has a duty to lead from where they are to where they want themselves or their organization to go. For better or worse, all people will take themselves and others somewhere during their lives. With a simple definition of leadership, more people can understand what Wilma Mankiller, the former principal chief of the Cherokee Nation, meant when she said: "Change is what you cause and not what happens to you."

The second lesson is: everyone is a leader. The question is, "Where are you going to lead us?"

CHAPTER 4

6S6°T

Point B
Where You Want to Go

Where there is no vision, the people shall perish.
PROVERBS 29:18

A creative man is motivated by the desire to achieve,
not by the desire to beat others.   AYN RAND

WHERE AND WHAT IS POINT B?

It seems simple enough that in order to lead, you must have an idea of where you want to go. But perhaps our greatest single weakness as people, organizations, and governments is not knowing where we want to go. We want to move but are unsure where. To some, the idea of having a vision seems altruistic, a bit like Don Quixote, the Man from La Mancha, charging windmills. To some, having a dream is a vision while asleep. But a vision is defined in the *Random House College Dictionary* as "imaginative conception or anticipation" and dream as "an aspiration; goal; aim." So for the purposes of this model, *vision* and *dream* are synonymous, even though vision has connotations of the spiritual and academic, and dream has connotations of the emotional and motivational. Visions and dreams for this discussion are logical and imaginative aspirations. Visions and dreams are the result of thought, design, and desire, not divine intervention. Visions and dreams require that we think forward and ask what is possible not only in the next few months but in the next few years or decades.

Which comes first, the determination of Point A (where you are) or Point B (where you want to go)? I don't know that it matters. Understanding where you want to go takes tremendous clarity of thought and drive. Sometimes, to get a glimpse of the future, you need to see the past.

History Course: Why Did We Believe We Could Not Do That?

In 1991, I worked for the late Principal Chief Wilma Mankiller. I was walking down the hall of one of our buildings, and I overheard one person tell the other, "We can't do that, the Bureau of Indian Affairs won't let us." It was a fascinating moment that piqued my curiosity; why did our people believe it, and when did such a fatalistic belief sneak into our national psyche? It was a prevailing thought among employees that the BIA had some strict supervision and veto power over the Cherokee Nation. It was not true. The Cherokee Nation was a sovereign government in the world community of governments before the United States (and the BIA) ever existed, and I believed in our history the Cherokee Nation had always determined its own course. So why did our people believe the Cherokee Nation was something less than the "dependent domestic nation" that the U.S. Supreme Court said it was as early as 1831? Coupled with the idea that our managers needed to know the past in order to make good decisions in the present, I asked Principal Chief Mankiller if I could develop and teach a Cherokee legal history course. Of course, she encouraged me to do so, and I began to assemble everything I could find as source documents: treaties, maps, articles, movies, slides, excerpts from books, random quotes, and more. The course book was organized chronologically and covered Cherokee history from 1700 to the present. In 1991, the 40-hour course was first taught in our historic capitol by me and Pat Ragsdale, who was a director of tribal operations.

After completing the class, one new employee said, "The first day, I got mad; the second day, I wanted to cuss and spit; and the third, I wanted to get a gun and shoot someone. The fourth day, I was just proud to be a Cherokee." The class became a life-changing experience for many. Although I had not believed in the concept of historic grief, I did after teaching the class several times, because by the third day of class, I could sense this cloud of grief rise from the class and dissipate. Those most reluctant about attending a 40-hour history course—because "It's been 30 years since I was in school" or "I have work to do" or "I never liked history anyway" or "I work in maintenance and don't need history"—were the most enthused after completing the class. Some would come to the class with a chip on their shoulder against the white man and the U.S. government because of their understanding of our history. The treatment of the Cherokee Nation by the United States, as laid out with primary documents in the class, was much more brutal than they ever imagined.

However, instead of leaving the class more embittered, the opposite occurred. People left the class understanding that if our ancestors survived horrific episodes—eradication of our people by disease in the 1730s, genocidal warfare by Americans in the 1770s, forced removal in the 1830s, abandonment in the American Civil War, coerced assimilation and liquidation of the Cherokee Nation's resources in 1906, the "Grapes of Wrath" exodus from Oklahoma during the Depression, relocation and termination in the 1950s, and bureaucratic imperialism today—then each of them had a legacy that inspired them with determination to carry on and do better. The result of the class on individual perception and behavior was quite moving. When I took office, we hired Julia Coates, PhD, an outstanding Cherokee college professor, to teach the class full time. Post-class surveys revealed 90 percent of the students reported it changed their lives. Coates received hundreds of personal testimonies from students whose lives the course changed. People took the class over and over. It was the only class I have ever heard of that the daily attendance increased rather than declined. Later, employees were required to attend. To date, more than 10,000 people have completed the course including employees, Cherokee citizens in urban communities, and the general public. It received a best practices award from Harvard

University. It also helped describe Point A for the Cherokee Nation, but even more importantly, it gave a glimpse of what Point B, the future, could be.

100 Year Plan: We Won't Even Be Here Then

How often do we think about the long-term future? As principal chief, the haunting questions were where I was supposed to lead our people and how I was supposed to build our nation. A good place to learn about the future is to study the past. I knew from our research and history class where the Cherokee Nation was economically, socially, politically, and culturally 100 years ago. So the obvious question was, "Where could we be 100 years from now?"

Shortly after my first election, we began discussing a long-term plan for the Cherokee Nation. It is common to have a five-year plan in business. I suggested regaining what U.S. Senator Dawes observed about us over one hundred years ago: every Cherokee owned his home, there was not a pauper in the Nation, and the tribe owed not a dollar. In 1888, the Cherokee Nation was economically self-sufficient; we had a strong sense of identity and culture; and we had cohesive communities that helped individuals in tough times and enjoyed the good times. Today, poverty and social well-being statistics are dismal, and epidemics of methamphetamine use, diabetes, domestic abuse, and other physical and social maladies are staggering. So why not come up with a plan that in a hundred years, we could be where we were one hundred years ago? During the course of a community talk, I mentioned having a 100-year plan. A community member had the gumption to raise her hand and ask the question that many had on their mind. She asked, "Why have a 100-year plan when we won't even be here then?" I answered, "Yes, that is true, we won't be, but who will?" It seemed like a light went on. Everyone in the room then understood that the very reason for having a 100-year plan was the fact that we would not be here. Our children, grandchildren, and generations yet unborn would be. We had a duty, an obligation, a responsibility, and an honor to pass on to our descendants a legacy that we inherited from our ancestors who died before we knew them. We received a gift from those relatives we never knew, because they came generations before us. We knew we must pass it on to those we will never know because they will come generations after us.

It was hard for people to think in 100-year terms, and who could blame them? So in 2003, Mike Miller, our communications officer, produced a videotape shot in a local television news station. It had two six o'clock newscasts portraying events twenty-five years in the future; it was called *2028*. The first scenario was based on the Cherokee Nation following the norms of non-Indian governments where political expediency, self-interest, and short-sightedness were the norms. The news anchors reported high rates of diabetes, crime, methamphetamine use, joblessness, and the death of the last Cherokee speaker. The sports guy reported on Indian stereotype mascot teams playing professional baseball and football. The second television newscast addressed the same issues but in a scenario where the Cherokee Nation adhered to its 100-year plan and made decisions based on cultural principles, what was good for generations to come, and visionary aspirations. The newscast reported Cherokees had a life expectancy five years longer than the majority population, the Nation reacquired one million acres of land, the Cherokee Nation's Delegate to Congress was instrumental in bringing lasting peace to the Mideast, there had been no reported case of methamphetamine use in five years, and a 100-member Cherokee youth choir sang to the President of the United States in Cherokee when he visited the Cherokee Nation. The sports guy reported on the national stickball championship with sellout crowds watching two Cherokee community teams play.

The message of the video was that we had a legacy as people who faced adversity, survived, adapted, prospered, and excelled. *2028* asked questions about what path we would choose. Could we transcend mainstream gang politics and have the discipline to live up to our legacy? Could we, over the course of several generations, come to face emerging adversities with calm, call upon our historical stamina to survive, use our intelligence to adapt, work for prosperity, and demand excellence of ourselves? Did we as a government and people want to have something to show for a day's work and a lifetime's effort? Could we continue our legacy with a 100-year plan?

I gave the 2009 graduation speech ("Want Something") at Sequoyah High School. Ninety of the school's 400 students were graduating. At that time, I thought that my speech was good, would challenge the students to want to be something, and would encourage them to achieve whatever it was that they wanted to be. Here is that speech.

Sequoyah High School Graduation: Want Something
Sequoyah High School Graduation Speech, 2009
Delivered by Principal Chief Chad Smith

What do you do?

Why do you do it?

Answer: It makes me feel good.

A standard graduation speech tells you that you can be anything you want to be. That is true. I suggest you *will be* what you want to be. If you really want something, you will make decisions, consciously and subconsciously, to get it. You will eat, sleep, and work to be what you want to be.

- If you want to be happy, you will do the things that make you happy.

- If you want to cover up pain, you will do the things that cover up pain.

- If you want to watch life go by and cope with the results, you will do the things to cope.

- If you want to excel, you will do things to excel.

For example, if you want be good in basketball, you will think about moves, plays, and strategy. You will practice hard, be at practice on time, study other players, and anticipate situations on the floor. You will live and breathe basketball.

Story: I saw a girl's T-shirt that said, "My boyfriend told me I had to choose between him and basketball. I hope he won't be lonely." One of my sons wanted a University of Oklahoma ring-tone on his phone. For two solid days he navigated through the menu on the phone, called the phone company over and over, and would not quit until he got that ringtone. He wanted it. He got it.

You will become a laborer, bus driver, doctor, or business-person because you want to be one and have made a host of decisions to take you to that occupation. Generally, it is not the big decisions that get you where you want to be but the multi-tude of small, ordinary, everyday decisions. If we know what we want, we will make the decisions to achieve that want. We will get up early, study, and organize our time and resources to learn about and practice becoming what we want to be. If you want a professional job, you choose the college, secure the scholar-ship, outline the curriculum plan, prepare early for class, buy the books early, ask questions, get up early to study, organize your day, engage the teachers, and truly learn about the profes-sion you want.

Leadership is going from point A to point B. Point A is where we are, and Point B is what we want to be. In between, there are opportunities and challenges, but we need the skills to deal with each.

My admonishment and challenge to you is "want to be something." It can be a laborer, a doctor, a teacher, an equip-ment operator, but want to be something! Want something that will allow you to be happy and healthy.

No one can tell you what you want or make decisions for you. Only you can decide what you want and what you will become. Only you will be responsible for your actions, decisions, and what you end up being. Many people never decide what they want to be. They are reluctant and often don't know what they want and as a result fall into traps of deception, of drugs, alco-hol, abuse, and poverty. Do people really want these lives? I sug-gest you begin to understand what you want. If you don't, you may end up with buyer's remorse and realize that you really did not want what you got when the new wears off. Look at what you want and choose to want things that will make you feel good and feel good for a long time. Feeling good is:

- Being happy rather than miserable
- Being healthy rather than being out of shape, addicted to drugs or alcohol
- Being confident rather than insecure
- Being self-reliant rather than living off others
- Being warm hearted rather than cold hearted
- Being large and strong in spirit rather than small and petty
- Being one who gives rather than one who takes

Want an occupation that will make you feel good, such as being:

- Satisfied
- Marketable
- Constructive
- Contributory

When you decide what you want, prepare. J.B. Hunt, who had a very successful trucking business, attributed his success to "filling up in the evening rather than in the morning." What he was saying was to prepare in the evening for the work tomorrow so you will get the most out of the day. At the end of the day, ask yourself, "Do I have something to show for the day's effort? Am I working toward what I want to be?"

Understand that what you think you want might not really be what you want—like buying a new truck and realizing the cost of gas, payments, and insurance is not worth it. But even if you discover what you thought you wanted to be is not actually what you want, don't be discouraged, because you have learned a lot in the effort. But please don't want nothing. Please don't settle.

Because then other people or happenstance will make decisions
for you. You will wander, waste your time and energy, and hope
things will be okay. If you want nothing, you will come to understand you wanted someone else to want for you, to make your
decisions for you, and to take responsibility for you. You will be
what you wanted: which is to be irresponsible.

As you want, you will do and you will become. Want well and
proceed undaunted.

When I wrote this speech, I was wrong.

Sort of.

It might sound odd, but the vast majority of those students, their
parents, and their grandparents did not imagine, much less understand,
all of the job opportunities, occupations, and professions they could pos-
sibly strive for and achieve. They had not seen those achievable occupations because they were often isolated in their communities; they did not
know anyone who held those occupations; their aspirations were often
limited to the minimum wage jobs that were familiar to them.

How could I challenge them to want to be something when they did
not know the range of possible careers? How do you pursue a dream you
have never seen? How do you learn what you do not know?

As principal chief of the Cherokee Nation, I held educational sum-
mits and discussed potential solutions to breaking the cycle of poverty with school administrators throughout northeastern Oklahoma. I
learned that as many of 60 percent of Cherokee children were raised by
their grandparents in core Cherokee areas, because of single-parent families or both parents working to make ends meet. Most of these students,
their parents, and especially their grandparents were not aware of the
career opportunities they could achieve. They felt intimidated and pow-
erless due to the changing economic and technological landscape. They
had little hope because they could not envision successful futures for
themselves and set goals to achieve success.

So what should the Cherokee Nation want? Do Cherokees want to
pass on the great Cherokee legacy? Should they want to regain what they
had 100 years ago? Did enough of our people know our history and cul-

ture to agree on a vision for rebuilding the nation? Did we as a group care about nation building? Was there something better out there for us and our families?

Public Defender: Glimpse of Life

As a public defender in Tulsa County, Oklahoma, in the late 1990s, I represented indigent people in criminal cases. I remember one young man I interviewed in jail when he was waiting to be sentenced by the judge for drug crimes. He had just turned 18 and had lived through a terrible childhood. As a child, he was passed from foster home to foster home, over one-third of his body was burned in an accident, and he had gotten into a lot of trouble stealing and doing drugs. He was the kind of kid that every policeman knew his birthday and was waiting for him to turn 18. He thought he could sway the judge by getting a job. He told me about getting a job at McDonald's. His face lit up as he spoke about being around people, helping others, and not looking over his shoulder wondering if a drug dealer was going to approach him for money he owed. He said with a sense of triumph, "My girlfriend and me don't fight as much." But when he talked about his days dealing drugs and hanging out with gangs, his face turned dark. It dawned on me that this young man had never seen anything in his life but crime, abandonment, and fear. His job at McDonald's gave him a glimpse of a life he never knew was possible: openness, the ability to earn, and security. After listening to him, I understood that many of us just don't know what good things are outside our immediate environment. So how do we find out about them?

First Lawyer I Met: If He Can Do It

In 1975, when I was 25 years old, I worked as a planner for Ross Swimmer, the principal chief of the Cherokee Nation. He was the first lawyer I ever met. I had always thought lawyers, doctors, and bankers were a class so far above me that I could never achieve such status. He was hard working, diligent, and intelligent; he led the Cherokee Nation well. After working for a year for Chief Swimmer, it dawned on me that if he could be a lawyer, I could too. He provided an example of leadership. He let me leave work an hour early each day so I could attend law school at night.

How do you see into the future? How do you envision a vision or dream a dream? Imagination is a good start. Seeing someone else succeed inspires. The sense of accomplishment of building something better is another. And asking the questions "Why not?" or "What if?" is still another way to look to the future. Having confidence or faith there is something better ahead is still another. Many great thinkers, visionaries, philosophers, and leaders understood George Bernard Shaw's statement, "You see things; and you say, 'Why?' But I dream things that never were; and I say, 'Why not?'"

Brainstorming: What If?

One way to answer the question "Why not?" is to ask the question "What if?" A great technique I learned four decades ago during a college class was brainstorming. It is a common exercise in which small groups of four to eight people gather in a circle and within a limited amount of time are required to come up with the greatest number of ideas for solutions to problems as a group with each member contributing. The ideas cannot be discussed on their merits. What happens is some off-the-wall, impractical, out-of-left-field ideas by one team member spawn very feasible and powerful ideas by others, and those spawn even more ideas. It is an exercise to challenge the imagination, not stifle creativity and intentionally not evaluate each idea at the moment. Sometimes we have to unleash and exercise our imagination.

It is difficult to appreciate what you could accomplish if you had a Point B: if you knew where you wanted to go, had a vision, held a dream, strove for a goal, focused your aim, or proceeded toward a destination.

Randy Pausch, the author of a moving book, *The Last Lecture*, evaluated the success of his life by whether he had accomplished his childhood dreams. He concluded that he had a full and meaningful life when he died at the age of 47 from pancreatic cancer because in some form or other he had achieved his childhood dreams. He accomplished being in zero gravity, authoring an article in the *World Book Encyclopedia*, being

Captain Kirk, winning stuffed animals, and being a Disney Imagineer. How many of us could say we had a vision and accomplished it?

We have to understand the value of a Point B and then discover what it is for us or our organization. Point B generally is found by the imagination springing from other ideas, examples, history, and even a glimpse of and desire for something better. It is a challenge to find or establish Point B, but it is rewarding. "Want to" seems to find a way.

ARTICULATE THE VISION

If you want to be successful, it is this simple. Know what you are doing, love what you are doing. And believe in what you are doing.

WILL ROGERS

One of the most important lessons I learned over 12 years as principal chief was to understand and be able to articulate the product I wanted. At first, product was a hard word for me to understand, since it came from corporate business vocabulary and conjured up images of an assembly line with workers packing office accessories into brown boxes. But it made sense when I thought about it, because a product is what you want to produce or achieve; it is the completion of your work. It is Point B. In the language of other disciplines, it is the vision, dream, goal, aim, mission, purpose, work, or achievement that you want to accomplish. It became very apparent that once there was clarity in defining the product, everything else would fall into place. As a result of clearly defining the product, I could determine whether there was value, demand, viability, and feasibility for the product. It was easier to answer the question of whether someone needed or wanted the product. Then I could frame sets of principles to guide decisions to produce the product. With a set of decision principles framed, the processes and activities could be developed. Fundamentally, once I knew the product, I could work backwards to establish the system to produce the product. In government and nonprofit work, there seems to be a tendency to focus on the activities rather than the ultimate goal.

For example, let's say a group of people trying to deal with a town's juvenile crime believe building a youth activity center would help resolve the problem. A building fixes nothing. A building is a means to an end. A building creates only shelter; it does not address the core problem of juvenile delinquency. Constructing a building without more of a plan would be to acknowledge that there is no understanding or articulation of the product. Perhaps after more research, it is discovered that only 20 junior high students are acting out because of tensions at home caused by their parents being part of a massive layoff from the local factory. If the students had constructive jobs after school, it would provide temporary financial help to their families as well as development of social and behavioral skills that the students could use for the rest of their lives. So the product, or Point B, would be responsible junior high students. The product could be measured immediately, in part, by a reduction in incidents of juvenile delinquency. The principle would be to channel the junior high students to constructive uses of their time. The activity would be after-school work for these 20 students, with mentors on the job who coached responsible behavior; pay the students, thus reducing the financial strain at home; and divert their attention from undesirable activities. The youth center building is unnecessary.

Cultural Tourism: Tell Our Story

Another example of understanding the "product," or Point B, was our initiative for cultural tourism within the Cherokee Nation. We had great cultural assets like the Cherokee Nation Female Seminary, the first institution of higher education for women west of the Mississippi River, established in 1846, opened for enrollment in 1851, and now the iconic building for Northeastern State University. There was the Cherokee Nation Supreme Court building, constructed in 1844, the oldest public building in Oklahoma; the National Capitol building, reconstructed after the American Civil War; and the Cherokee National Penitentiary, built in 1877, which required vocational training of its inmates. Also, in the Tahlequah area, there were other historic assets like a "New Deal" Public Works Progress Administration building constructed in 1930; the antebellum Murrell home, which survived the American Civil War;

and the John Ross Cemetery The history of the Cherokee Nation cuts across the spectrum of American history from a unique perspective and displays that history with its tremendous cultural and tourism properties. We understood that cultural tourism was a growing industry in the United States and the world. Here was an opportunity to teach our history to our local neighbors and to our own people. It would stimulate other businesses such as food and beverage, arts and craft, and other hospitality operations. But it was an industry that required a large initial investment for renovation of historic properties, marketing and advertising, and integration of amenities.

What is the product of cultural tourism? Several months of discussions, drafting, and redrafting yielded no satisfactory result. Long paragraphs of "whereas," "at the same time," "while," and other language connectors convoluting any meaning were drafted, redrafted and discarded. After some frustration, we adopted a rule: if we could not state the product of cultural tourism in 10 words or less, then we missed the point. Finally, the product was determined. It was so obvious, it came as an epiphany. A simple answer is often a sign that you are successful. The product of cultural tourism was to "tell our story." With the product articulated, everything else fell into place. It provided the answer to questions such as how and which cultural properties were to be restored or remodeled; how to design the tour and travel bus routes; how to draft brochures, scripts, and advertising; and who to hire. To "tell our story" was Point B for cultural tourism.

DECLARATION OF DESIGNED PURPOSE: WHAT WAS POINT B FOR THE CHEROKEE NATION?

For no man nor race is endowed with these qualifications without a Designed Purpose.

REDBIRD SMITH

After I was elected in 1999, I felt like the dog that chases a bus: what does he do when he catches it? The government was in such disarray that it was difficult to know where to start the reconstruction. I had to answer three key questions: What was the Cherokee Nation? Where did we want it to go? What was best for our Nation?

Having studied our history, I found the first question relatively simple. The Cherokee Nation was a government, as expressed in the Act of Union of 1839, that existed "before the memory of men." The Cherokee Nation was also a cultural group, a regional economic development agency, a social service provider, a family of families, and a community of communities.

Where did we want the Cherokee Nation to go in 1999? It seemed clear that we should publish a plan outlining where we should take the Nation. We needed to articulate our product, or Point B. After months and months of work groups, community participation, review by native speakers and thinkers, common sense, and the guidance of Kyle Smith, we developed the outline of a long range plan. It articulated our vision, guiding principles, desired outcomes, attributes, statement of work, organizational structure, history, short-term objectives, and budget cycle processes. It was titled "Declaration of Designed Purpose."

We came to understand that becoming a "happy and healthy people" was Point B was for the Cherokee Nation. The preamble and overview of the "Declaration of Designed Purpose" that was provided to each of our employees explained the "designed purpose" and served as the manual for reaching Point B.

Declaration of Designed Purpose:
Preamble

Sometimes people ask me, "Why have a Cherokee Nation? What purpose does it serve today?" For me, the simple answer is that the Cherokee Nation and its history and culture are our legacy, and it enriches our lives, families, and communities. It gives us strength in times of challenge, it gives us comfort when we are weak, and it gives us a sense of identity and value. It sustains us and gives us direction and a vision for the future. As citizens of the Cherokee Nation, it is important that we listen to the wisdom of the Creator, our ancestors, and our elders to gain a better understanding of where our vision should take us. And the wisdom of our ancestors tells us that Cherokees are a special people, with a special purpose.

"I have always believed that the Great Creator had a great design for my people, the Cherokees. I have been taught that from my childhood up, and now in my mature manhood I recognize it as a great truth. Our forces have been dissipated by the external forces, perhaps it has been just training, but we must now get together as a race and render our contribution to mankind. We are endowed with intelligence, we are industrious, we are loyal, and we are spiritual but we are overlooking the particular Cherokee mission on earth, for no man or race is endowed with these qualifications without a designed purpose."

REDBIRD SMITH

1918

Our designed purpose is to become a happy and healthy people, and to pass that on as our legacy to future generations.

The Legacy of the Cherokee Nation

A legacy is often defined as a gift from our ancestors—our parents, our grandparents, our ancestors—all the way back to time immemorial. We, as citizens of the Cherokee Nation, have received a legacy that has cost thousands of lives, millions of acres of land, and immeasurable grief, suffering, turmoil, and tribulations. The Cherokee legacy is that we are a people who face adversity, survive, adapt, prosper, and excel.

We see that legacy in the many episodes of our history. In the 1730s, we lost half our population to smallpox because of exposure to disease carried by commercial traders from England and France. In the 1770s, we faced the genocidal wars of Great Britain and the United States, which were intended to wipe us from the face of this continent.

In the 1830s, we faced the political and legal battles to save our homeland and existence. That episode resulted in the Trail of Tears, on which we lost 4,000 of our 16,000 people on the 850-mile death march from Tennessee to Indian Territory in the middle of the winter of 1838–1839. We faced those adversities, survived, and adapted. After the Trail of Tears, we built a sophisticated society and restored our government to serve our needs. We had two passions of self-governance: law and education. In furtherance of our belief in the law, we adopted an Act of Union and a Constitution in 1839. In 1844, we built our Supreme Court Building, the first public building in Indian Territory. We went on to build a National Capitol Building, a National Prison, and nine district courthouses. To advance our other passion of education, we built the first institution of higher education for women west of the Mississippi River, the Cherokee Female Seminary, which opened in 1851. We then built the Male Seminary and went on to build 150 day schools throughout the Cherokee Nation. Ninety percent of our people were literate in our own language.

The Civil War was devastating to the Cherokee Nation. Two-thirds of our people fought for the North and one-third for the South. More than 2,500 Cherokees died, leaving behind 4,000 widows and orphans. The Cherokee Nation suffered greater human and property loss than states in the Deep South per capita. We recovered from that episode even after the United States enacted a retribution treaty against us in 1866. Then came the ugliest chapter in our relationship with the United States government: allotment. It was the design of the United States to forcibly assimilate us and terminate our government so that Cherokee lands could be opened up for non-Indian settlement. Historically, the Cherokee way was to hold land as a tribe, but in 1906 the common title of Cherokee lands was divided among individual Cherokee citizens as individual allotments. By 1920, the American policy to get our lands was so successful that we had lost 90 percent of our land. No longer did we have the protection of common title to our lands. We became dependent on a cash economy.

We suffered, again, in the Great Depression and the Oklahoma Dust Bowl. Between 1930 and 1940, half of our Cherokee population left Oklahoma for Texas and California. The "Grapes of Wrath" migration was an economic Trail of Tears for Cherokees. There were also the relocation programs in the 1950s and 1960s designed to further the policy of forced assimilation and termination.

In 1975, we adopted a superseding Cherokee Nation Constitution and began our efforts to revive the Cherokee Nation. In 1976, a federal judge found that the Bureau of Indian Affairs had practiced a policy of "bureaucratic imperialism" since 1906. The BIA had wrongfully prevented the Cherokee Nation from exercising its governmental rights. The political Dark Ages of the Cherokee Nation came to an end.

The Future of the Cherokee Nation

That's where we come from. But where should the Cherokee Nation go? In what direction are we headed? The answer is to become a happy, healthy Nation and pass on our legacy.

That legacy carries with it a duty, a burden, a responsibility, and an obligation to carry on and give those gifts to our children and future generations. But far greater than that duty is the immeasurable honor we have to carry on this legacy. This legacy inspires us to achieve our designed purpose of becoming a happy and healthy people.

One hundred years from now, our great-grandchildren will judge our decisions of today. Either we will be economically self-reliant (supporting ourselves, our families, and our communities), enjoy an enriching cultural identity (knowing our history, arts, culture, language, traditions, and wisdom), and be cohesively bound to the community in a spirit of ᎦᏚᎩ (gadugi), or we will pick up a dusty history book and find a footnote, "Once there was a great Cherokee Nation, but it is no more." We must make that choice now, as a people, about which future we choose.

This is our legacy, this is our challenge, this is our honor, and this is our designed purpose: to be a happy, healthy people and pass our distinctly Cherokee way of life on to future generations. We must decide whether to embrace this great legacy and pass it on with all the value ascribed to it. Or, by choice or default, we could allow this legacy to lapse. This declaration is a plan to pass on our legacy and achieve our designed purpose so that in 100 years we will have descendants who joyfully and gratefully receive that legacy, individually and as a Nation, to face adversity, survive, adapt, prosper, and excel. We hope they, too, will work to create a happy, healthy Cherokee Nation for the generations that follow.

Chad Smith
Principal Chief

Following the preamble was the overview, which clarified and articulated the "what and where" of Point B. I believed that the "designed purpose" and vision was for Cherokees to become a happy and healthy people. This declaration provided a clear understanding of where the Cherokee Nation should go in the next 100 years and how to get there. To provide clarity, we offered a series of statements and steps that went from broad and general to narrow and specific.

Declaration of Designed Purpose:
Overview

A Happy and Healthy People

"Where there is no vision, the people perish."

PROVERBS 29:18

The DESIGNED PURPOSE OR VISION for the Cherokee Nation is what we ultimately want to achieve: to become a happy and healthy people. The vision begins with a look at the past. A little more than 100 years ago, the Cherokee Nation had a sophisticated government with a Supreme Court Building, a National

Capitol, a penitentiary, nine courthouses, an outstanding educational system with two higher education institutions, 150 day schools, and 90 percent literacy in the Cherokee language. U.S. Senator Henry L. Dawes, at the Lake Mohonk Conference in 1883, stated:

The head chief told us that there was not a family in that whole nation that had not a home of its own. There was not a pauper in that nation, and the nation did not owe a dollar. It built its own capitol, in which we had this examination, and built its schools and its hospitals. Yet the defect of the system was apparent. They have got as far as they can go, because they own their land in common. It is Henry George's system, and under that there is no enterprise to make your home any better than that of your neighbors. There is no selfishness, which is at the bottom of civilization. Till this people will consent to give up their lands, and divide them among their citizens so that each can own the land he cultivates, they will not make much more progress.

How could a society improve upon a system that had no poverty, every family had a home, and the government had no debt? If we are to be a happy, healthy people, 100 years from now our great grandchildren will have what we had 100 years ago: no poverty, every family in their home, and a debt-free Cherokee Nation. These are symbols of a happy, healthy Cherokee society.

"Happy" means living a fulfilled life and becoming strong and self-reliant as a result of responsible and self-confident decisions, where we use our Cherokee language and practice our Cherokee life ways. It is also a life in which we practice ᏍᏉ (gadugi) and enjoy family, friends, community, Nation, and country.

"Healthy" refers to the soundness and vibrancy of body, mind, heart, and soul. We live in safe homes and communities, surrounded by family, friends, and community members who look out for the well-being of others.

In many ways, we want to repeat the success of our past and use our cultural attributes to guide us in the future.

A happy, healthy Cherokee Nation does not have to be distant, vague, or abstract. It is as present and concrete as one's own life. The vision is achieved by practicing ᏍᏓᏳ (gadugi) and other cultural values. In a happy, healthy Cherokee Nation, Cherokees are satisfied with their own personal achievements and have happy and functional families, strong and supportive communities, and a vibrant and enduring tribal government.

In a happy, healthy Cherokee Nation, Cherokees have the careers they choose, they wisely determine their own destinies, and they have families who enjoy each other's company and share in each other's challenges. Communities in a happy, healthy Cherokee Nation are growing places with nearby career opportunities, so we can keep our close-knit bond and cultural identity strong. Our tribal government in a happy, healthy Cherokee Nation is one our citizens can be proud of and want to take part in.

Every individual Cherokee must do his or her part for us to be a happy, healthy Cherokee Nation, and the Cherokee Nation government and its employees must do their part as well.

Just recently, I came across a quotation from Beatles founding member John Lennon (1940–1980): "When I was five years old, my mother always told me that happiness was the key to life. When I went to school, they asked me what I wanted to be when I grew up. I wrote down 'happy.' They told me I didn't understand the assignment, and I told them they didn't understand life." Perhaps "happy and healthy" is a Point B not just for Cherokees.

We can see our opportunities in the study of civilizations past and present. As we decide our future, there are lessons to guide and teach us if we choose to heed them. How do you validate a vision or goal? Perhaps the most essential goal for all mankind is to become a happy and healthy people. In Turkey, often referred to as the cradle of civilization, the Turkish have been ruled by four empires: Greek, Roman, Byzantine, and Ottoman. Now Turkey is a democracy. The Turkish are industrious and hospitable. How do we evaluate the success of a civilization? There is no better place to start than Turkey. What happened in each of those civilizations that caused them to grow but then die? What were the influences that fostered success but then failure? What was the quality of life under each civilization? What were the principles each was based? What mistakes can we avoid if we study them? Should we measure the value of our society, our government, our Nation, and our civilization not by how many empires have risen and fallen, how many mansions we have, or how many of our jet airplanes can fly 300 people 600 miles? I believe great civilizations are measured by whether the population is happy and healthy.

In Turkey and other civilizations, we have seen the rise and fall of a number of societies and governments. We can learn from records and architectural ruins what worked and what did not work for the last 3,000 years. We see things built to last not five years but thousands of years. The answer to these questions can give us guidance for our decision making today.

At times our situations seem overwhelming, but it is small decisions that will determine what we, our families, and our Nation will become for generations. No matter how small or trite they may appear, every decision directs our path. Do we eat wholesome food at the table with our family, or do we pick up fast food and eat it in the car on the way home? Do we do our homework and prepare for the next day, or do we rush about in the morning unprepared for our daily tasks? Do we tell our children goodnight and remind them of values that will give them confidence, patience, and happiness, or do we yell "goodnight" across the house while watching television?

The combination of small, ordinary, everyday decisions creates fulfilling lives and great civilizations that can last for hundreds of years.

Right to Succeed: Define Ourselves

Is it the goal of all great civilizations and societies to become happy and healthy? As we articulate our vision, it is a marvelous but sometimes frightening concept that we and we alone must hammer out our future.

"The Right to Succeed" was my January 2008 column in the *Cherokee Advocate* addressing the fact that deciding Point B is our decision and no one else's.

"The Right to Succeed"
By Chad Smith, Principal Chief

Perhaps the greatest choice we make is how to define ourselves and decide our future. Every one of us determines who we are and what we do with our lives. No one else does. We cannot blame anyone else for our personal identity and what we do with our opportunities and challenges.

We are all alike and born equal in the sense that each one of us gets up each day with the right to decide what we are going to make of that day and what we are going to do with our lives. We can define ourselves as self-reliant or as a victim. The person who takes responsibility for his life and is self-reliant has a happy and more productive life. He accepts opportunities and challenges and makes the best of them. He spends his time figuring out how he can make the best of a situation rather than blaming someone else.

On the other hand, a person can choose to be a victim and surrender his opportunities and challenges to someone else and blame everyone—his family, his neighbors, the Cherokee Nation, or even the Creator—because he does not have what he wants or expects.

People with a victim mentality become weak and bitter because they have not taken the time and expended the energy to understand a situation and to deal with it. I hear people complain and blame others every day when they have not taken the first step to help themselves or others.

The whole idea of the Cherokee Nation as a tribal nation is to help people help themselves, to help them take control of their lives and not to succumb to a victim mentality. Sometimes elected officials want to throw money at people and claim to be helping them, but the way to really help takes more work than spending the tribe's money on social services.

Our efforts today focus on creating jobs so our people can support themselves and their families, revitalizing our language so we can be directed by our cultural wisdom, and promoting a sense of community.

I was at one of our gaming operations for a meeting, and as I left I was greeted by a large young man who was full-blood Cherokee. He worked for Cherokee Nation Enterprises and was very pleasant. I did not know what he wanted to talk about, but as he began, he beamed with pride.

He said, "You know, you talked to me four years ago and told me to apply myself. Well, I took your advice and did. Then I was making $8 an hour. I applied myself, worked hard, and got promotions. I am a manager today and make $20 an hour. I can pay my house and car payments and buy any shoes for my kids that they want. I enjoy my job. I want all my family and kin to know that if they apply themselves, they can make something out of themselves."

He was one of a thousand success stories that the Cherokee Nation has helped by helping him to help himself. He defined himself as a success, not a victim. With the great Cherokee history and culture and Cherokee examples of success, how can we accept something less than defining ourselves as self-reliant and not a victim? We should define ourselves as strong, not weak; self-reliant, not dependent; happy, not miserable; successes, not failures; survivors, not victims. We have lived too long with low expectations for ourselves and our children.

As Joe Grayson, our deputy principal chief, said, "You give a Cherokee a chance and he can do anything he wants. We can even put a Cherokee on the moon writing Cherokee in the dust, if we set our mind to it."

Perhaps with this New Year we need to define or reaffirm our definition of ourselves similar to what Redbird Smith said

100 years ago. He said, "We are loyal; we are industrious; we are intelligent; and we are spiritual." None of those values include playing the victim or blaming others for our choices. In 2008, we should help each other put aside victimhood and choose to define ourselves as the self-reliant people that Cherokees have been for centuries.

Is "becoming a happy and healthy people" anything more than fancy words in a bound report on the third shelf in an office at the Cherokee Nation? It is not only a vision that can be articulated, but it is one we capture on occasion.

Christmas All Year Long: It Is the Small Things

My brother, Shane Smith, and I wrote a screenplay decades ago titled *WXMS*. It was about a father who ran a radio station and had lost the appreciation of his family and community. After a traumatic experience that caused him to gain a better perspective, he decided to run a radio station whose format all year long was Christmas music so it would lift people's spirits and encourage them to embrace their family and friends. A glimpse of what a happy and healthy people looks like is found in "Moments of Christmas," my letter to employees of December 23, 2004 (see sidebar).

"Moments of Christmas"
Letter to Employees
By Chad Smith, Principal Chief

Dear Employee,

I want to wish each of you a Merry Christmas and Happy New Year. Holidays change for us as we grow older. When we were young, it seemed like an eternity before Christmas came around as we anxiously anticipated holiday gatherings, family reunions, and, of course, presents under the tree. As we get older, Christmas has a tendency to sneak up on us.

Now, at this time of year, we begin to see things in a different light, one that reminds us of the true Christmas spirit. I recall at Fairfield church a young Cherokee girl, probably 12 or 14, sitting in the front row of the church, putting her arm around her grandmother during the services. At the Sequoyah High School chapel during their Christmas pageant, I heard Cherokee children all around me, lifting their voices in songs in our Cherokee language. Along the routes of the nighttime Christmas parades, I saw excitement in young children's faces, peeking out of blankets and hooded coats, hoping to receive bits of candy and anticipating the arrival of Santa Claus. It is meaningful to see our Cherokee Nation employees and their children riding on the floats, walking alongside handing out candy, even leaving the parade boundaries to make sure the little ones received a piece of candy. Of course, it's the small things—a smile, a handshake, and kind words—that are most meaningful and remind us that Christmas is about peace on Earth and goodwill to men.

Sometimes it is hard to get past the shopping, the hustle and bustle, and the consumer-driven advertising to catch these wonderful glimpses of the Christmas spirit. I encourage each of us to look for Christmas spirit as we go about our everyday chores, to appreciate these glimpses of kindness, and to actually pass some of those meaningful moments on by expressing our appreciation of our families, friends, communities, tribal citizens, and to each other.

Yes, happy and healthy does not have to be seasonal.

POINT B IS REACHABLE

Actual knowledge of the future was never lower, but hope was never higher. Confidence will beat prediction anytime.

WILL ROGERS
Sept. 19, 1923

Who Would Have Thought?

One of the great blessings I had as principal chief was that I saw visions attained and dreams come true. I would not have believed 10 years ago what our staff could accomplish in that time.

In 1999, when I was running for principal chief, I attended a community meeting where my opponent quickly put together a handful of young Cherokee students to sing in Cherokee. Their appearance was shabby, they were disorganized, and the performance was poor. I felt bad for the students pushed into such a situation. Could we do better than that? Could we have a Cherokee youth choir to be the counterpart to the Mormon Tabernacle Choir, even though it may not be as large? After all, gospel music sung is nice, and when sung by children it is beautiful, and when gospel music is sung by children in Cherokee, it is angelic. As one elderly Cherokee woman remarked, "I was surprised God spoke English; I thought he spoke only the most dignified Cherokee." Although there were no Cherokee speakers under 50 years old, could we teach young people to sing in Cherokee?

Youth Choir: Positive Unintended Consequences

We knew our Cherokee language was dying, and language is the vessel of cultural intelligence. How could we revitalize our language? We hired a choir director and Cherokee speaker to recruit children for a youth choir, teach them to sing Cherokee, and perform at community events. We challenged the director and her assistant to develop the "Cherokee Mormon Tabernacle Choir." As with all things in development, the first several years were slow, and the choir faced challenges. But soon they grew from 10 members to 40, the quality of their singing improved, they appeared more places, and more requests came in. Individual choir members grew in confidence and leadership. We produced and published 10 CDs of Cherokee gospel and patriotic music; we finished a CD of Motown in Cherokee language just for the fun of it. The Cherokee National Youth Choir has won numerous Native American Music Awards, was inducted into the Oklahoma Music Hall of Fame, and has performed at the White House for President Bush and at Ground Zero, the Kennedy Center in Washington D.C., the National Museum of the American Indian, and the Macy's Thanksgiving Day Parade in New York City. They performed with Dolly Parton, Vince Gill, The Oakridge Boys, the Tulsa Pops Symphony, and others. Their CDs are played in Cherokee households and at daycares and funerals. A positive unintended consequence that should have been obvious when I started the choir was that the choir was not only a means to revitalize our Cherokee language and advance cultural attributes, but it also developed leaders. Every trip the choir took, the bus drivers, hosts, attendees, and casual observers remarked how polite, positive, and pleasant the members were. There are 120 students who have been in the youth choir, and they offer story after story of how singing Cherokee before audiences, visiting new places, representing the Cherokee Nation, and taking responsibility for their musical part and as ambassadors has changed and improved their lives.

Choir director Mary Kay Henderson tells a story about the time a full bus load of the choir was driving toward Stillwater, Oklahoma, and stopped at a roadside mom-and-pop grocery store for the choir members to go to the bathroom and get snacks. The cashier was the owner and only attendant in the store when the 30 choir members, age 12 to 18 years old, came in. Mary Kay said the owner was not happy, and you could see the stress on the older lady's face; she was thinking that this pack of kids would shoplift her blind and mess up her bathrooms. After 15 minutes of milling around in the small store, the choir members got all their snacks and drinks and boarded the bus. As Mary Kay was doing a "nose count" to make sure everyone was on the bus, the owner came out of the store looking mad and knocked on the bus door. Mary Kay said her heart sank thinking that the owner was going to complain that one of the choir members had done something wrong. The owner had Mary Kay step out of the bus, and the owner told her, "You know, I get a lot of people and kids through here, and yours were the most polite good kids I have ever seen. I just wanted to let you know." The lady turned with a smile. Such stories were not the exception; they were the rule.

When students join the choir, they receive a medal recognizing them as ambassadors of the Cherokee Nation, and each member has performed that role well. So an off-the-cuff idea grew into a project that changed the lives of scores of Cherokee youth, touched the hearts of thousands of Cherokees who listened to the music of the choir, and promoted the learning of our language. People often ask, "Who would have thought 10 years ago that the choir would be what it is today?"

Hard Rock: On the Back of a Napkin

Hard Rock Tulsa is one of six Hard Rock hotel-casinos in the world. It is the premier destination resort in Oklahoma. It is owned by the Cherokee Nation. A decade ago, the Cherokee Nation's gaming operation was high stakes bingo, making $3 million a year and employing 500. It was run like a mom-and-pop business. In 2000, I asked David Tippeconnic to become the chairman of the board of the Cherokee Nation's gaming operations. The Cherokee Nation separated businesses from the government for operations and management. Tippeconnic was the former CEO of Citgo, and a Cherokee and Comanche. He knew how to run a major business, to demand business cases for decisions, and to recruit business talent. We moved David Stewart, a Cherokee CPA who was the CEO of Cherokee Nation Industries, an aerospace and wire harness business that the Cherokee Nation owned, to run the gaming operations. Literally, on the back of a napkin were plans drawn to improve gaming operations and build the Tulsa, Oklahoma, property into a regional destination resort property. By 2011, the businesses of the Cherokee Nation had 5,500 employees and made an annual profit over $100 million. What started out as a 60,000 square foot sheet metal building became Oklahoma's premier resort destination with a 400-room hotel, 1,200 slot machines, six restaurants, a world-class golf course, and a premier concert hall. Again, people often remark, "Who would have thought 10 years ago you could pick up a travel magazine on an airplane and see our Tulsa Hard Rock?"

Sequoyah High School: Become the School of Choice

Sequoyah Schools (grades 9–12) is a Bureau of Indian Affairs boarding school located in Tahlequah, Oklahoma. Its history goes back to the

American Civil War when the Cherokee Nation established an orphanage due to the loss of life by Cherokees fighting on both sides, which displaced many Cherokee children from their families. In 1906, the federal government took over operations and established it as an orphan training school and then later as a boarding school. My dad graduated from Sequoyah in 1940 and was pleased to have three meals a day, a warm place to sleep, and an opportunity to learn a machine shop trade. He would fondly tell stories of his friends who worked in different parts of the school. Everyone was required to do chores and learn a trade. On Saturday night, he would meet one friend at the bakery and sneak out a loaf of freshly baked bread, meet another friend at the kitchen and get a pot of beans, and then they would go by the well house where milk was stored from the milking operations and sneak out a quart of milk. They would all climb Bald Hill, take the center out of the loaf of bread, pour the beans in the hollowed-out loaf and, as my dad would say, "have a meal fit for a king." It was a home for hundreds of children who, because of the Depression or dysfunctional families, would have otherwise had no hope for a safe and comfortable life.

By the time I took office as principal chief, the school had been contracted by the Cherokee Nation for operation but had gained a reputation as a school of last resort. People remarked that you went to Sequoyah if you got kicked out of other schools. Capacity was 350 students, but it had an enrollment of only 205. I wanted to build a leadership academy out of respect for my dad. We recruited staff and coaches, imposed admission guidelines, and invested in facilities and curriculum. Since that time, Sequoyah has become a "School of Choice" (the school's motto), and enrollment is over capacity with 150 students on a waiting list. By 2011, the school's sports teams had excelled with state championships, 44 students had received Gates Millennium Scholarships, and students enjoyed current interests such as robotics, music, art, and drama. Today every student works on an Apple computer, and there is no armed security or fences. Sequoyah enjoys a sense of family and leadership. Thousands of family and community members attend football and basketball games in support of the students striving for excellence. Alumni and community people say, "Who would have thought 10 years ago that Sequoyah would be what it is today?"

Each of these successes occurred because we shared a vision and strategy, memorialized in the "Declaration of Designed Purpose," and we had "horses and fishes."

Determining where and what Point B is becomes a rewarding challenge. It goes to simple fundamentals. It is often difficult to articulate. What is it that you really want, and is it clear enough in your mind to articulate? Tommy Tucker, a college campus minister and pilot of the Cherokee Nation's twin engine plane for 39 years, said there were three rules to getting something done. One: externalize the idea by getting it out of your head and writing it down. Two: visualize the idea by posting the writing somewhere that you will see it often each day. And three: give it to someone else to have them hold you accountable each week to get it done. Tucker's rules are a good way to clarify your thoughts and articulate Point B.

The third lesson is to envision where you want to go. The question is, "Can you see where you want to be in several years?"

ized they did not know where they were or how to get back to camp in the dark. They had to know where they were in order to get back to camp. That was one of the skills scouting taught. Someone must know where he is to begin to lead.

ROAD MAP: JOURNEYS START WITH A GPS

We must know where we are to find the path to where we want to go. We must establish Point A, a beginning, to navigate to Point B, an end. Just like getting directions from a global positioning system (GPS) in the car or using a smartphone, you must enter a "start" and an "end." For individuals, identifying Point A involves a humbling self-assessment of one's physical, intellectual, and creative status, as well as an external environmental assessment. Aspects of Point A include place, time, social position, economics, spirituality, views of family, hometown, community of friends, relationships, etc. Determining Point A includes knowing your strengths, weaknesses, opportunities and challenges. The humility reached in determining Point A gives you the confidence of knowing all about yourself and how you connect with your environment.

For institutions, determining Point A is not much different; it requires making an assessment and taking an inventory of the strengths and weaknesses of the organization, including its competitive advantages and intelligence, and then determining its market position and the nature of its market. Often that determination is called a SWOT analysis (strengths, weaknesses, opportunities and threats).

Point A is not only a snapshot of where you or your organization is at this moment in time, it also is the recognition of where you have been and what experience, knowledge, education, and intelligence you carry with you. For the Cherokee Nation, it was critical to know our history to determine where we were and where we wanted to go. The adage "If you don't know where you have been, how do you know where you are going?" has wisdom. Our history course gave a clear and often graphic picture of where the Cherokee Nation had been and established a sound identity for its citizens.

Crossroads Letter: What Are the Epidemics We Face?

For the Cherokee Nation, it was critical to study our history to have a clear understanding of Point A, the national character of the Nation, and where it fit into the social, governmental, cultural, and economic environment. "Crossroads" is a September 2003 column I wrote for the *Cherokee Advocate* that addresses socially and culturally where many of our people were. To some degree, it reflected our Point A.

"Crossroads"
By Chad Smith, Principal Chief

Today, I believe that we are at a critical crossroads as a Nation, as communities, and as individual citizens. We must come face-to-face with a serious weakness that has become epidemic. We see symptoms of the trouble in the growth of diabetes, the clamor for free housing and social services, and the devastating effects of methamphetamine production and use.

This epidemic has blinded many of us to our own abilities, responsibilities, and opportunities. Our vision is cloudy, and we often stumble and grasp for things to help us stand. But the things that we take hold of are not things that build us up. They are props that hold us up, barely keeping us from falling.

Over the past four years, I have observed many things. Too many of my observations didn't reflect what I've always held to be true characteristics of the Cherokee people.

Instead of seeing strength, I often see weakness.

Instead of responsibility, I often see people blaming each other.

Instead of self-reliance by planning to improve, diligently working, and doing a good job, I often see a sense of dependency on subsidized housing, free health care, scholarships, and donated foods.

Instead of leadership, I often see confusion.

Instead of tribal patriotism, I often see efforts to destroy the Cherokee Nation's sovereignty.

Instead of ᏍᏚᏯ (gadugi), I often see destructive selfishness.

I have heard people immediately after getting their Cherokee citizenship card ask for the list of free things they are entitled to as tribal members.

This is not the Cherokee way. It will lead to the demise of the Cherokee Nation.

Last year, I met with a 22-year-old college student and mother of one. She expressed to me how she wanted an Indian house while she was going to school and how disappointed she was that I could not give her one. She began to cry. I explained that usually students go to school to get an education so they can get a better job to earn enough money to buy a home. She did not understand. She thought she was entitled to a free home—right now.

Thankfully, not everyone who comes to the Cherokee Nation feels or acts this way. But stories like this show us that some of us have an odd perspective. That perspective is: "I am entitled to free things simply because it is my right as a Cherokee citizen." This perspective becomes an attitude that has devastating effects on our Nation. If we continue enabling a dependency mindset, we will become weaker and weaker as a people.

But let me also say, there are Cherokees who need our help. We as a Nation, as a people, and as their Cherokee kin should help them. But those who can help themselves should help themselves. We need to be in the business of helping people help themselves. Nothing real or worthwhile is gained by doing for those who can do for themselves.

I've heard our Cherokee people say "No one owes us a living," and that is true. Not the federal, state, or tribal governments. Not the business world or society in general. Not our parents, children, or relatives. How many of us have forgotten that a living is earned? Jobs, houses, scholarships, and quality lifestyles are not given to us, they are earned.

While the picture of the Cherokee Nation I see contains warnings, it also abounds with promise. The greater picture begins with images of the past; it is freshly painted with the present and is unfinished for the future. It is full of people, places, and acts. ᎦᏚᎩ (gadugi) is working together for the benefit of the community. And ᎦᏚᎩ (gadugi) is the critical tool and skill we must practice today to reach the tomorrow we all want.

The Cherokee Nation is a family of families, community of communities, and a nation of people. The Cherokee Nation must choose to be economically self-reliant, to have an enriching cultural identify, and to have a healthy tribal government. History and the well-being of our children provide only one answer. I submit to you: we must proceed with the vision of rebuilding our Nation.

My 10-year-old daughter, Anaweg, loves to climb the magnolia tree on Capitol Square. What a great experience. She and her siblings and friends will climb high into the tree, giggle, and enjoy themselves in their adventure. It makes my heart light to see our children full of life, energy, and anticipation—enjoying themselves on the sacred ground of our historic capitol. It is the history and future of this ground that makes it sacred. And 25 years from now, my daughter and her generation of Cherokees will judge us on what we did to pass on our great legacy.

ᎦᏚᎩ (gadugi). We must live by it. Not because it is the right thing to do—even though it is. Not because it is the strategic process to save the Cherokee Nation—even though it is. But because it is the principle, the perspective, and the opportunity for us to pause and enjoy ourselves, our lives, and our kin by doing something worthwhile. By sharing, we receive. By coaching, we build. By working, we become stronger. By listening, we understand. By respecting each other, we endure.

The assessment of where we are as people and organizations and our relationship to our environment or market must be thorough to understand clearly Point A. Such an inventory and evaluation will tell us not only where we are starting a journey but what improvements we need to make, what tools we need to acquire, what intelligence we need to gather, and what map we need to draw.

Responsibility: Accept Responsibility with Pride

Just as it is our responsibility to determine where we want to go, it is also our responsibility to determine where we are. Personal responsibility drives leadership as addressed in "Getting Their Stories Straight," my letter to employees on June 29, 2001.

"Getting Their Stories Straight"
By Chad Smith, Principal Chief

Dear Employee,

You are aware that every day we receive many visitors to the Cherokee Nation. Some of these visitors are here on business and others just passing through. Recently, an employee was overheard complaining to a visitor of changes in her department. It seems that her working environment had been reorganized, and she did not like the changes. The visitor asked what recommendations or suggestions she had to make the work go better. The employee looked dumbfounded. She was surprised that in response to her complaints someone would expect her to make a constructive recommendation.

Several years ago, we were visiting an Indian family when a 20-year-old nephew and his wife arrived, parking behind us. When we got ready to leave, I asked them to move their car. The nephew went outside, opened the hood of the car, connected the battery, and started the car. I asked him what was wrong. He said the engine would not turn off when he turned the key off, so he had to disconnect the battery. When I asked if they had tried to fix it, his wife spoke up, saying that they had called two mechanics on the phone and gotten different answers. She then said, "They can't even get their stories straight!" I thought, "Why in the world would this young couple think that mechanics, over the telephone, without even looking at the car, could give them a proper diagnosis? And why would the mechanics, not even knowing one another, need to 'get their stories straight?'"

Both of these stories illustrate a willingness to blame someone else for our own lack of responsibility. It is easy to sit back and complain, but it is a different matter to take responsibility for a situation and resolve it. To solve a problem, one must identify the problem and then find a solution. Complaining without a recommendation for a solution is only half an effort. Many times, people want something fixed but want someone else to do it for them.

At a conference recently, I heard a full-blood, traditional Navajo speak to a group of 250 Navajos. He and his wife, who also was a Navajo-speaking full-blood, had raised four children who all went to college and maintained their traditional lives. The group was lively and comical. At the end of his talk he said, "You know, some people think someone owes them a living; but they don't. No one owes any of us a living." His comment was well received by this traditional group.

I firmly believe the traditional Cherokees believe the same. *No one owes us a living.* Understanding that, and acting upon that understanding to fix or accomplish things ourselves, is the definition of accepting responsibility. When we find ourselves faced with problems, it is our duty to find a solution, to make a recommendation or suggestion to make things better. Change is going to happen whether we control change or it controls us.

Each of us has the duty to set goals for ourselves, achieve those goals, manage change, solve problems, and to make our work better. Our responsibility is to serve the Cherokee people, not our own interests. One does not build confidence in our government if the community only hears complaints. Let's take the initiative and accept that responsibility with pride.

Understanding Point A, where we begin, brings humility, perspective, and confidence from which we can start a journey, build responsive and effective institutions, achieve a dream, and reach Point B. The Google Earth satellite maps that zoom down to your backyard offer a vivid example of understanding Point A geographically. With the touch of a button, you can sense your relationship with the world. The pop-art poster of the food chain of fish—in which a small fish is about to be eaten by a larger fish, and that larger fish is about to be eaten by an even a larger fish—humorously illustrates the fact that you must have a broad perspective to understand Point A. Determining Point A means understanding yourself, organization, and environment.

The fourth lesson is to evaluate where we are, or to determine Point A. The question is, "Do you know where you are in time, place, and personal abiltities?"

CHAPTER 6

DᏰC D4Ꭺ ᏝᎢᎶ4ᏐᎠᏟ ᏓᏟᎠᏆᏐᎠᏝᎶᏅᏥ

Between Points A and B
Planning

We all want to get to town and stir up a rooster tail of dust behind us, but we have to slow down for the turns, detours, potholes, and bumps in the road."
HASTINGS SHADE, DEPUTY PRINCIPAL CHIEF
1999–2003

How do we get from Point A to Point B? The sequencing is:

Point B. The product, where we want to go

Point A. The place where we start

Principles. Criteria that drive our decisions

Plan. The outline of steps from Point A to Point B

Process. The practical steps to carry out the plan

Preparation. The skills necessary to go from Point A to Point B

Progress. The metrics of determining that we are executing the plan

Plant. Planting and growing the seed of inspiration

Proceed. Proceeding undaunted

ROAD MAP AND GPS:
HOW DOES A MAP WORK?

How do we navigate from Point A to Point B? We prepare a plan. Back in the day, if you wanted to travel to a new place, you got out a map. If it were within driving distance, you pulled a paper road map out of the glove box that could never be folded back to its original condition. You found your destination on the map by hit and miss, or you looked at the index and found the vertical and horizontal coordinates. Then you looked at the various routes and highlighted the best one with a crayon. Today, you turn on your GPS and respond to several questions: What is your destination? Do you want to start with the current location? Do want to travel by air, bus, automobile, or foot? Do you want a route with the most interstates, least construction, quickest time, shortest distance, fewest tolls?

The GPS asks for guidance (principles) that will determine the route. The decision maker is the GPS and navigation computer. You know you want to go from Point A to Point B, but there will be different routes. How do you know which one to take? How do you deal with the turns, detours, potholes, and bumps in the road? There will be more decisions to make along the route. If we want to go to Norman, Oklahoma, from Tahlequah, Oklahoma, what are the principles that guide our decisions? If the principle is to get there as quickly as possible, then we take Interstate 40. If we want to stop, shop, and eat at our leisure along the way, then we will take a different route through Tulsa and then down the Turner Turnpike. If we want to enjoy a historic drive with the top down in a vintage Corvette, we head down U.S. 66, the Mother Road. Setting out principles will guide our decisions not only during the initial planning but whenever we must make decisions along the way. If we come across a detour, knowing the guiding principles will direct us back to the path or route we desire. It could be said that leadership is drawing a map and following it.

For the Cherokee Nation, the Declaration of Designed Purpose (DODP) explains the steps of going from Point A to Point B. Redbird Smith used the phrase "designed purpose" over 100 years ago to express the future challenges, opportunities, responsibilities, and honor of the Cherokee people because he believed they were endowed with the blessings of intelligence, industriousness, spirituality, and loyalty. The Cherokee Nation's "designed purpose" was to become a "happy and healthy people." The DODP memorialized Redbird Smith's designed purpose and provided instructions on how to get from where we were to where we wanted to go: Point A to Point B. The DODP was not just a planning document; it was a manifesto of philosophy, an articulation of decision-making principles, a refinement of outcomes, and description of leadership attributes. The DODP was the handbook of the Cherokee Nation's principle-based leadership model. Its purpose was to encourage and empower every employee to be a contributing leader and to align the Cherokee Nation's human and physical resources to reach the designed purpose. The DODP was the Cherokee Nation's GPS.

PRINCIPLES

Live in such a way that you would not be ashamed to sell your parrot to the town gossip.

WILL ROGERS

There must be a clear understanding of decision-making principles for one's own life and for an organization. The DODP records a set of principles derived from extensive discussions with Cherokee-speaking people, thus capturing the cultural intelligence of traditionalists. Of course, principles for individuals and organizations vary based on the Point B desired. Principles are culturally based. The Cherokee language was the most accurate repository of the Cherokee worldview or culture. The Cherokee worldview certainly has a unique perspective.

Four Directions: Emulate the Messengers

An example of how Cherokee principles differ from those of other organizations can be found in the story "Messengers of the Four Directions," told by Benny Smith, an amazing Cherokee teacher, traditionalist, and speaker. It is common for philosophies and cultures to reflect the significance of cardinal directions and the belief that opposite directions represent opposite or balancing considerations. The Keetoowah Society is a Cherokee society of traditional spiritual thought. As Benny Smith tells us according to the Keetoowah Society's teachings, the Creator sent four Messengers from the cardinal directions, the East, North, West, and South, to mankind with gifts and instructions to emulate the Messengers. The first Messenger from the East brought "guardianship" of the creation; the second from the North brought "analytical intelligence"; the third from the West brought "wisdom"; and the fourth from the South brought "great emotion." In Cherokee thought, there is a great distinction between "analytical intelligence" and "wisdom" and between "guardianship" and "great emotion," because each is afforded a cardinal direction. In English-speaking thought, intelligence and wisdom would have a closer relationship.

The principles of the Keetoowah Society result in different decisions than the principles of other cultures. A Nazi Germany culture, for example, would derive different decisions from the same set of options. In Keetoowah Society, a principle is to "hold everyone sacred"; in Nazi thought, the Aryan race was superior, and innocent Jews were to be exterminated. Point B was very different for the Keetoowah Society and Nazi culture: one was happiness and health, and the other was world supremacy. Each established a set of principles to direct decision making to achieve their respective Point B.

Patriot vs. Looter: Be a Patriot

> It is one's pride in his heritage that makes him give up
> his all for his government.
>
> Redbird Smith
> 1917

The importance of principles cannot be overstated, as seen in the difference between a patriot and a looter. Redbird Smith defined a patriot as "someone who gives his all for his government." Most often we think of patriots in terms of military veterans contributing and sacrificing—sometimes even their lives—for their country, the community of American citizens. American Indians, including Cherokees, are highly patriotic to the United States. No ethnic or racial group has a higher enlistment rate or number of combat decorations per capita in United States military service. Since Desert Storm, there have been at least seven Cherokee citizens who have given their lives in the Middle East. The Cherokee Nation built an impressive Cherokee Nation Patriots Memorial in Tahlequah to recognize the sacrifice and contribution of veterans and other patriots. On occasion, someone will ask why Indians are so patriotic in light of their harsh treatment by the United States government over the last several hundred years. The answer is that the United States is also our country, and this is still our homeland.

The opposite of a patriot is a looter. Loot as defined by the *Random House College Dictionary* is "anything taken by dishonesty, force, stealth." The word conjures images of riot mobs in the inner city fighting police, burning cars, breaking into stores, and stealing any merchandise they can carry off. Looting is less dramatic when people demand things of others and their government that they have not earned such as welfare, subsidies, unearned services, and government supported products. A patriot's decision is one of personal resolve; a looter's decision is one of gang mentality driven by others. A patriot earns and willingly gives what is his and valuable to him; a looter takes without permission what someone else has earned. The looted property is valuable to the owner but has less value to the looter. A patriot is humble and keenly aware of his actions; a looter is arrogant and moves for reasons unknown to him. A patriot builds; a looter destroys. The analogy is harsh, but evidence of this debilitating trend today is the repeated complaint, "The government has done nothing for me." Some tend to believe the government is a substitute for God, that it knows all and will provide for all our needs, and when it does not, they are disappointed and bitter. The government is merely an amalgamation, a conglomerate, a massive community, a corporate body of citizens or people. It is easy for some to loot the government because it has no face, and there is a belief that the government has an unlimited supply of money behind it. The reality is that the government, especially of Indian tribes and nations, is composed of families and neighbors who share the responsibility to care for themselves and those who cannot care for themselves.

I heard one tribal politician at a community meeting tell the group as his staff was passing out a questionnaire, "We want to know what we have done for you lately and what we can do for you in the near future." An Indian couple sitting close to me whispered one to the other, "He sounds like a white man."

Of course, very few people are purely patriots or purely looters in all things they do. Each of us has some patriot and some looter tendencies, but in the process of identifying, building, and recruiting people, those with a patriotic philosophy will lead, and those who yield to a looter's mentality will devour and disintegrate the organization.

Politicians or Statesmen: Ag'iners Have One-Track Minds

The difference between a patriot and looter is similar to the difference between a statesmen and politician. The *Random House College Dictionary's* distinction between politician and statesman is interesting: "POLITICIAN is more often derogatory and STATESMAN laudatory. POLITICIAN suggests the schemes and devices of a person who engages in politics for party ends or his own advantage. STATESMAN suggests the eminent ability, foresight, and unselfish devotion to the interest of his country." My column "Politicians or Statesmen" appeared in the *Cherokee Phoenix* newspaper on June 5, 2006.

"Politicians or Statesmen"
By Chad Smith, Principal Chief

My desire for future elections is that the Cherokee people will select more and more statesmen, not only in Cherokee elections but also in state and federal elections. I look forward to the day when only statesmen will run for office.

A statesman is a servant leader who is not concerned about his political future but about what is best for the people. Former Deputy Principal Chief John Ketcher is a great example of a statesman. A statesman is open-minded, logical, intelligent, and compassionate. A statesman reconciles conflict and looks into the future.

Unfortunately, many elected officials are not statesmen or even leaders. They are in office to make themselves feel important, to gain power, and sometimes to get money. This kind of elected official is caustic, negative, and hateful. He stirs up messes, acts self-righteous, gets personal and calls other people names; he is the first to claim he is not a "politician" and that he "is working for the people." Some think success is getting their picture in the paper handing out a check. Some elected officials think their job is to be against the chief.

This type of elected official is not a statesman. A statesman does not buy votes with "quick fix" handouts. A statesman makes the tough decisions. He considers all his constituents. He has a vision and a long-term plan.

My mother told me there are some people who, if you gave them a gold mine and stood on your head, would still complain. In eastern Oklahoma, "ag'iners" is a slang word for those who are against everything. These ag'iners are rubber stamps who, regardless of the issue, say "no." In politics, everyone is an expert, especially the ag'iners. They boast they can do a better job even though they have never done anything themselves. The ag'iners are the first to complain and criticize but never have a thought-out answer or solution. They don't want to build up; they want to tear down. Recently, someone told me of one ag'iner who takes pride in filing frivolous lawsuits. Ag'iners have one-track minds—to "be against." Disagreement doesn't make someone an ag'iner. Statesmen can disagree with each other respectfully and make their points politely and rationally.

We need statesmen who can be positive, work with one another and with each branch of government. I listen to the Cherokee people and am convinced they want statesmen as elected leaders. I ask you to think about what is good for the Cherokee Nation and our children, not just what we can get for free now. Please think about the kind of people we need in public office to make good decisions for the present and the future. We don't need ag'iners; we don't need self-serving politicians. We need positive leaders and statesmen.

The world is not black or white; it is not just patriots or looters, politicians or statesmen. People comprise a matrix of feelings, understanding, and motives. I was an assistant district attorney prosecuting crime in the mid-1980s. Law enforcement personnel became jaded: everything was black or white. You were either a good guy or a bad guy. I was surprised it took only six months for me to see the world the same as them. My next criminal law attorney job was on the other side of the courtroom as a public defender. On that side, everything is gray with no black and white. People have mixed feelings and motives; principles are absolute. Principles have to be clearly expressed so decisions can be made effectively and efficiently to get to Point B.

Job Growth: A Kindly Man Cannot Help His Neighbor

Principles drive decision making, which produces consequences. The columnbelow ("Job Growth: Best Use of Resources for Cherokee Families"), which appeared in the *Cherokee Phoenix* on December 30, 2005, discusses the result of principle-driven decisions.

"Job Growth: Best Use of Resources for Cherokee Families"
By Chad Smith, Principal Chief

Some elected officials think the only way to help our Cherokee people is to give them more things for free or at reduced cost whether they are needy or not. Some of our people think the only reason the Cherokee Nation exists is to give them "benefits." I have even heard some say: "Why have a Cherokee card if we get no benefits?"

The greatest service the Cherokee Nation can provide for its citizens is the opportunity for them to support themselves. Meaningful jobs give Cherokees the means to support themselves, their family, and their community.

A hundred years ago Redbird Smith said, "A kindly man cannot help his neighbor unless he has a surplus, and he cannot have a surplus unless he works." We know it is a long-standing Cherokee value to be independent and strong. With the modern economy, we know that self-reliance is accomplished by working at a job or running a business. At the end of the day, we know it is good for individuals to have a sense of achievement and the pleasure of providing for their families.

We also know that for the same amount of money necessary to provide all the social services of housing, assistance, donated foods, and medical care for one family, we could help eight families develop skills for a job or create jobs.

Throughout history we have seen the Cherokees enduring a series of "Trails of Tears." The first was when we were forced from Georgia to Indian Territory in the winter of 1838. We lost one-fourth of our citizens. The next "Trail of Tears" was economic removal, when one-half of the Cherokee population left Oklahoma during the Depression for Bakersfield, California, and other parts of the West.

We want to prevent a third "Trail of Tears," one where our children and grandchildren must leave the Cherokee Nation in order to find work and develop careers.

The greatest need across the country is jobs. It is perhaps even more important for rural areas like the Cherokee Nation's 14 counties. Jobs mean income to provide food and shelter. For Cherokee Nation citizens, local jobs mean that we are able to stay near our ancestral homes, our communities, and our loved ones.

Job growth is creating more jobs and offering our people the training to prepare them to compete for those jobs. The future of our Cherokee Nation depends on the strength of our people.

One important goal we must keep focused on is to provide a stable financial future for our grandchildren. This means developing businesses that have growing power and will be here for many years to come.

The Cherokee Nation has grown to become one of the largest employers in northeastern Oklahoma. We now employ nearly 6,000 people. While most of the growth has come from our entertainment and hospitality businesses, we also employ many people in manufacturing, healthcare industries, and in our government. We need 10,000 more jobs in order to fully employ our Cherokee people in our jurisdiction. Too many of our people are unemployed or underemployed.

People with jobs benefit everyone. They pay taxes; they purchase homes; and they spend at their local retail stores. They participate in and give back to their communities. With your help, The Cherokee Nation is pursuing a better and financially solid future for our children.

My brother Kyle Smith, who assisted in the initial organization design of my first administration, used the word *strategy* a lot. Since I am a lawyer by trade, it takes a long time for things to sink in. *Strategy* was a foreign word with little meaning. It finally hit home when he explained strategy this way: "If you know where you are going, strategy is when to turn left or right; it is when to say yes or to say no." If the Cherokee Nation wanted a happy and healthy people, you would say yes to building meaningful employment initiatives and no to efforts that did not promote self-help. Principles guide decisions, and decisions result in consequences.

Guiding Principles: What Directs Your Decision Making?

Mothers are the only race of people that speak the same tongue. A mother in Manchuria could converse with a mother in Nebraska and never miss a word.

WILL ROGERS
May 11, 1930

Principles can be articulated and communicated with various levels of detail and application. The Cherokee Nation published guiding principles as part of the DODP to be applied to decision making. These guiding principles directed Cherokee people and the Cherokee Nation toward achieving a designed purpose.

Guiding principles are what we use to help us make decisions and choices so that we can create more jobs, growing communities and a strong culture. If we make our decisions based on these principles, then we will be well on our way to being a happy, healthy people. Here are the guiding principles from the DODP:

ᎦᏚᎩ (*gadugi*). "Work together to help one another." This type of work does not demand or expect return or payment for work. Our reward is the satisfaction of accomplishment. We are building a stronger nation by serving one another.

ᏕᏣᏓᏙᎯᏳᏎᏍᏗ (*detsadadohiyusesdi*). "Believe in one another." Our product is our people, the citizens of the Cherokee Nation. We should believe in that product, that we can succeed—that our Creator has a Designed Purpose, an ever-renewing, ever-expanding, upward progress of life.

ᏗᏣᏓᏏᎾᏍᏗ (*ditsadasinasdi*). "Live and work in a resourceful way." We cannot be lazy or complacent. We will be industrious, identifying and using each of our valuable resources. We will invest in our people and our communities to advance the Cherokee Nation.

ᏕᏣᏓᎵᎨᏅᏗᏍᎨᏍᏗ (*detsadaligenvdisgesdi*). "Be responsible for each other." We will take care of one another, as individuals and as a Nation. We will protect our governmental rights of sovereignty. We will determine our own identity.

ᎬᎾᎨᏒ ᏅᏁᎵᏙᎲ ᎡᎶᎯ ᏄᏍᏗᏓᏅ ᏕᎦᏕᎶᏆᏍᎨᏍᏗ (*gvnagesv nvnelidohv elohi nusdidanv degadeloquasgesdi*). "Learn from all I observe." We will live Cherokee culture by using language, history, custom, wisdom, art, music, and traditional values in everyday activities. We will inform and educate our people so that they can make wise choices.

EGⱣꞆ ᏗᏥᎮᎤᏗ ᎢᏤᎲᏗ (*gvwalitsv ditsadayohisdi itsehesdi*). "Live and never give up." We must be determined that we will succeed. We are the ones who determine our successes or failures. Obstacles and adversities can present challenges and opportunities, but our determination mandates that we will face adversity, survive, adapt, prosper, and excel.

This set of guiding principles offered the basic guideline for all Cherokee Nation employees on how to make decisions to take us to where we wanted to go. Lesson: the articulation of principles will determine how decisions are made. The question is, "Can you write down what influences your decisions?"

PLAN

When planning for a year, plant corn. When planning for a decade, plant trees. When planning for life, train and educate people.

CHINESE PROVERB

The purpose of a plan is to record or memorialize the steps of going from Point A to Point B. Recording a plan may be sophisticated or simple as long as it provides sufficient next steps.

Graduate Assistant: Treat Me Like a Child

I was a sophomore at the University of Georgia and part of a program called the Indian Teacher Training Project sponsored by the U.S. Department of Education. It was a cohort program of 15 Indian students; we student taught in an Indian community one semester and attended classes on campus the next semester. The first day on campus, I met Dr. Marion Rice, the project director, who introduced me to a graduate assistant for orientation. The graduate assistant was a mature PhD candidate. We sat down and discussed what needed to be done for housing, enrollment, my student ID, and so forth. He wrote out a checklist with the places I needed to go and how to get there using a very matter-of-fact method. I thought he was treating me like a child, and I was somewhat offended since I was a college sophomore. He finished the list of eight things to do, and I begrudgingly took his handwritten notes out the door and headed to complete the activities we had discussed. As I walked 40 feet outside the building and looked around at the huge campus, I felt lost. In another 40 feet, I remembered the checklist with instructions to the offices and buildings where I needed to go. In another 40 feet, I was thankful for the graduate assistant, his patience, and especially his list. That was a plan, a step-by-step record of activities designed to take me from Point A to Point B. It was memorialized in his handwritten checklist. It was a map of where I needed to go.

Desired Outcomes: What Do You Want at the End of the Day?

For the Cherokee Nation, the plan for going from Point A to B required more definition and clearer directions on how to get to Point B. Desired outcomes are broad objectives for achieving a vision. The desired outcomes for the Cherokee Nation identify the elements needed to become a happy, healthy people. Our success is measured by these outcomes. *Three characteristics of a happy, healthy community were summed up in three words: jobs, language, and community.* If we create jobs in or near our Cherokee communities, those communities remain strong, which allows us to keep our unique language and culture alive. The exercise of sovereignty and leadership were additional desired outcomes.

Jobs is the word that best sums up our economic strategy. In a happy, healthy Cherokee Nation, we have economically self-reliant individuals, families, and communities, and therefore a self-reliant Nation. This means creating new jobs through starting and expanding tribal businesses, recruiting new businesses, and developing entrepreneurs, as well as helping citizens become self-reliant through education, skill development, and career planning. Jobs are the key element to holding our communities and culture together. In fact, the idea of working hard to keep our communities strong is a cultural value generations. As Redbird Smith stated over 100 years ago: "A kindly man cannot help his neighbor in need unless he has a surplus, and he cannot have a surplus unless he works. Our pride in our ancestral heritage is our great incentive for handing something worthwhile to our posterity."

Language is what allows us to communicate the ideas of learning to think, act, speak, and write Cherokee. This includes exercising cultural attributes through fluency, literacy, art, music, sports, ceremonies, and everyday activities.

Community is a word tied closely to jobs and language. We bind ourselves together in cohesive communities in a spirit of ᎦᏚᎩ (gadugi) in such a way that our culture thrives. The concept of Cherokee community includes places such as Bell, Peavine, Tahlequah, and Jay, as well as communities of interest such as professional, sports, educational, or religious communities. Cohesive communities encourage people to help each other help themselves when challenges arise and to enjoy the company of others.

Sovereignty is the word we use when we talk about protecting and preserving the Cherokee Nation's right to choose our own future, exercise self-government, and strive as a Nation to become a happy, healthy people. Sovereignty includes defending the rights of the Cherokee Nation from outside threats and building a statesmanlike government to pass on our legacy.

Leadership is the ability to take ourselves, families, communities, and our Nation from where we are to where we want to be: a happy, healthy people. Leadership includes making sound decisions and providing the initiative to execute our plans.

The desired outcomes may be referred to as objectives. Each of the desired outcomes for the Cherokee Nation was an element to achieve being a happy and healthy people. If a program initiative did not accomplish one of our desired outcomes, then we did not do it. It was not that the initiative was not necessarily good or worthwhile; it was just one to be undertaken by someone else, because it did not take us to our Point B. We once turned down a $50,000 grant to neuter stray dogs because it did not advance one of our desired outcomes; rather it would have detracted from our priorities and was work someone else could do.

The Pod: Nothing over 32 Inches High

An example of the application of principles and desired outcomes is shown in the story of how we came to organize our executive staff using a "pod." We had 20 functioning disciplines such as education, health, law enforcement, commerce, accounting, legal, etc., that we called "groups." The 20 members of the executive staff were titled "group leaders" and had ultimate responsibility for their disciplines. Each group was decentralized and located some distance from other groups. Communication was poor. The group leaders focused on their disciplines, not on the desired outcomes. There was excessive office gossip and drama because the group leaders saw each other only every other week at a two-hour group leaders meeting. In 2008, group leaders had offices at different locations throughout the Nation's main headquarters building or in the general area of the city of Tahlequah. Some groups were as small as 35 employees, and one had 1,200 employees. At that time, communication was slow and often inaccurate, group leaders fussed among themselves, and there was little collaboration to achieve the desired outcomes of the DODP even though each group excelled in its respective discipline. After a number of discussions with the group leaders asking how we could improve communication, collaboration, and cooperation, Melissa Gower, the group leader of health, the largest group, suggested that we put all the group leaders in one place—a pod. The rest of the group leaders reacted with disbelief and frustration. Over a period of several months of deliberation, they came up with all kinds of reasons and/or excuses not to work in a centralized location with other group leaders. One excuse was, "Who is going to look after my employees if I am not there with them?" My answer was, "If you need someone to babysit your employees, you are not doing your job of leading them." Another question was, "How do I stay in contact with my subordinates?" The answer was staff meetings: bring them into the pod, and get out in the field more often. One group leader asked if he could have two offices, one each in the new and old areas. The answer was "No!" One indignant challenge was, "Everyone could see me come and go." So? One desperate challenge was, "What if a gunman came and shot all the group leaders?" The same safety measures would apply in the new area as in their prior offices. The question was addressed by another staffer who said, "I guess we then would get new group leaders." The question really was not about safety; it was about their concern that the new area would take away executive status that had been previously reinforced by large, separate, isolated offices. The loss of a known environment and the fear of change was very real to them. However, one group, communications, wanted its entire group to relocate to the Pod so they would have easier access to administration, but there was no room.

The nickname "pod" stuck because we could not come up with a better one. The pod was a practical application and symbol of the principle-based leadership model we employed at the Cherokee Nation during my tenure. We took a large area of the main office building, gutted the inside, installed glass in the perimeter offices facing the open center area, and installed sound-damping acoustic tile and carpet. It was one large open room surrounded by 19 glass-fronted offices that housed 55 people: my immediate office staff, 20 executive staff, and their assistants. The pod had six meeting areas in glass-fronted rooms and an open area with noise suppression that would accommodate 8 to 100 people. It had a small kitchen and coffee maker. The pod was so open, you could almost see everyone from any angle in the large room. The only rule was that you could not obstruct the view across the pod, which meant no posters on the glass fronts of the offices and no furniture or other items higher than 34 inches in the open area.

The day came for group leaders and their assistants to move in. Group leaders each got one small glass-fronted office and space in the open center of the pod. They were permitted to bring one staff person with them. The next question was, "Which office do I get?" I anticipated a turf battle over who got what office. My response was, "I don't care. You get an office and square footage in the open area of the pod; you decide who goes where. But by the way, what are the principles to make the decisions as to who goes where?" Even as simple an exercise as locating offices can be effectively managed by agreeing to principles before the decision is made. Some of the principles that emerged from discussion among the "not so happy" group leaders were controlling sound, locating close to other group leaders they worked with often, taking into consideration the learning and communication style of the staff, and so forth. On the day of the move, the glass offices were assigned using sticky notes; some group leaders agreed to change offices, and blue masking tape on the carpet demarcated a grid for desks and chairs in the open area. I walked in with some staff planning where their furniture would go; we pulled up the blue tape grids. It reminded us of the 1970s sitcom *WKRP in Cincinnati*, where newsman Les Nessman enforced imaginary property lines around his desk. The pod was designed to be an organic, democratic, fluid, and dynamic environment, and if it were up to me, all the furniture would have been on rollers so it could be moved easily. After several weeks, staff began to move their furniture around. The education and leadership group leaders created a mini-quad with their desks to facilitate communication. The lawyers, accountants, and information technology people generally wanted their assistants sitting outside their glass offices. Those group leaders who dealt with services and built programs sat in the open area in an assortment of mismatched desks and chairs brought from their old offices. It was great. Group leaders, secretaries, interns, and visitors were all working in a large open area. There was absolutely no pretense or air of status.

Instead of it taking days to get a response to interoffice mail or hours to get a reply to an e-mail, and instead of playing phone tag, the group leaders and I would quickly address and resolve issues in minutes or seconds by going over to one another's desk, conferring in the pod, or catching up in the kitchen. After a month of adjustment, few group leaders would have suggested going back to the old way.

The pod was designed as a result of and for principle-based leadership. Every group leader was a bureaucratic entrepreneur and was charged with identifying the problem or opportunity, marshaling the human and physical resources, and executing the initiative. They could do it in the pod with all the decision makers in one place. My assistant, who did all of my scheduling, had a loud voice, so she got the glass office, and I got a desk in the open area. I was readily accessible to group leaders, staff, interns, and visitors. If we needed privacy, we went to a glassed-walled meeting room. If someone was on the phone, you came back later. The environment was fluid and dynamic.

For me, a great consideration was the fact that systems operate by default. If you have to nurse, repair, or energize a system, there may be a design flaw. By default with decentralized offices, the group leaders did not collaborate, communicate, or cooperate with each other. Every discipline excelled tremendously over the decade, but by default, group leaders focused on their discipline, not the designed purpose and desired outcomes. By default, the peers of the group leaders were their subordinates, who tended to agree with group leaders and not challenge them. With the centralized pod configuration, by default group leaders had to communicate, collaborate, and cooperate because they had to look at each other daily. They would not hold a grudge because they would see each other the next day. They could deal with issues while their memories were still fresh. They could bring closure to projects quickly, simply, and economically because an expectation of performance was reinforced by proximity. If you saw people all day long, you quickly ran out of excuses for not delivering on your commitments to them. In the pod, the group leaders' peers were fellow executives who could challenge and police each other. The designed purpose was reinforced in the pod environment; our work was not about someone having a nice office or a particular department looking good and growing; it was about the Nation becoming a happy and healthy people, and our focus was on the desired outcomes. The pod demonstrated the practical and effective consequences of principle-driven decision making.

Structure: Take the Court Clerks Flowers

Organizational charts should reflect real management operations. If you want to know who gets things done in the courthouse, it is not the judge or bailiff, it is the court clerks. If you are working regularly at a courthouse, take the court clerks flowers on occasion. They deserve the appreciation and will give you the patience and information you need to get your job done. If you drew a chart to map out who got things done in a court system, the court clerks would be at the top, and the judge would be somewhere down the chart.

How do you structure an organization to get you where you want to go? During the first two years of my tenure, I was extremely concerned with the management structure of the Cherokee Nation. An organizational chart seldom represents a true map of leadership; it rarely shows who gets things done in an organization and what its true priorities are. Staff, secretaries, assistants, line workers, and others with common sense and a strong work ethic find ways to get things done in spite of organizational impediments. Just like the court clerks.

An organizational chart should reflect the system necessary to produce the product. We must start with the product and work backwards to design the system to produce the product. It's simple but true. In a classic bureaucracy, the structure is a pyramid hierarchy with a "span of control" of five subordinates per supervisor. Such an organizational structure is not only arbitrary but ineffective. The product or Point B of the Cherokee Nation was to achieve a 100-year plan of Cherokee people being happy and healthy as indicated by desired outcomes. If the system did not produce those results, there was a design flaw. As Paul Gustafson, a consultant during those two early years, stated over and over, "Systems are perfectly designed to get the result they get." The organizational structure should not only be a map of the system designed to produce the product, but it should also reflect real authority over apparent authority; budget authority and resources; access to policy decision makers; and supervisory responsibility. The structure not only produces a product, but the design of the structure is also a product of the organization's principles.

A leadership and management organization structure is often limited by legal and industry constraints. The legal structure of the Cherokee Nation is based on a constitution similar to that of most states and the United States. There are three branches of government: executive, legislative, and judicial. As the United States Supreme Court in the 1803 case of *Marbury v. Madison* held, the legislature enacts the law, the executive enforces the law, and the court tells you what the law is. The executive, as the name implies, executes the operations of the Nation. The Cherokee Nation by statute endeavored to separate government functions from business functions. Decision-making principles of government and business are unfortunately different. Government decisions are political decisions by elected officials. Many elected officials make decisions based on the political expediency of satisfying at least 51 percent of their voters during an election cycle. To look good and "do something for the people" are often the political drivers. In this instance, doing something for the people often involves instant or short-term gratification rather than a positive long-term benefit. "Political winds" is a good description of how many elected officials make decisions. Sometimes elected officials make decisions just because they are elected officials: decisions based on arrogance and with short-term effect. The measure of a sound decision for this class of elected officials is reelection. I am being a bit cynical, but that is how political systems are designed. There are some good elected officials who make decisions not on what is politically expedient but on what is good for generations to come. Often they are called "statesmen." Business decisions are made according to a different set of principles. Generally, business decisions are made on whether profit and/or asset values increase. Governmental decisions are made on what the project costs; business decisions are made on what the project returns.

The Cherokee Nation by statute separated its businesses from its government. A corporation is set up under tribal law, the principal chief appoints the board of directors for four-year staggered terms, and the legislature ratifies the appointment. The principal chief is the shareholder's representative, but the employees work for the chief executive officer (CEO) of the company. The CEO works for the board, and the principal chief provides input from the Nation. The policy maker and ultimate decision maker is the board of directors. One good example of the difference between political and business decisions came in 2007, when a proposal was made to build a $4 million marquee sign outside the Cherokee Nation's flagship casino in Catoosa, Oklahoma. The tribal council members complained that the $4 million could be used for social services such as cancer treatment and housing. The tribal council members could not understand or appreciate there was no $4 million pile of cash lying around to build the sign; the money would be borrowed and repaid from the $19 million in new business the sign would pull off the highway. The politicians screamed, "We have better things to do with $4 million, like buy eyeglasses and cancer treatments." The business board members thought, "This is a no-brainer: invest $4 million and get $19 million back in revenue in one year." Since the Nation's business and government operations are separate, elected officials had reason to defer to board members and staff when challenged by constituents. The elected officials could point out that they could not intervene in purchasing, employment matters, and business disputes of the corporation. The board members had no constituents to satisfy and could measure their performance by the performance of the business.

The Cherokee Nation was divided by principles: the government side by political principles and the business side by for-profit principles.

Principle-Based Leadership Organizational Structure: Lack of Control

The executive branch of the government had the greatest organizational design opportunity to take the Cherokee Nation to the designed purpose, or Point B. The organizational design of the legislative and judicial branches was set by the constitution, and they did little proactive work. The judicial branch responds by deciding cases brought to it, and the legislative branch responds to constituent demands or desires. The businesses followed a standard corporate model influenced heavily by the rules of the Sarbanes-Oxley Act of 2002. The principal chief's office was the center of policy making and had the platform to advocate, influence, and negotiate the principles and policies for all aspects of the Nation. The question was how to structure the executive branch of the Cherokee Nation to enjoy the long-term vision of a happy and healthy people by creating jobs, revitalizing language, and developing cohesive communities.

We identified the functional disciplines of the Nation, assigned them to groups, and put the groups into teams based on who their primary clients were. The service team's clients were Cherokee people or communities and consisted of health, education, social services, housing, law enforcement, community services, and commerce. The direction team's clients were the service team groups and consisted of legal, accounting and procurement, human resources, management resources, property management, and information systems. The direction team's client was also the Cherokee Nation as an entity, including other teams that consisted of the office of the principal chief and deputy principal chief, communications, government relations, strategy, solutions, and leadership. The regulatory team's client was the Cherokee Nation to insure statutory compliance by Cherokee Nation operations using independent regulatory commissions and boards including gaming, tax, election, registration, newspaper, environment, and healthcare.

The three operational teams included the direction team, the service team, and the resource team and two other teams were the regulatory team and business team. The business team was primarily Cherokee Nation businesses. The team structure chart from the DODP appears in Figure 6.1.

These five teams, coordinated by the principal chief, must work together to meet their goals and to help Cherokees help themselves.

Direction Team

The direction team provides staff advice and assistance in the overall administration of the government. Team members provide leadership for the Nation in terms of vision and direction. Their clients/customers are the other teams.

> **Office of the principal chief.** Responsible for conducting the business of the Cherokee Nation, establishing policy, carrying out the laws of the Cherokee Nation, and administering day-to-day operations.
>
> **Office of the deputy principal chief.** Empowered to act as directed by the principal chief. Responsible for conducting the business of the Cherokee Nation, establishing policy, carrying out the laws, and administering day-to-day operations.
>
> **Government relations.** Provides direction to the executive branch by working on a government-to-government level with the United

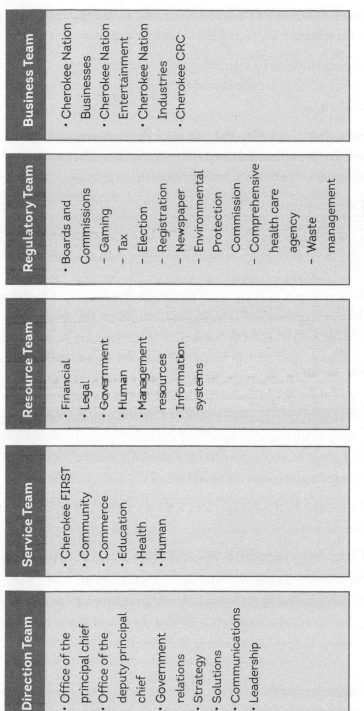

FIGURE 6.1 *Cherokee Nation government executive branch team structure.*

Direction Team
- Office of the principal chief
- Office of the deputy principal chief
- Government relations
- Strategy
- Solutions
- Communications
- Leadership

Service Team
- Cherokee FIRST
- Community
- Commerce
- Education
- Health
- Human

Resource Team
- Financial
- Legal
- Government
- Human
- Management resources
- Information systems

Regulatory Team
- Boards and Commissions
  - Gaming
  - Tax
  - Election
  - Registration
  - Newspaper
  - Environmental Protection Commission
  - Comprehensive health care agency
  - Waste management

Business Team
- Cherokee Nation Businesses
- Cherokee Nation Entertainment
- Cherokee Nation Industries
- Cherokee CRC

Tax. Pursuant to statute is charged with ensuring the Nation complies with federal, state, and tribal tax law.

Election. Pursuant to statute is charged with conducting tribal elections.

Registration. Pursuant to statute is charged with administering enrollment of Cherokee citizens.

Newspaper. Pursuant to statute is charged with providing editorial guidance and independence to the *Cherokee Phoenix* newspaper.

Environmental Protection Commission. Pursuant to statute is charged with enforcing tribal environmental law.

The group leaders from each team periodically met to discuss the progress we'd made toward achieving our desired outcomes and operational performance. The most notable aspect of this structure was that each of the groups in the service, resource, and direction teams was on one tier and reported directly to the principal chief. As principal chief, I had 20 direct reports. The secretary of state acted as a part-time chief of staff. Group leaders were given charge of their discipline, taught the DODP, established annual goals, negotiated budgets, and were instructed that the principal chief had an "open door" policy. Group leaders knew that my style was "bottom line"; I wanted to know what decisions they needed made. I would inquire if I needed their background facts, subordinate policies, and feasibility assumptions. They also knew it was their job to marshal resources, involve other group leaders, and resolve issues before they came to me for a decision. An organization is only as good as its people, and its people are only as good as their leadership skills. There were lots of informal conversations in the pod between me and group leaders. I was known for inviting a half dozen group leaders, staff, and Cherokee speakers to impromptu discussions where we'd sit around a table to address a question or issue. It was common to pull out the dictionary to ensure everyone shared an understanding of the terms we were using in English and to ask our Cherokee speakers how they would look at the issue from a Cherokee speaker's point of view.

When this flat organizational structure was introduced in 2000, several of the group leaders welcomed the responsibility and autonomy, several were uncomfortable, and several were lost. Those uncomfortable and lost were accustomed to someone instructing them on how to run their discipline or group and having someone to blame if things went wrong. Group leaders were never punished for making an honest mistake after having done due diligence; mistakes were part of the process of maturing and growing as a leader. During my tenure, I terminated the employment of only a few people, usually because they micromanaged their groups.

The principle-based leadership model was evidenced by our very flat organizational structure and the very informal and dynamic pod. The design was not to control staff but the opposite: to encourage them to use their talent to reach Point B.

PROCESS

Individual responsibility could be masked in corporate personality, which . . . had no body to kick nor soul to damn.

H. CRAIG MINER
in *The Corporation and the Indian*

Process is the practical and often recurring application of principle-based decision making. Once you have made a decision with the same facts or variables, process is replication that is often recorded as policy or in operational manuals. For those decisions where there is no precedent, policy, template, or manual, the first decision is, "Whose decision is it?"

Whose Decision Is It: One of Two Piles

Some people have asked why I appear to be so laid back, don't get rattled, and seem calm during stressful times. The answer lies in identifying what decisions are mine and what decisions should be made by others. Sorting out decisions this way should not be confused with the notion that one just doesn't make decisions. You must, with every decision that comes within your realm, first decide whether it is yours or someone else's to make. If it is someone else's decision, you must encourage them to make it. And deciding whose decision it is should not be confused with the excuse, "It is not my job." The work, project, or job may very well be yours or may be shared with others. In every work effort, there are decisions to be made that are not yours, and if you try to take them away from others and make them yourself, the result will likely be disruption in the workplace and poor decisions. At the Cherokee Nation, it was common for tribal council members to want to make administrative decisions about who got hired and fired, who was eligible for programs, and who should establish nonstatutory policy. Those were not legislative decisions, and it was disruptive and unproductive when council members attempted to insert themselves into the decision-making process.

In short, I sorted all decisions into two piles: those that were not mine and that I should transfer, delegate, or farm out to the appropriate people, and those that were mine. The next step was to determine if a decision was really necessary and, if so, when it had to be made. Then came another question: what degree of confidence did I have in the existing information to make a sound decision? I feared making decisions that had unknown and unintended consequences. Due diligence was required. I would encourage staff and others to challenge and test decisions and to think them through to their logical ends. I never wanted a decision to go out of the office that would later embarrass us. If it was a controversial decision, I wanted to know the complete ramifications, including the reliability of the data, the premise assumptions, and the principles driving the decision. And sometimes decisions had to be made then and there, so I made them and took responsibility.

For some leaders, it is hard to delegate decision making. There is always the temptation to take back a decision because of lack of confidence in the delegate or the urgency of the decision. Of course, on rare occasions, a leader must take back a decision, but once that happens, the delegate is undermined and the relationship is potentially damaged.

Leaders must train delegates to make sound decisions and hold them accountable for a sound decision-making process. There is little value in second-guessing a delegate's decision. Some decisions are not right or wrong; some decisions may cost more, take longer, or be less clear than better alternatives. My subordinates made many decisions that I disagreed with, but I would not change them if they had followed a sound decision-making process, collected sufficient facts, and relied on intelligent premises. In the end, my subordinates were often right. Perhaps one of the greatest rewards for a leader is to have confidence in the decision making of his staff.

Autocracy and micromanaging have short-term value, particularly for compliance issues, but over the mid and long range, such practices will stifle growth, chill discretionary effort by staff, create poor morale, and drive away the most talented and creative employees.

The fifth lesson is that principles, planning, and processes create the plan or map to go from Point A to Point B. The question is, "Do you know what drives your decisions?"

CHAPTER 7

DᏏᏟ D4Ꭺ ᏝᎣ4ᎴᏠ DᎣᏁᎯ

Between Points A and B
Doing

We do this today so the children can do for themselves tomorrow. ᏗᎯᏟ ᎤᎾᎵᏍᏕᎸᏙᏗ
(DINIYOTLI UNALISDELVDODI)
CHEROKEE CULTURAL CONCEPT

After we plan how to get from Point A to Point B, then we do.

PREPARATION

But how do we prepare for the road in between? Preparation is acquiring the intelligence, tools, and training to execute a plan. We must learn to think and make good decisions, understand what drives people, recognize the value of experience, and communicate using all of our resources.

Think in Other Languages: Five Fingers

What do you call someone who speaks three languages?
Trilingual. What do you call someone who speaks two
languages? Bilingual. What do you call someone who
speaks one language? American.

AUTHOR UNKNOWN

For a leader, helping others to make good decisions is a challenge and a reward. The process of sound decision making includes identifying pertinent facts or data, isolating variables, and then applying the proper principles. Doing so requires intelligence. We can educate ourselves and improve our intelligence by learning and thinking from different perspectives. Language is not only the method to communicate intelligently, but it also captures the concepts of different perspectives and new knowledge and preserves them. Fluency is the degree of speaking proficiency, and literacy is the degree of reading proficiency. Literacy develops abstract thought because consistency and the ability to manage many concepts can be easily and effectively shared and stored.

Language is the vessel of culture. Nothing else can express and preserve the attributes and concepts that make cultures different and people unique. Language allows us to understand new information, data, and knowledge; to see from different perspectives; and to improve our judgment in applying proper principles. Preparation requires pertinent education and training. At every level of an organization, you want people who can make good decisions. The more education, knowledge, and wisdom, the better. Language is the vehicle for each.

In 2010, I gave a brief talk at a National Guard air and space camp certificate ceremony. I held up my hand, showing each finger and thumb, and asked the seventh and eighth graders to promise me they would learn to speak five languages before they graduated from high school. They looked at me indifferently. The five fingers I held up represented the five languages. I went on to say the first language was English; the second, math; the third, music; the fourth, art; and the fifth, Cherokee. Our perspective changes and decision making improves when we think outside our normal frames of reference and vocabulary.

Say No to English-Only: Promote Intelligence

I staunchly object to the English-only efforts in Oklahoma and other parts of the United States. By design, such efforts challenge a major ethnic group, Hispanics. They also send a doofus message to our children that English is omnipotent and superior. Isn't it odd that Americans speak the foreign language of English rather than an American language like Cherokee, Sioux, or Navajo? Furthermore, why would you want to thwart a child's desire to learn all she can? The English-only policy is myopic, and the damage done to children is evidenced by the English-only policies of the Bureau of Indian Affairs (BIA) punishing Indian children in boarding schools for speaking their native languages. At the same time that the BIA was washing Indian children's mouths out with soap for speaking Cherokee and other tribal languages, World War II Indian code talkers were helping defeat the enemies of the United States by using tribal language in battlefield communication. Languages are intelligence; why would you ever want to outlaw intelligence? Instead of Oklahoma wanting to limit language to English, the state should be promoting the learning of every type of language imaginable: Slavic, romantic, native, music, art, math, science, etc.

English-only efforts are like book burning, a deliberate attempt to promote ignorance as opposed to championing learning. How could we prepare ourselves and our children for facing the challenges before us without intelligence?

Don't Let Oklahoma Be Bullied by English Only: Language Is Intelligence

My column in the May 2008 *Cherokee Phoenix*, "Say No to English Only," addresses the issue of English-only efforts.

"Say No to English Only"
By Chad Smith, Principal Chief

Students who speak and think in multiple languages are at an advantage over those who speak only one language. But decades ago, our native ancestors were punished for speaking their tribal languages at Indian boarding schools they had to attend where "English only" was the policy. Their stories of abuse are well documented. Cherokee, Choctaw, Creek, Kiowa, and Seminole students were punished by physical beatings and isolation. Their mouths were washed out with soap for speaking their own languages.

On a personal note, my father attended a BIA boarding school at Sequoyah in Tahlequah, Oklahoma, and my uncles and aunts attended the BIA boarding school Chilocco near Newkirk, Oklahoma. Each had stories of oppression for speaking the Cherokee language. None of them ever forgot what they endured, and today we should remember their experiences as we see the state government proposing English-only policies.

State Representative Randy Terrill introduced a bill to make English the official language of Oklahoma, the "Native State." Our past proves that this kind of regime is damaging to our tribal languages, to our elders, and to our communities. No one can explain how this kind of policy, which failed miserably under federal edict, would bring any kind of benefit to Oklahoma. Even though Representative Terrill tried to pacify Indian nations by exempting the teaching of tribal languages, the effect of this bill is to punish any American citizen, Oklahoma resident, or taxpayer who does not speak English by denying them state services.

This bill is a slap in the face to people like my wife's father and countless other elders who speak no English. Our respected and precious elders who retain our Cherokee language would be shunned by the state under this bill.

A sensitive topic that each of us should never forget is that English only, under federal and state regime, was designed to assimilate us and destroy our culture. The English-only policy has done untold harm to our culture. Our lands are gone, our language is forgotten by generations, and we are just now beginning to recover from decades of English-only policies.

Now, the same policy is shamelessly being pushed upon another group of people, primarily Hispanics. The most appalling provision is the fact that the bill is based upon simplemindedness. This bill is not oppressing Oklahomans based on tribal citizenship or color or race or religion, but because they have additional intelligence that the authors of the bill don't have.

"Bilingualism and multiculturalism are divisive," said Representative Terrill in a press release. *Divisive* means *troublesome* or *disruptive*, so according to Representative Terrill's statement, if an individual comes from an ethnic heritage or religious group, or if an individual can speak more than one language, then that individual is unruly, disorderly, and inharmonious. In short, Representative Terrill is saying that people who can speak more than one language are somehow harmful to this state.

We should oppose Representative Terrill's way of thinking. Instead, we should encourage every Oklahoma child, Indian or not, to learn as many different languages as possible. We should teach our children our tribal languages. We should cheer on our children when they want to learn classical languages, Romance languages, or any language from across the world. Every language has its own intelligence, its own innate knowledge that can't be found anywhere else. Societal values and concepts that are unique to different cultures are imbedded in language and often cannot be translated well. Teaching our children the value of many languages can only enhance their personal intelligence and their understanding and compassion for other cultures.

The phrase "history repeats itself" is more true now than ever. Native Americans heard the demand for "English only" 60 years ago during the termination period, 100 years ago with forced assimilation and allotment, and 150 years ago with forced acculturation initiatives.

The United States is based on diversity, and Oklahoma is a state of great diversity. The foundation of this diversity was created by our 39 tribes and various immigrant ethnic and religious groups. We are a state of abundant languages and cultures. The very intellectual richness of Oklahoma is what makes us so good.

I encourage each and every one of you, as well as each and every tribal leader and council member, to oppose English only. We should promote intelligence, not support ignorance.

My column in the March 2009 *Cherokee Phoenix*, "Don't Let Oklahoma Be Bullied by 'English Only'" went on to address the inherent bigotry of English-only efforts.

"Don't Let Oklahoma Be Bullied by 'English Only'"
By Chad Smith, Principal Chief

What would Will Rogers say about Oklahoma legislators wanting to pass a law that makes English Oklahoma's official language? Will might reply, "Thank God we don't get all the government we pay for." It's been said that declaring English as our official language would be like declaring that hotdogs are the official food at baseball games. Maybe that's what our legislature should address first.

Will Rogers said, "There is nothing as short-sighted as a politician." Ironically, even some of the biggest proponents of "English only" openly admit there is no question that it's advantageous to be proficient in other languages in addition to English. They also admit that the last three U.S. census figures show that more than 97 percent of people in the U.S. speak English well. So why fix a problem that does not exist?

Will also said, "When ignorance gets started, it knows no bounds." Speaking other languages should be encouraged. Our children should speak Romance languages, American Indian, technical, and art languages. After all, we want them to do better than us and have a better life. There are other choices such as "English plus," which promotes the concept of proficiency in English plus a second language. States such as New Mexico, Washington, and Oregon have passed English-plus laws, while Hawaii and Louisiana have passed measures that preserve language and culture. Last month, the city of Nashville soundly defeated proposed English-only legislation because it did not want to be viewed as intolerant and cold-hearted. We should follow its example. To paraphrase Geoffrey Nunberg, a senior language researcher at Stanford University, "English only" is a bad cure for an imaginary disease. "My ancestors did not come over on the Mayflower; they met it," said Will Rogers. Oklahoma's tourism slogan is "Native America" and draws on multiculturalism. The first thing many visitors ask upon arrival is, "Where are the Indians?" "English only" creates a business and social black eye for our state and its residents and visitors. In a state that already has faltering tourism, industries, and businesses, do we really want to present the image of Oklahoma as a backward place that endorses ignorance over intelligence, intolerance over openness, and force over education?

Unfortunately, the real crux of this issue is not saving money or unifying people. "English only" is really about the political fear of someone being different or smarter because they can speak a language that others cannot. It is political bullying, firmly rooted in intolerance, hatred, fear, and the federal English-only policies that led to my dad having his mouth washed out with soap for speaking Cherokee in federal boarding school.

Will Rogers, a fellow citizen of the Cherokee Nation, knew Oklahoma values and especially human values. One of the most powerful things Will ever said was, "We will never have true civilization until we have learned to recognize the rights of others." The ability to speak another language is a form of intelligence. Should not intelligence be a right we recognize rather than something we legislatively prohibit?

Oklahomans don't like bullies, especially when it is the government. When Randy Terrill introduced "English only," he called me about excluding Indian languages and said the bill was "only directed toward Hispanics." Our native people have been the victims of this type of bullying for centuries. I can't stand idly by and watch it happen all over again to others, and I urge Oklahomans to join me and the leaders of many other Oklahoma tribes, state business leaders, and educators in this fight.

The *Random House College Dictionary* defines bigotry as "stubborn and complete intolerance of any creed, belief or opinion that differs from one's own." "English only" represents a graphic example of promoting ignorance rather than intelligence. We can lead only by reason developed using intelligence, not dogma embedded in stubborn ignorance.

Cherokee Messenger: Exercise Leadership

Here is a story in which thinking in another language gives a better perspective, promotes reasoning, and results in a better outcome: Most Indian tribes have adopted the Miss America model of a young female representative for the Indian tribe or nation, and they are generally called "royalty." The tribes hold pageants based on selection criteria similar to that of the Miss America pageant. In 2000, the Miss Cherokee pageant held its forty-seventh competition for young women ages 18 to 24. The categories included talent, evening dress, traditional dress, interviews, and onstage impromptu questions. It was a mess. The young women started accusing each other of shacking up with guys and threatened to sue one another. Didn't we as a nation want something more meaningful? We got together several of our Cherokee speakers and asked them what they would call our Miss Cherokee in "Cherokee thought." After several weeks of discussion, they concurred that in Cherokee they would call her a "messenger." That made perfect sense because she is a representative of the Cherokee Nation. Then the question became: by which principles would you choose a messenger? You would choose a messenger by the contents and presentation of her message. A talent, swimsuit, and evening dress competition provides little insight into one's ability to represent the Nation with a meaningful and impactful message. As a result, the Miss Cherokee Contest was changed to the Miss Cherokee Leadership Exercise. Each candidate selected and presented a platform issue that would be her main topic during her tenure should she become Miss Cherokee Leadership. Other categories—such as impromptu questions onstage, traditional clothing, and the sharing of cultural presentations—were included in the exercise. The result was absolutely amazing. The young women delivered powerful and insightful statements on important issues, problems, and resolutions. It was inspiring for the audience to witness the participants' intelligence and leadership. It was truly a leadership exercise that benefitted each participant and the audience.

Just as a footnote, the Miss Cherokee pageant started in 1950 as part of the Cherokee National Holiday. Cherokees routinely hear from people talking about their "great-great-grandmother who was a Cherokee princess." The only Cherokee "princesses" were winners of the Miss Cherokee pageant. So unless the great-great-grandmother was a Miss Cherokee, the claim is highly suspect.

Had we not examined the purpose of the Miss Cherokee pageant from a *Cherokee language perspective*, we would not have had the insight to reframe it from a pageant to a leadership exercise. Thinking in another "language"—be it Cherokee or one of the different perspectives offered by fields such as math, music, and art—can help each person learn better from all he observes.

Interest Analysis: What Drives People?

We can prepare ourselves to lead by learning better reasoning skills; we can navigate difficulties, frame controversies, and lead others by understanding what drives people. It is not what people say but rather their motivating interests that best reflect why they do what they do.

I grew up watching television programs of Daniel Boone and Davy Crockett, the brave "Indian fighters." As a child, it did not dawn on me that they were fighting and killing my people. Charlie Hill, the Oneida comedian, had an act ragging on Davy Crockett. Regardless of the popular stories of Crockett's Indian fighting, there is a different story that best reflects what really drove him. In the late 1820s, Georgia was leading the southern states to get Indians out of the southeastern United States. Andrew Jackson ran his presidential campaign on a platform to remove Indians west of the Mississippi to Indian Territory, where they would be out of the way of southern whites. In 1830, Congress was considering the Indian Removal Act, which would give the president authority to remove the Cherokees and other southern tribes to Indian Territory and to exchange their lands in the South for those in Indian Territory. The debate in Congress was divided North and South and by party. Davy Crockett was a U.S. congressman from Tennessee and a member of Jackson's political party. Contrary to Davy Crockett's historical reputation as an "Indian fighter" and apparently an "Indian hater," his core interest is seen in his stance on Indian removal. James Adair reports in his book on the history of the Cherokee Nation that David Crockett

> . . . denounced the treatment to which the Indians had been subjected at the hands of the Government as unjust, dishonest, cruel, and short-sighted in the extreme. . . . He had been threatened that if he did not support the policy of forcible removal his public career would be summarily cut off. . . . But while he was desirous of pleasing his constituents and of coinciding with the wishes of his colleagues as any man in Congress, he could not permit himself to do so at the expense of his honor and conscience in the support of such a measure. . . . He believed that American people could be relied on to approve their Representative for daring, in the face of all opposition, to perform their conscientious duty, but if no, the approval of his conscience was dearer to him than all else.

The Indian Removal Act was passed by a vote of 102-97 in the House of Representatives after Andrew Jackson lobbied three among his party to change their votes. Crockett's constituents did not appreciate his conscientious duty. David Crockett lost his next congressional race and ended up going to the Alamo, where he was killed. The Cherokees and four other tribes were forcibly removed to Indian Territory; the Cherokees lost one-fourth of their population in the winter of

1838–1839 on the infamous "Trail of Tears." Davy Crockett was not an Indian hater; he was driven by a compelling sense of right and wrong.

What people and institutions do is based on their primary interests, regardless of personality, reputation, appearance, or standing. For Davy Crockett, it was his own conscience; for Andrew Jackson, it was political gain. Davy Crockett was willing to sacrifice his political career for his conscience, and he did.

One exercise we did in our Cherokee history course was to brainstorm a list of all the groups of people and institutions who were involved with Indian removal. They included Georgians, the state of Georgia, missionaries, the president, the Congress, surrounding states, national political parties, religious organizations, the Treaty Party, the National Party, businesses, etc. Then we identified the interest of each group or institution in the controversy over Indian removal. There were those external groups who wanted the land and assets of the Cherokee Nation, including a low-grade gold found at Dahlonega, Georgia; groups who wanted political control over Cherokee territory; groups on either side of states' rights issues; groups promoting human rights; and internal groups within the Cherokee Nation that differed on the issues of governmental autonomy, survival, property rights, etc. This information was placed on a matrix including the strength and sustainability of the various interests. Next the class brainstormed all possible actions the Cherokee government could have taken in response to the threat of forcible removal and concluded by evaluating every action, discarding those not feasible and prioritizing the balance. Each time the exercise was performed, the result was the same; the resolution by the class was similar to what the Cherokee leaders did in the 1830s, which was to lobby and litigate. Unfortunately, greed and the lust for power consistently won over principles of right and wrong in the Cherokee conflict. Identifying the driving interest of a party or organization is the best way to predict its future behavior.

One method of solving a problem between two parties is to reach an "integrative resolution." The process begins with A-listing the interests or desires of each party to determine what they really want (i.e., which issues are really important to them and which are not). Often, each side can have what they really want and give up only ancillary issues, creating a win-win resolution. By contrast, a compromise involves each party giving up something important and leaves both sides with a grudge, which jeopardizes the resolution. A compromise is a forced lose-lose situation.

In resolving conflict, the same exercise is helpful: Define the controversy. Determine the participants. Identify their interests. Evaluate how the interests can be reconciled. Many controversies can be resolved by identifying and framing what may appear to be conflicting interests but are not. I seriously doubt there was any possible integrative resolution in a case such as the Trail of Tears, but the intelligence gathered in the process can nonetheless assist in developing alternative plans.

Tippeconic's Doctrines: Don't Fall in Love with an Asset

We can also prepare ourselves as leaders by learning from the experiences of successful people. David Tippeconnic was the former CEO of Citgo, a major oil company. He is Cherokee and Comanche. I met him in 2001 and subsequently asked him to be chairman of Cherokee Nation Enterprises, now Cherokee Nation Businesses, the Cherokee Nation's business corporation. Prior to his tenure, the gaming operations made $3 million a year and had 500 employees. The business was run like a mom-and-pop operation. He instituted corporate governance and strict business case analysis. We recruited outstanding Cherokee businesspeople to serve on the board and created a culture of performance. Within a decade, CNB had 5,500 employees, declared $130 million in profits, and expanded its portfolio to other businesses including environmental protection, information technology, aerospace assembly, and hospitality amenities. Tippeconnic coached the business staff with a list of observations, admonitions, and tips that we often used on the government side.

Dave Tippeconnic's Doctrines

- **Get our house in order.** This pertains to making sure we have made an assessment of our business, what we are. What are our strengths and weaknesses? What are our key issues? Do we have sound business work processes in place? If not, what do we need? What are key challenges and opportunities? What are our priorities? Do we need to make any staffing/organization changes? To do what we need to do, is it best we centralize or decentralize?

Once the assessment is made, we need to develop plans to make improvements (i.e., to get our house in order). This is especially true of a growing business like CNE. Now is the time to get it right so we can be ready to effectively manage a larger business.

- **Challenge everything.** Always question why we do something the way we do or why it is one way when it could be another way. Always search for a better, more efficient, and more effective way to do things.

- **Lead by example.** Don't spend your time and energy telling people how good you are—let them make up their own minds (they will anyway) when they see how you go about doing your job and the results of your efforts.

- **Set roles/responsibilities/expectations.** It is important for you to have a clear understanding with your employees and others in the company as to what their roles/responsibilities are and what you expect of them on the job. It is especially important to cover interfaces with other organizations—communicate with each other. Over time organizations will learn that they can depend on you to fulfill your role, or they will wire around you, which is what you want to avoid. When setting roles/responsibilities/expectations, let this be a discussion with your employees. When your employees have input into the process, they will be more committed to meeting your expectations.

- **Function as a team.** After roles/responsibilities/expectations are set, work to get the organization to function as a team. The desired result is what we want to achieve. It is not important to be able to say, "I did it." What is important is that we achieve what we want to accomplish in an efficient, effective, and timely manner. Actually getting the organization working as a team is all-powerful, and success will follow.

- **The role of executive leadership.** The role of executive leadership/management/supervision is to set direction, establish roles/responsibilities/expectations, set priorities, and provide the needed tools to your people (the organization). Direction is set at a high level with vision, mission, and values. Roles/responsibilities/expectation/priorities set direction at a day-to-day level. Setting priorities is critical. Generally an organization has more on its plate than it can work on at any point in time. If priorities are not set, you run the risk of getting bogged down and will not accomplish very much in a timely manner. Once you have set the course and established priorities, you have to be sure your organization has the tools to do the job in a way that meets your expectations. Tools include staffing, information, training, funds (money), etc. However, we all have to understand that we will not be able to provide all the tools the organization needs/wants.

- **People are important; business is common sense.** When you get down to it, business is not mystical—it is generally common sense. Treat people like you would like to be treated. Be demanding but fair and consistent. Give people a chance to be successful by making sure they know their roles/responsibilities and your expectations. Support them with tools and guidance. Reward good performance and deal with underperformance. Sometimes you need to think about what you would do if this were your money or your company. This will bring the decision closer to home.

- **Decision making.** Decisions should be made based on the facts of the situation. It will take time and effort to dig out the facts, including the risks associated with the decision. Work to develop the business case, i.e., the economics of the decision. In dealing with risk, identify the economic sensitivity if something adverse were to happen, and then determine how you can manage or avoid the risk. It is very important in evaluating a situation that you stay focused on the business aspects and keep personalities out of the decision. The facts and analysis will generally lead you to the right decision. Don't forget to monitor the results of the decision. Sometimes we do not make the correct decision, or we have to make adjustments along the way— that's OK, just learn from each decision as it will help you make better ones in the future. The main thing is to make a decision using facts and your best judgment. Avoid feel-good decisions.

- **Develop the business case.** When developing the business case, it is important to dig out all the facts you can about markets, customers, capital costs, expenses, risk, environmental issues, alternative scenarios, sensitivities, etc. Translate the facts into economics, and highlight associated risks by developing economic sensitivities/alternative cases. The more we learn about the situation, the better our decision will be. It is easy to fall into a trap of study, study, and study; we have to balance the effort so that we can get to a decision point in a timely manner.

- **Analyze the financials.** Everyone should try to understand why the financial numbers are what they are; however, the financial organization should take the lead in digging behind the numbers to identify variances and opportunities. In this effort, they should ask questions of operations and others. Don't always take operations' answer; have the curiosity to understand what drives the numbers and what opportunities exist to improve the business. What are the drivers of top performance in each segment of the business?

- **Build credibility and trust.** Credibility and trust are important in any business relationship. Both are difficult to develop, but both are easily destroyed. Once destroyed, it is very, very difficult to rebuild credibility and trust. Your actions must be honest, legal, ethical, and forthright. Stay away from hidden agendas; stay focused on the business aspects of the deal.

- **Maintain effective communication.** Effective communication is essential to achieve a successful business. Communication with employees must be open and honest. Effective communication is not one-way; it has to be a two-way dialogue. Effective communication will not just happen; it takes time and effort. Follow-up is critical to close the loop, as people will hear what you say but won't necessarily believe you until you demonstrate you are good to your word.

- **Appearance is important.** If you are sloppy in how you dress, act, or maintain your facilities, it will affect how your customers and business associates perceive the quality and professionalism of your business. Getting to work or to appointments on time is also important.

- **Set priorities.** A critical responsibility of management is to set priorities. We all have limited staffing and other resources, so we can only do so much. Stay focused on priority items. Complete them one at a time, and move on to the next one. Otherwise, if you spread yourself too thin, nothing will happen.

- **Recognize and reward performance; move away from entitlements.** No one is guaranteed a job or pay raise. Employees who have an entitlement attitude become obstacles for the rest of the organization. One has to earn his way (by fulfilling his roles and responsibilities) if he wants to keep a job and progress in his career. People should be given the opportunity to demonstrate what they can do. Management has the responsibility to be sure people understand their roles, responsibilities, and expectations on the job and to provide the essential tools needed to perform. In addition, management has the responsibility to reward performance and to deal with underperformance.

- **It's results that count.** All the talk, planning, who did what, etc. doesn't mean anything if the desired results are not achieved. It's the results—and only the results—that count.

- **Inherent risks.** It's important to identify and deal with the risks inherent in a business. Sometimes you can put measures into place (like a gaming compact) that deal with risks; other times you will need back-up plans; and in other cases you will accept the risks as part of doing business. With our gaming business, we must have legal, ethical, and enforcement (surveillance, security, compliance) activities that cover everyone. We cannot assume that just because I'm CEO or whatever, I am above reproach.

- **Negotiations.** Prepare thoroughly for negotiations. Think through your position and the position of the other party. No one else will watch out for your interests; that is your responsibility. Patience is critical in any negotiation. If you get in a hurry or are trying to beat a deadline, it will more than likely work against you. It is also critical to identify alternatives so, if necessary, you can walk away from the deal. The alternatives may cost you in the short run but pay in the medium to long run. When you have the deal, confirm it in writing right away; otherwise positions may change when the parties talk to others. Also, when you have a deal, honor it.

- **Don't fall in love with an asset.** One all-too-common mistake in the business world is that companies fall in love with an asset, so they hang on and continue to invest in the asset when it is to their business advantage to sell or do something else with the asset.

- **Training.** Training is important, but it can also be a distraction if not properly managed. It can be a time and resource robber. Training should be directed to the company's highest priority need. For example, in our case, we have a priority issue around employee turnover. This could mean we need training specifically directed at new employee orientation, job training, and supervisor training. Once the need is identified, "rifle shot" training should be provided to those individuals who have the need in their current job. Once all the specific current job-training needs are addressed, you can provide more training for development purposes. When general training is made available and you have to call around to fill seats, that's a red flag.

David Tippeconnic's doctrines gave corporate staff specific direction and guidance. His first point, "Get our house in order," is similar to Point A, a general current assessment of the organization. Another class of his doctrines deal with leadership, the process of going from Point A to Point B. He admonished his team to challenge everything, lead by example, set roles/responsibilities/expectations, and function as a team. He explained the role of executive leadership and stressed that people are important and that business is common sense. He encouraged his team to build credibility and trust, maintain effective communications, and set priorities. He then addressed sound business practices: decision making, developing the business case, analyzing the financials, identifying inherent risks, and negotiating. His tips included: don't fall in love with an asset, it's the results that count, recognize and reward performance, move away from entitlements, and train employees. And he reminded us that it is still important to dress and present yourself in an appropriate manner. All of these doctrines or pointers help create productive business leaders.

Tippeconnic's doctrines also illustrate a very important point: rote memory of leadership characteristics is not important; what's important is understanding each working concept, assigning each the language that best expresses for you the meaning, and using it as needed. For example, "Don't fall in love with an asset" clearly expresses for me that an asset merely is a means to an end, and it is the end that matters. It reminded me not to lose focus on the product, or Point B, and get distracted by activities, institutions, or programs. Assets are a means to an end not an end unto themselves.

Branding: Do You See What You Get?

Another way for you as a leader to prepare for the journey from Point A to Point B is to communicate where Point B is and how you are going to get there. Just as Tommy Tucker suggested, visualize what you want to get done by writing it down and posting it somewhere you will see it every day. We need to be reminded of where we are going and how we are going to get there. Monuments remind us of what is important. To visualize Point B, an iconic image, logo, motto, or statement is often helpful. In marketing, this is called branding or identity management.

Branding is generally thought of as a marketing icon that identifies a product. The value of branding is demonstrated by the exercise of bringing refreshments to a meeting. Lay side by side Oreo cookies in their package and generic knock-off cookies in their package. Watch which cookies go first. The Oreos will. Branding communicates what is known and expected of a product and company. Just think about McDonald's, Walmart, and Kentucky Fried Chicken—there are no surprises with their products; we know what to expect. The brand also is the symbol and summary of the essential work of an organization. You know what you are going to get when you see the brand. Branding is not only the visual symbol but the music, slogan, and other images closely associated with the visual symbol. Does the image portray the identity of the product and organization? If there is no branding or identity policy, then you, your staff, and the public see nothing but visual noise. To build a brand, you must identify the essential attributes, aspects, or qualifications of your business. It is a similar process to being able to articulate a product.

A great value of branding is its ability to reinforce an organization's attributes and goals with its employees and customers. Think of every surface, interior and exterior, every audio file or broadcast, every piece of paper, every electronic file, and every video clip as a medium to strengthen your brand, to solidify and claim an identity, to tell your organization's story. Part of communicating and sharing Point B with employees and constituents is branding, or identity management. Often it is a great opportunity that is lost.

What was the image that we wanted to broadcast to the world when I took office in 1999 after an administration of chaos and confusion? We took down the multitude of security cameras at our office complex that had been used by the previous administration to watch employees and the general public as they came and went in our public building. We kept cameras for only those areas where there were security issues or cash management. The message was that the office complex was open, free, and friendly. The previous administration had hidden itself away in an office maze in the corner of the building with several security doors and gate-keeper secretaries. It took an appointment to get into the inner sanctum of the principal chief's office. We immediately removed the security doors and gate-keepers and even took down some walls to open access. The message was clear: we intended to have an accessible and approachable administration. The previous administration had reserved private parking in spaces closest to the building. We had those reserved parking signs removed and replaced with handicapped parking. The message was that my administration was there to help constituents, not ourselves. Taking out surveillance cameras, changing floor plans, knocking down walls, creating more physical access, and repainting signs helped to brand our style of openness and accessibility.

Governor Bill Anoatubby of the Chickasaw Nation is known for beginning every speech with a litany: "Greetings from the unconquered and unconquerable Chickasaw Nation known for its intrepid warriors never known to lose in battle." Later in his career he added, "and its dynamic women." His speech branded the Chickasaw Nation; he captured its chosen identity.

We sought to similarly brand the Cherokee Nation in our cultural tourism initiative.

Each state is entitled to be represented by two statues in the United States Capitol's statuary hall. Oklahoma's two statues are of Cherokees: Sequoyah, known for developing a Cherokee written language and syllabary, and Will Rogers, known for being a humorist, newspaper columnist, radio commentator, and movie star. They also represent the broad attraction for cultural tourism in the Cherokee Nation by providing geographical bookends: Sequoyah's home place in the southeast of Cherokee Nation, near Sallisaw, Oklahoma, and the Will Rogers Memorial in the northwest of Cherokee Nation, near Claremore, Oklahoma.

Cultural tourism appeals to individuals who want to explore history, culture, and their own heritage, and it appeals to communities that want to share their history and character. For an Indian tribe such as the Cherokee Nation, cultural tourism offers the chance to tell our story in our own unique way. Cultural tourism can preserve culture and language and stimulate economic development by creating tourism-related jobs. Additionally, taking the lead in regulating cultural tourism development allows us to ensure its integrity and authenticity.

People have a deep, emotional connection with their heritage, especially if they are Indian. In Oklahoma, where the Cherokee Nation is the largest of 39 tribes, it only makes sense to build on Oklahoma tourism where the state slogan is "Oklahoma: Native America." Creating a positive image for the Cherokee Nation is beneficial not just for tourism but for local businesses and for social goodwill.

The product of cultural tourism in the Cherokee Nation is Cherokees telling their story. The impact of the story depends on how well it is told. The story can be told orally, by customer service, by property interpretation, by literature, by audio-visuals, by mass communication, by architecture, and by designing tour and travel. The ability to tell a story well is essential in bringing individuals into the empathy and emotion of the Cherokee Nation and its cultural experience. It is fundamental to the cultural tourism effort that each employee—regardless of whether she is a bus driver, waitress, or operations manager—understands and practices good storytelling.

Cultural tourism is based on a mosaic of places, traditions, art forms, celebrations, and experiences that portrays the Cherokee Nation and its people and reflects the diversity and character of the Cherokee Nation. Cultural tourism helps accomplish three strategic initiatives: jobs, language, and community. Jobs is the initiative to become economically self-reliant. Language is to exercise and revitalize the arts and crafts, cultural attributes, and values that enrich Cherokee lives. And community is to help form and reinforce cohesive Cherokee communities. Cultural tourism, very simply, allows Cherokees to tell their story. That story can be told a number of ways; the content and the process is well defined by Cherokee history and culture, but the medium changes. The story conveys the wisdom, challenges, and aspirations of the Cherokee people. The first step in developing the cultural tourism system was to premise it on storytelling.

In addition to its power as an oral art form, storytelling also influences the design and architecture of historic properties, the organization of tour and travel, the presentation of meals at restaurants, the design and flow of retail stores, and the layout of art studios in historic districts. Understanding the process of storytelling and being able to communicate the content of the Cherokee story is the organizing concept for Cherokee cultural tourism.

The Cherokee story is first shared with an internal market—the Cherokee people. Unfortunately, many Cherokee people have lost cultural attributes, knowledge of their history, and the positive impact of a Cherokee way of life. Cultural tourism creates an incentive to relearn the language, to develop the arts and crafts to a higher level, to learn and tell stories, and to study the history of the Cherokees. In essence, cultural tourism helps reinforce the language, culture, tradition, and heritage of the Cherokees.

The second market is an external market—non-Indians. Cherokees have learned from history that public policy, embodied in law, changes every 20 to 40 years. In order to moderate or influence public policy, the Cherokee Nation must influence public sentiment so that the general public views us favorably or, at the very least, neutrally. We influence public sentiment by telling the Cherokee story. The time is ripe for the Cherokee story to be accurately told to non-Indians in the area, region, and nation in order to build social and political capital. The Cherokee Nation must ensure that crass, harmful stereotypes and misinformation regarding the Cherokee Nation are not perpetuated by Hollywood nonsense and other adversaries.

Our cultural tourism uses a holistic approach. Travelers can stop almost any place within the Cherokee Nation and get a sense of the cultural ambiance and history. For example, a family flies into Tulsa, stops at the Catoosa casino property, and then drives 65 miles to Tahlequah, the capital of the Cherokee Nation. On the way down on Highway 82, they stop for gas in the small town of Peggs. They go to pay for the gas and ask about Zeke Proctor, who is known to them as an infamous Cherokee outlaw. The gas station attendant says, "Well, let me tell you the true story about Zeke Proctor. He was not an outlaw but a great patriot . . ." The gas station attendant uses Cherokee greetings and goodbyes. On the building, the word for *gas station* is written in the Cherokee syllabary. The gas station also offers historic and cultural materials at the counter and sells authentic Cherokee arts and crafts. The family resumes its journey to Tahlequah, where they find 10 cultural properties including the Capitol building; the Supreme Court building, the oldest public building in Oklahoma; and the Female Seminary, the first institution of higher education west of the Mississippi for women. Downtown Tahlequah is themed with historically accurate decor and products, and the Cherokee syllabary appears on each storefront. Traditional Cherokee products and food are available in small boutiques and cafes including kanuche, wishi, fry bread, and quality arts and crafts. The family can also choose from a range of tourism and travel packages that include a drama, float trips, horseback trips, reenactments of the Trail of Tears, visits to historic cemeteries and churches, and so forth.

We branded Cherokee Nation cultural tourism with the phrase "Osiyo means in Cherokee, it is good to see you." First you introduce yourself, and then you tell your story.

Our administration boiled down the desired outcomes for our brand to one word each. Themes for events, signage, outlines for speeches, introductions, and even employee orientation all focused on jobs, language, and community. The message was that we should create jobs to become economically self-reliance, use our culture and language to think and act Cherokee, and build cohesive communities. Branding is a tool to communicate the identity and direction of an organization.

Thinking in other languages, discovering what drives people, learning from the experiences of successful people, and understanding branding offer lessons that prepare us to be leaders.

PROGRESS

Even if you are on the right track, you'll get run over if you just sit there.

WILL ROGERS

Metrics: Are We There Yet?

Along the path from Point A to Point B, we have to ask ourselves: Are we on the right road? Are we getting closer to our destination? Metrics and measurements answer those questions and give us feedback not only about where we are but about how effectively and efficiently we are getting there and when we should arrive. Take the analogy of driving from Tahlequah to Norman, Oklahoma: We can look at the road map, GPS, and road signs to verify that we are on the right path including the road we are on, the town we are entering, the next town ahead, the number of miles to the next town, the presence of a detour or construction zone, etc. We have the speedometer and odometer to tell us our speed, average speed, estimated time of arrival, how far we have come, and how far we have to go. We also have the fuel gauge and engine service indicators to tell us if we have the energy and mechanical ability to reach our destination. All of these metrics and measurements help us get where we are going. If we take a wrong turn or get lost, there is information that corrects our route to reach our designation. It is an information-rich environment for a 150-mile Oklahoma drive.

Successful operations also use metrics and measurements. As Kyle Smith tells me, "What you measure gets done." The critical question is are you measuring work that takes you to Point B, your destination? For instance, diabetes is a terrible epidemic, especially in Indian country. American Indians have a 100 percent higher incidence of diabetes than other racial or ethnic groups, and it is increasing. The Cherokee

Nation received a federal grant for the treatment and prevention of diabetes. As part of the grant, a public awareness campaign was conducted with billboards, literature, newspaper ads, etc. The measure of a successful campaign is not the number of billboards put up, the placement of newspaper ads, or the volume of literature distributed; rather, the pertinent question is, "Did the incidence of diabetes go down in the clinical test group?" Diabetes is measured by blood sugar. If blood sugar remained the same or increased in the test group, funding billboards, newspaper, and literature was a waste of time and money. The goal (Point B) of reducing diabetes as measured by decreasing blood sugar should direct the design of the program (i.e., to educate and create incentives in the clinical population to change their diets and increase physical activity).

For my administration, we adopted a balanced scorecard. It focused on the five desired outcomes and was developed in detail so that each group and department had a scorecard that rolled up to the national scorecard. Employee compensation was based on scorecard performance, attributes, and improvement.

Balanced scorecards developed by Art Schneiderman are very sophisticated and deserve adequate attention. It is not only the resulting scorecard that is important but the process by which the staff develops and interprets work and metrics. There are other methods of metrics, but regardless of method, the feedback information must focus on how well you are progressing or how close you are getting to Point B.

Cherokee Nation Businesses adopted a traditional corporate set of performance measures based on financial performance. We recruited 15 board members; each was Cherokee and had outstanding business credentials. They included Jay Hannah, David Tippeconnic, Adolph Lechtenberg, B.J. Dumond, Mitch Adwon, Mick Webber, Dennis Dowell, and others. They clearly understood the necessity of business case analysis and sound business decisions; they understood and enforced strict corporate governance, compliance, and integrity. Each believed the measure of business success was bottom line profit; they viewed labor as an expense and considered reinvestment critical. I, however, viewed the businesses as a means to an end: achieving our designed purpose and accomplishing our desired outcome. As the shareholders' representative,

I asked the board to evaluate the businesses using five criteria: make a profit, employ Cherokees, outsource to Cherokees, develop long-term capacity, and promote goodwill for the Nation. The board understood clearly the first criterion and was very comfortable focusing on profit since that was the driver for their work in the private sector. Their debate centered on what should be the threshold rate of return or profit necessary to expand or acquire a business. My belief was the businesses should at least break even and carry themselves, but creating jobs was the primary goal. If economic self-reliance was a desired outcome both for the Nation and individual Cherokees, employing and outsourcing were the primary products. For me, employees became an asset of the businesses rather than an expense. Expanding the employment of Cherokees and increasing their self-worth and their value to the businesses through training and leadership development was a desired outcome to be measured. "You do what you measure." We reported on the number and percentage of Cherokee current employees, new hires, terminations, and promotions at each tier of management and at each property or business location. We measured outsourcing based on the number and percentage of Cherokee firms bidding and winning awards, the dollar amount of contracts or services, and improvement of outsourcing to Cherokee firms. The number of Cherokee employees increased, and the goods and services outsourced increased dramatically. The measurement of developing long-term capacity and goodwill was more difficult and was reflected in a dashboard report. Long-term capacity was reflected in employee training and the acquisition of technical companies. Goodwill was reflected in community participation by staff and the dollar amount of earned media reports.

Leadership requires knowing where you are on the path from A to B and being able to answer the question, "Are we there yet?"

PLANT

You know, I used to think the future was solid or fixed,
something you inherited like an old building that you
move into when the previous generation moves out or

gets chased out. But it's not. The future is not fixed; it's
fluid. You can build your own building, or hut, or condo
... The world is more malleable than you think, and it's
waiting for you to hammer it into shape.

BONO

Plant and Grow the Seeds of Inspiration

There are many way to inspire people to envision and execute a plan. The most productive people have aspirations to contribute to a legacy, to leave something worthwhile for their children, to make a difference, to leave their mark, or, in more folksy terms, to leave the woodpile higher than when they got there. Many metaphors work, but the one I find most compelling is the "planting of seed corn." The concept is that you don't eat all of your harvest; you keep some back to plant the next year. The more you hold back for next year, the more you have to plant, and the more harvest you have for successive years. The idea of planting also suggests a natural cycle of seasons and the necessity of planting, weeding, nurturing, and protecting. Planting requires patience, discipline, diligence, and knowledge of the environment. It was easy for me to attract Cherokee leaders to help guide the Cherokee Nation because I shared with them a vision for the Nation and a desire to create a legacy. My executive staff could have earned more money than what the Cherokee Nation paid them, but at the end of every day, each of them could go home and say to themselves: I helped a person, family, community, and/ or the Nation to grow today. We knew the next morning we had the same rewarding opportunity. We got to build something meaningful. We got to build a nation.

President Obama captured the inspiration of legacy. At a memorial service to the victims of the Gabby Giffords shooting in Tucson, Arizona, he said, "All of us—we should do everything we can to make sure this country lives up to our children's expectations." And during a prayer vigil at Newtown, Connecticut, he said, "For those of us who remain, let us find the strength to carry on and make our country worthy of their memory."

We study our history. In spite of a great Cherokee legacy, I knew as we prospered that there would be a clamor for more free services or even per capita payments or revenue sharing that smaller tribes with better gaming markets paid. There was a great lesson to be learned from 1895. The United States made a payment of $7.8 million to the Cherokee Nation for the coerced sale of the Cherokee Outlet. Seven million acres of northwestern Oklahoma known as the Cherokee Outlet were taken by official extortion for $1.25 an acre in 1893 and opened for a land run. The Cherokee Nation had a decision to make in 1895: what to do with the money? The Nation decided to pay a per capita payment; every Cherokee citizen got a pro rata share, which amounted to about $390 each. That was a lot of money, but it was gone in a matter of months, and the Cherokee Nation was still vulnerable to encroachment by the United States on its remaining 7.5 million acres. Within three years, the United State liquidated the assets of the Cherokee Nation including its buildings, funds, and other assets and pro rata distributed its land as allotments. If the Cherokee Nation had made the decision to preserve itself in 1895, it could have retained enough money from the Outlet payment to lobby or even buy the United States Congress to prevent liquidation and allotment. Probably half a million dollars would have been enough to buy Congress in 1895. If the Cherokee Nation could have retained its lands in 1895, where would it be today with 7.5 million acres held in common? The recurring rental and royalties from oil, water, timber, and easements could have provided enough funding for the best schools and medical systems.

The Cherokee Nation lost a great opportunity in 1895. Its people fell prey to immediate gratification, and as a result, the federal government almost completely destroyed the Nation in 1906. It took Cherokees 70 years to begin to rebuild.

It is important to plant the seed corn. In his book *Built to Last*, Jim Collins discusses how corporations that not only succeed but last for decades have a clear sense of "mission or identity." Similarly, the inspiration for pursuing a long-range vision must be seeded and grown. My column in the February 2008 *Cherokee Phoenix*, "Tradition of the Seed Corn," addresses this concept.

"Tradition of the Seed Corn"

By Chad Smith, Principal Chief

One hundred years ago the Cherokee people reaped rich harvests of corn. At that time every Cherokee had a home and they all worked together for the common good. These Cherokees were wise. They knew to save their seed corn for next season's crop. They knew that if all Cherokee communities saved their seed corn, there would be plenty the next year to feed themselves and their neighbors if someone's crop failed.

Today, Cherokee Nation recognizes the wisdom of its ancestors and is continuing this tradition of saving, working together, and planning for future generations. We do this strategic planning in many ways, but our focus is on culture, jobs, and community. We know that our Cherokee language, culture, and heritage are what make us unique. We know that our culture thrives in strong Cherokee communities, where Cherokees can interact with each other daily and pass on our traditions. We know that keeping those communities strong for the future means that we have to create jobs so our citizens will be able to provide a good life for their families and don't have to move out of state, or even out of our communities. That is why we must wisely plant seed corn to create opportunities for jobs, communities, and culture to grow and thrive.

Culture

Cherokee Nation is investing in the uniqueness of its people and culture. We encourage our youth to learn Cherokee culture by teaching our language, history, art, traditions, games, and way of life. We can see the results of planting the seed corn of culture when we hear our elders talking to young children in Cherokee and hear the kids answering them back. We see it at our traditional grounds, where centuries-old ceremonies continue to this day. We must plant seed corn for culture by put-

155

ting our time, energy, and money into creating an environment in which our culture can thrive.

Self-Reliance

The tribe is strategically reinvesting in its businesses to create jobs in the Cherokee Nation that keep families close and enhance the quality of life for our people and our communities. The best service the Cherokee Nation can provide to our citizens is a job. With good jobs located in or near Cherokee communities, our people can provide for themselves and their families. For 100 years, we waited for jobs to come to the Cherokee Nation. When that didn't happen, we saw family members scatter and lost valuable citizens to faraway states where job opportunities were more plentiful. It's become quite apparent that unless the Cherokee Nation creates jobs in Cherokee communities, jobs won't be there. That is why we consider a job the best service we can provide a Cherokee citizen. Good jobs with benefits let Cherokee citizens provide for themselves and their families and give back to the community. When the Cherokee Nation invests money to create jobs, we are planting the seed corn that will help future generations of Cherokees live and work in Cherokee communities and keep our culture strong.

Strong Communities

The Cherokee Nation is a family of families and a community of communities. In our strongest communities, people still work together in a way that is ingrained within the Cherokee culture and language, the concept known as ᎦᏚᎩ (gadugi). We work together for the benefit of the entire community. By investing time, money, and other resources in Cherokee communities, the Cherokee Nation can help communities come together to help each other and themselves. We see the success of this approach with some of our self-help housing programs, where groups of Cherokees work together to build each other houses. They not only end up with new homes, they end up with a strong sense of community. These are the kinds of bonds that will keep the Cherokee Nation strong for centuries, but we must help by investing in that process today so we can see the results in the future.

I hope that all the citizens of the Cherokee Nation and our neighbors join us as we revive the tradition of the seed corn and work together for a better future for all.

The idea of the seed corn from a Cherokee perspective is further explained in my column in the April 2008 *Cherokee Phoenix*, "Planting the Seed Corn for Our Children's Future."

"Planting the Seed Corn for Our Children's Future ᏗᏂᏲᏟ ᎤᎾᎵᏍᏕᎸᏙᏗ (diniyotli unalisdelvdodi)"
By Chad Smith, Principal Chief

For centuries, Cherokees have focused on the legacies we will leave our children and grandchildren. Our culture and our nation exists today because our ancestors had the foresight to ᏗᏂᏲᏟ ᎤᎾᎵᏍᏕᎸᏙᏗ (diniyotli unalisdelvdodi): "We do this today so the children can do for themselves tomorrow." This reflects a tradition of planting seed corn year after year, preparing the ground, reaping and sowing, and saving the seed for future crops, for our children and their future. People who do this are held in great esteem by their communities because their neighbors understand that whatever they do—buy a car, go to work, plant a garden—it is all done for their children's future. Every Cherokee citizen can do it, and almost all of us do. Whether it is working on a community self-help project, assisting an elderly neighbor, or teaching our youngest ones the stories and traditions that have been passed down to us, we all can ᏗᏂᏲᏟ ᎤᎾᎵᏍᏕᎸᏙᏗ (diniyotli unalisdelvdodi), plant the seed corn.

This concept works on a personal level, as we all want happiness and health for our families. The Cherokee Nation government is here because patriots of our great nation, dating back more than 200 years, have made sacrifices of their time and skills to help the Cherokee Nation and our people grow stronger. Many family trees trace generations of service to the Cherokee Nation.

You may have heard me quote my great-grandfather Redbird Smith: "It is pride in one's people that makes a man give his all for his country." Cherokee patriots today have the luxury of giving their time instead of their all for their country, because earlier generations ᎫᏂᏯᏟ ᏓᎣᏢᏬᏛᏴᎶᏛᏗ (diniyotli una-lis delvdodi), thought to plant the seed corn for us. Planting seed corn is one motivator to reinforce the values of the organization and to motivate employees to invest extra effort into their work.

Planting seed corn is but one metaphor to illustrate the value and need to inspire people to complete the journey from Point A to Point B. There are many other good ones.

One of the great patriots and mentors during my tenure as principal chief was Julian Fite, our Cherokee Nation general counsel, who passed in 2005. He was Cherokee and had been a U.S. attorney. In 1993, he wrote an essay, "Starts with Identity," that provided valuable insight as we gained and grew inspiration to rebuild the Cherokee Nation.

Starts with Identity
By Julian Fite

Life is a difficult task to approach. We might do well or poorly in the eyes of the world, and it probably makes little difference what the world thinks. A major precept might be to screw up our own lives and others as little as possible. The opposite is the concept of the positive, of "doin" good.

I. Long ago, during college, I came to think of four positive characteristics—strength, wisdom, love, and tolerance. The terms are well understood and require little explanation . . .

II. Years later, while considering what positive activity is, I came to consider three areas of useful and positive activity—learning, achieving and helping . . . It seems three areas of positive activity are the basis for civilization and mankind's progress. The levels of learning, achievement, and helping others in a society tell us much about the success of that society. The opposites of these positive activities are certainly not desirable—ignorance, lack of achievement, lack of concern for others.

III. A favorite author and anthropologist, Robert Ardrey, in discussing the nature of man gave a most challenging analysis. Ardrey contended that there are three driving influences—identity, stimulation, and security. Identity was described as a clear sense of who one is and what one's role is—of relative importance and meaning. Stimulation means excitement, challenge, or even diversion. Security is protection of vital needs, of house, family, and country. Ardrey ranked identity as most important, stimulation second, and security as third . . .

IV. There are a number of precepts or rules that I have come to think are very important.

1. You can't fix others, only yourself.

2. Do not permit the mistreatment of others or the abridgment of free speech.

3. All are sick, and love is the medicine. We all have fears, weaknesses, troubles, and insecurities. If we give love, or act lovingly, we make others' lives a little better.

4. No man is an island.

V. You are what you think. I am a believer that thought precedes action and even reality. If we know that we cannot do or accomplish something then we certainly cannot. If we know or believe that we can, then we usually do. We create reality in our minds and then it becomes so. A child doesn't learn unless she thinks she can.

VI. You are what you do. Our lives tend to derive meaning, purpose, and a sense of self-worth from our activities. Thought without action is meaningless. We can think or dream of many things. But, unless we act, thought has no meaning or purpose.

VII. The "Woodpile Theory." We should leave the woodpile a little higher than we found it. We live a fairly short life, compared to history. If we can, we should make things better for our families, for everyone. That gives purpose and meaning to life.

"Planting the seed corn" or "leaving the wood pile higher" are similar motivational metaphors because they don't elicit an immediate emotional response but confirm that staying focused on the journey from Point A to Point B is a long-term process. It is a natural process. Planting the seed corn reminds us in graphic ways that understanding and appreciating long-term achievement ensure that the organization will endure, that legacy is passed on, and that Point B is reached.

The great wisdom book at Galatians 6:7 reads, "Whatever a man sows, that shall he also reap." It certainly applies not only to individuals but to organizations as a driver to motivate people to adhere to a plan or strategy.

A powerful lesson for me was that a greater inspiration to plant the seed corn and pass on a legacy was not to honor your ancestors but to love your children.

PROCEED UNDAUNTED

An invincible determination can accomplish almost anything, and in this lies the great distinction between great men and little men.

DR. THOMAS FULLER
1608–1661

If you stop to throw a rock at every dog that barks at you, you will never get to town.

HASTINGS SHADE
Deputy Principal Chief

Proceed Undaunted: Don't Throw a Rock at Every Dog that Barks at You

From my high school wrestling days, I picked up the saying, "Proceed undaunted." If you know where your Point B is and have a path mapped out, there is little reason not to proceed undaunted. Sometimes it is as simple as "throwing your hat across the creek and going after it," or as Jay Hannah, the chairman of our business board, would say, "It is time for the getting on with the getting on."

Before I took office in 1999, the Cherokee Nation had undergone a constitutional crisis, because the previous principal chief had stated he would decide which decisions of the Cherokee Nation Supreme Court were constitutional and which ones he would abide by. Absolute chaos ensued. The first six months of my tenure were terrible as we sorted out the good from bad and productive from counterproductive, assessed systems, and set up foundational systems as simple as proper accounting. Every day an antagonistic press and hateful political opponents would challenge me publicly on personal and policy issues. My dad told me a story a long time ago about how he could tell what kind of day he was going to have as he was walking to school. It depended on whether he saw a rabbit or squirrel first. A squirrel meant a bad day, and a rabbit meant a good day. He then chuckled and said that if he saw either, it would be a good day, because he grew up during the Depression, and seeing either meant he would have something to eat. For me, the daily press coverage was foreshadowed by first seeing a rabbit or a squirrel.

Linda Lewis, a marketing consultant, gave great advice: "Outperform your criticism." In public relations, you often don't respond to false allegations and unfounded criticism directly because it gives the public a second opportunity to hear the negative assertions. For six months, I bit my tongue and worked harder. It was amazing—soon the negative press and criticism began to subside. Linda's adage does not work in political campaigns, but it worked for building an organization.

Often when I get frustrated that things are not working out according to my plan A, B, or C, I think of my uncle Tim Beck at Christmas time in Oklahoma when I was 12 years old. He and my cousin, who was a couple of years older than mes, were trying to put together a pole lamp he got my aunt as a Christmas gift. After studying the instructions, they still could not get it to go together right. Uncle Tim, in the midst of his frustration, turned to my cousin and said, "You know someone was smart enough to make this lamp. We ought to be smart enough to put it together." Sometimes proceeding undaunted requires some patience and encouragement.

Five Minutes That Can Change a Life: Ten Things at Bedtime

Proceeding undaunted often comes from a foundation of confidence, patience, and encouragement. Sometimes it is confidence in your talent, and sometimes it is confidence that you make sound decisions. My column in the June 2009 *Cherokee Phoenix*, "Five Minutes That Can Change a Life," discusses how confidence grows.

"Five Minutes That Can Change a Life"
By Chad Smith, Principal Chief

Have you ever considered that a five-minute investment of your time can change someone's life? It can change the lives of children in your family. It can change for the better the future of the Cherokee Nation.

Sam Bradford, a Cherokee Nation citizen, Heisman Trophy winner, and University of Oklahoma football team quarterback, is living proof of the power of five brief minutes. Those who only know of Sam as a football player might be surprised he is a college honor student, a participant in the Fellowship of Christian Athletes, a golfer, and a cello player. Sam can also tell you that all his awards, including his Heisman Trophy, are not what make him a leader.

Sam told us that in his freshman year at OU, he almost quit the football team. He almost quit on his dream. As you can imagine, the amount of time spent on practicing and on studying can be overwhelming for a young freshman. Sam said that he got up at 5:30 in the morning for practice, worked hard in practice every day, and got yelled at by the coaches for everything he did or did not do; his efforts were getting him nowhere. He was red-shirted and did not get to play, a strange situation to find himself in as a young man who had always been a starter on every team in every sport at which he tried his hand. He was tired, confused, and seriously contemplated quitting.

In my interview with Sam, I asked him, "How did you overcome that?" His reply was simple. He said, "I never quit in anything I'd done in my life. I sure didn't want to quit now." So Sam made a choice. Behind his choice were many reasons. He chose to continue on his path and to pursue his dream.

He did not give up because of five minutes.

On stage here at Sequoyah, I asked Sam if he had any advice for young families. He said he did not, but he did know that every night, his dad came into his room and told him 10 things. One was that he could be anything he wanted to be. After years of hearing every night from a very young age his dad saying that he could be anything he wanted to be, he believed it. During times of challenges, despair, hardship, and personal doubt, he believed his Cherokee dad, Kent Bradford. His dad believed in him and every night validated valuable attributes. It took only five minutes a night.

Instead of quitting and settling, Sam Bradford became the first Cherokee Heisman Trophy winner.

You, too, can go to the room of your children, grandchildren, nieces, and nephews every night and tell them they can be anything they want to be, that you support them, that they need to get an education, that you love them, that they are responsible for their decisions, and that they have a great Cherokee legacy to guide them. You can repeat and tell stories of Cherokee attributes. A child hearing that affirmation, affection, validation, and support every night for 10 years, or 3,650 times, before he goes to sleep means he will believe it and will make it through the challenges and tough times. As you take these five minutes with your family's children, your words should also remind you that you, too, can be anything you want to be. We then lead not only by voice but by example. Five minutes can change not only a single child, but also a community and a Nation.

Raising the Bar: Leave a Legacy

Sometimes we need reinforcement or validation as we proceed undaunted. Even though we have confidence, others' expectations can reinforce our confidence as we navigate and overcome difficulties. As Tommy Tucker suggested, to get something done, have someone else hold you accountable. I recall as a child at the kitchen table with my three brothers my Dad's look of disappointment when hearing a report on our behavior; it was worse than a spanking. He did not have to say a word for us to understand what he expected. We wanted to live up to his expectations. In sports, they call it "raising the bar." My column in the April 2009 *Cherokee Phoenix*, "Raising the Bar," discusses how creating expectations improves our performance even though we may not hit the target.

"Raising the Bar"
By Chad Smith, Principal Chief

The girls team was young and had some big shoes to fill, with the graduation of the talented starters from the previous seasons' three-time state championship teams. While they played hard and gave it their all, the girls did not make it to the state tournament. My daughter is a sophomore on the team, and she and the other players were devastated.

As a parent, you hurt for them and feel their disappointment. You might think it's a bad thing, but in this instance, there is a lesson of great value in knowing that they expected more out of themselves and felt bad that their season was over. Why is that good?

There was a time when Sequoyah was satisfied with mediocrity, but no more. Today, students and staff at Sequoyah Schools expect an outstanding season. The boys basketball team has been to the state championships eight times, winning one state championship and three runner-up titles. The girls team has been to the state championships five times, winning an impressive three consecutive state championships and one runner-up title.

Other sports also have impressive records, and our students excel academically. Sequoyah athletes have raised the bar and, with pride and confidence, have increased their expectations of themselves and their school. In falling short of their expectations, the girls felt extreme disappointment.

They now expect to go to the state tournament each year, knowing that they can win that title. They know how to lead themselves, work hard, be disciplined, and proceed undaunted. They have learned that the trials and tribulations of heartache and hard work pay off. In this, they have succeeded. By virtue of the fact that they are exceedingly disappointed in failing to advance to the state tournament, they have come a long way. They no longer settle for mediocrity, and we know that next season they will again give it their all and work even harder to reach their goal.

Their heartfelt lessons should inspire all of us. We believe in these athletes and are there to support them, whether they win or lose. We challenge them to excel, support them in that effort, help them with the discipline, and encourage them when they become disappointed. While supporting them in reaching their goals and expectations, we should be making efforts to do better ourselves. We should increase our own expectations. Too often, we just settle, take what is easy and expedient, and do not expend that extra effort. But when our expectations increase, we have succeeded. We know that those who have gone before us can do it; we know that we can, too.

Proceeding undaunted, repeating encouragement, and expressing expectations are all motivating factors when we meet challenges along the journey. My dad told me a story: It was 1950, and I was only a month old. He and my mom were going to leave Pontiac, Michigan, and look for work in Denver, Colorado. He had a 1950 Chevrolet and a small travel trailer that we lived in. He set about putting a heavy-duty trailer hitch on the Chevrolet to tow the trailer. There was a retired older man who lived in the trailer park, and he spent the entire day helping my dad fix that trailer hitch. At the end of the day, my dad asked how much he owed the man. The man responded, "Nothing. Do something for someone else and it will get back to me." My dad always remembered that, and I remember his story of encouragement not in words but by deeds.

On my first day of graduate school in 1973 at the University of Wisconsin at Madison, I went into a drugstore that still had a long, old-fashioned soda counter and grill. I walked by a guy in his thirties hitting his head with the palms of his hands. I sat in the seat farthest from him and asked the waitress, who seemed to be ignoring his behavior, what was going on. She said he had said something off-color to the waitresses. He was literally beating himself up for this mistake rather than apologizing, learning from the experience, and moving on. Even when obstacles, difficulties, challenges, or problems are of our own making, it is best to move on and proceed undaunted.

Proceeding undaunted is pretty much just an attitude. My wife, Bobbie Gail, is a full-blood Cherokee whose first language is Cherokee. Her family's first home had a dirt floor. She is pleasant, reserved, and sees the world through Cherokee eyes. Generally, people expect her to be meek. But she knows how to proceed undaunted. She went to events with me as first lady of the Cherokee Nation. One event was First Lady Laura Bush's Festival of Books in 2003 at the Congressional Library in Washington, D.C. At the dinner, with 200 people, were President Bush and Laura Bush, Secretary of Defense Donald Rumsfeld and his wife, General Colin Powell, and Julie Andrews. We were invited as guests of Gayle Ross, an outstanding Cherokee storyteller, who performed at the event telling a masterful story of the Cherokee Nation. Bobbie wanted Julie Andrews's autograph. I said, "I don't know if you can do that." At a break, Bobbie proceeded undaunted to Julie Andrews, introduced herself, told her how much she liked her in *The Sound of Music*, and got her autograph. I was shocked. After visiting with other people, I lost Bobbie and found her talking to Mrs. Donald Rumsfeld at their table. Bobbie found out the Rumsfelds had a place in New Mexico, and they were talking about Indians. I approached them and Mrs. Rumsfeld turned and introduced me to her husband, Secretary of Defense Donald Rumsfeld. After we visited with them for awhile, Mrs. Rumsfeld turned to her husband and said, "Donald, Bobbie wants to meet the president. Will you introduce them?" I was dumbfounded. Donald Rumsfeld took Bobbie and me across the room and introduced us to the president and first lady of the United States. Later I asked Bobbie why she had been so assertive; I had seen how friendly she was in community meetings with people and especially Cherokee speakers, but I was taken aback that she got us introduced to the president. She said, "They are people too."

Of course, she was right. Proceeding undaunted is a bit like the Nike commercial: "Just do it." Proceeding undaunted is perseverance. Proceeding undaunted is ᏂᎤᏍᏗᏅᎥᎦ "determined/persistent: never give up."

SUMMARY

How do we get from Point A to Point B? The short answer is, "Proceed undaunted." However, every journey has it turns, detours, potholes, and bumps in the road. There will be disappointment and confusion. Keep in mind the steps along the journey:

Point B. The product, where we want to go

Point A. The place where we start

Principles. Criteria that drive our decisions

Plan. The outline of steps from Point A to Point B

Process. The practical steps to carry out the plan

Preparation. The skills necessary to go from Point A to Point B

Progress. The metrics of determining that we are executing the plan

- Work well done: you can bring dignity to any job if you do it right.

- Indomitable spirit: it is the attitude, not the prowess, that results in success.

- We won't even be here then: work to leave something worthwhile for your descendants.

- If he can do it, I can: the power of an example.

- Want something: the worst thing that can happen to you is apathy.

- Glimpse of life: epiphanies are wonderful.

- What if: imagination should run wild.

- Tell our story: what is the product?

- I have always believed the Creator: we have a designed purpose.

- Whose decision is it: delegate decisions when appropriate.

- Define ourselves: we choose our identity.

- Produce the product: start from the end and work backwards.

- What are the principles: what drives our decisions?

- Where have we been: know our history; it will reflect the future.

- Nothing over 32 inches high: create a productive environment that works by default.

- Think in other languages: know there are other ways to see things.

- Patriotism: find and give meaning to your work.

- Are we there yet: what you measure gets done.

- Five minutes at bedtime: consistent encouragement and validation works.

- Seed corn: look to the future.

- Proceed undaunted: don't let things distract you.

The success of each of us and our institutions and organizations lies in learning valuable lessons so they are not forgotten.

We remember valuable lessons by a unique label, image, code word, or story in much the same way a cliché captures a broader concept. I know there is so much more to learn and that every adversity creates opportunity even though I may not welcome it.

On occasion I am asked, "What do you remember most about being principal chief?" There are several moments that stand out, and each reflects a sense of hope and promise. Several years ago, soon after opening the new gym at Sequoyah, the "Place Where They Play," the basketball teams were playing. The girls team had won several state championships, and the boys team was doing well. The gym was packed, and people were watching the game and walking around talking; the gymnasium was designed to encourage family and community visiting. There was a great sense of community and pride. Two young girls from our immersion school came up to me and were talking Cherokee. They were fluent. The students in our immersion school were the only Cherokees under the age of 50 who were fluent and literate in Cherokee. The moment captured many great things about the Cherokee Nation that I strove to preserve and promote: a sense of community, leadership (as shown on the floor by the ball teams), and the reassurance that our future had promise with a class of children knowing our language.

I confess that one of the great lessons I keep forgetting is one my mother, Pauline, told me over and over, though it never set in properly. She was the salt of the earth and would give you the shirt off her back. She said, "Take some time to smell the roses." Of course she was right.

It was a great honor to serve as principal chief. The leaders I recruited and those who emerged when given the chance made the Cherokee Nation grow exponentially for 12 years. The lessons we learned were simple but effective.

Craig Miner's book, *The Corporation and the Indian*, is about the Allotment Era of the Five Civilized Tribes and the federal government's forced assimilation policy in 1898. Miner characterized well the challenge, calling, and opportunity for the Cherokee Nation: "A sovereign people must determine its own citizenship, wisely or unwisely, it must provide for its own military defense, it must execute its own laws (by force if necessary), and it must produce patriots to protect itself against the corruption of its legislative apparatus." Governments, businesses, communities, families, and individuals all have the choices to determine their futures, and leaders will make those choices.

When I took office in 1999 as principal chief, we did not know where we could take the Cherokee Nation. The lessons learned during that time worked for the Cherokee Nation. For 12 years, we built rather than destroyed, planted the seed corn, and left the wood pile higher.

So the last lesson is that leaders will take us from Point A to Point B. The important question is, "Where are you going to lead us?"

PART 2

DSGℓℐᎾᏒℐ TEWhℓᎯᏋᎯ

LESSONS
APPLIED

APPLICATION OF
LESSONS LEARNED

THE SPEECHES THAT make up the second part of this book reflect the progression of my learning during my tenure as principal chief, and they record some of the progress we made at the Cherokee Nation from 1999 to 2011. Most were state of the nation speeches required by the Cherokee Nation Constitution in which I report on the status of the Cherokee Nation for that year. I saw these speeches as an opportunity to share inspirational stories, to outline a course of action for the Cherokee Nation, and to remind people of the "designed purpose" that Redbird Smith spoke of 100 years ago. Change is not linear, and the velocity of change is not constant. During the first year of my administration, as we were trying to clean up the accounting, legal, and operational messes of my predecessor, progress was maybe two steps forward and one step back. Soon it became more steps forward before one back.

Change in organizations and in people's lives resembles a frequency chart or a map of statistical sampling. Once responses are recorded on a chart, it looks like a shotgun blast on a sheet of paper, and with a regression analysis, you can chart a line or path. The chart comprises a scattering of frequency points along an ill-defined band and a series of outlier points. It is never simple and pretty. In the following speeches, themes emerge and progress is seen amidst individual events that often look random. These speeches share the lessons I learned after becoming principal chief. I wish I had learned them well before my tenure, but I am still learning lessons daily. Only after steady growth by me and my staff did our designed purpose become clearer, a leadership model emerge, and our vocabulary about positive change become more articulate.

Commitment Message at the Inauguration of Chad "Corntassel" Smith as Principal Chief of the Cherokee Nation—1999

INTRODUCTION

My father grew up in the heart of the Cherokee Nation during the Depression in Oklahoma and had 10 half-siblings. He helped raise the family by hunting, farming, and working. He was a full-blood Cherokee and graduated from Sequoyah High School, a Bureau of Indian Affairs boarding school. There he learned discipline and mechanics as a trade. He was handsome, athletic, and spoke Cherokee as a first language. He married my mom, who lived 10 miles away from where he grew up, after World War II. She was non-Indian and had 10 siblings also. He was a tail gunner in the Army Air Corp, and she was a "Rosie the Riveter" during that war. They were married in 1947, and I was born in 1950. Because of the desperate economy in eastern Oklahoma, they went looking for work. They ended up in Denver, Colorado, and my dad started a 33-year career with Gates Rubber Company, beginning as tool crib helper and working himself up to an industrial plant maintenance manager. In 1959, he was transferred to Nashville, Tennessee, where he supervised 130 employees. They moved back to Oklahoma in 1973, and I came back to Oklahoma in 1975 after graduate school. That year I began working at the Cherokee Nation as a planner for Principal Chief Ross Swimmer. That lasted several years, and I went to law school.

Growing up, we would visit Rachael Quinton, my Cherokee grandmother, in Oklahoma, attend her one-room church, go to stomp grounds, and swim in the creek. I have three brothers and two half-siblings. I remember when I was 12 years old, after visiting my grandma, I was determined to teach myself to speak Cherokee. I found a bible in the Cherokee language and a Cherokee dictionary and put them in a briefcase because I was going to teach myself to speak Cherokee. My dad did not teach us because, like many in his generation, he accepted the myth that speaking Cherokee was less important than speaking English. I never did learn.

I married Bobbie Gail Smith, a full-blood Cherokee, in 1978, and our oldest son was born in 1980. When he was 12 years old, I watched him do something I'd never discussed with him. He got a bible in the Cherokee language and a Cherokee dictionary and put them in a briefcase because he was going to teach himself to speak Cherokee just like I did 30 years prior.

My great-grandfather, Redbird Smith, was a Cherokee Nation senator in the 1890s and was jailed by the United States for protesting its forcible assimilation policy of land allotment. My grandmother was a grassroots advocate for the Cherokee people. Working for the "tribe" was something I wanted to do since college. I was an ironworker during high school and college, putting up the structural steel for buildings and bridges. At the end of a day, I enjoyed seeing something I'd accomplished. In the early 1990s, I returned to work at the Cherokee Nation for Principal Chief Wilma Mankiller, who had a nurturing strength and believed in building communities.

Those were influences that encouraged me to run for principal chief in 1995 when Wilma Mankiller retired; I lost to Joe Byrd. His tenure between 1995 and 1999 was disastrous. He stated he could decide for himself what orders of the Cherokee Nation Supreme Court were constitutional and then proceeded to fire the entire marshal service for serving a search warrant to get copies of attorney fee records that he would not release. He then fired the newspaper editor and the court clerks and enlisted his loyalists on the tribal council, including Bill Baker, to impeach the entire Supreme Court for issuing the search warrant. It was called the Constitutional Crisis. As a result, the Cherokee Nation's reputation was shot, Cherokees were embarrassed by the resulting press, the Cherokee Nation had no budget for three years, 600 employees were furloughed, and another 200 were laid off. The Bureau of Indian Affairs put the Cherokee Nation on a monthly allowance because of mismanagement of cash flow and books that could not be audited.

In 1997, I protested my predecessor forcibly taking over the Cherokee Nation courthouse with his security force where the Cherokee Nation marshals were stationed as ordered by the Cherokee Nation Supreme Court. I was arrested and the charges were dismissed seven years later.

In 1999, I ran again and won, but the Cherokee Nation was in shambles. These were the circumstances when I was inaugurated as principal chief on August 14, 1999. That is when the learning of lessons began with great intensity.

COMMITMENT MESSAGE

August 14, 1999

Greetings. I have taken the oath of office of principal chief and commit to you my dedication to fulfill my oath to the people and the constitution of the Cherokee Nation.

The Cherokee Nation has suffered turmoil, crisis, chaos, and pain for the past several years. All agree that healing, rebuilding, and renewal are needed. Where do we turn for the guidance to bind our wounds, design our future, refresh and re-create our energy? Where does our journey go from here?

We must look to our history and culture to determine what values and attributes were responsible for carrying us through trials, tribulations, and challenges of the past. What carried us through the 1720 smallpox epidemic, the 1760 frontier wars, the Trail of Tears, the Cherokee Civil War, the American Civil War, allotment, the Depression, and 70 years of disenfranchisement when our right to govern ourselves as a people was denied? What trait gave us the reputation of being a people with the ability to survive, adapt, and prosper as a unique nation?

From where do we derive our human and tribal strength? What is the commonality of our diverse people? What is the tie that binds us as a people whether we are full blood, mixed blood, or thin blood; whether we live in Coffeyville, Nicut, Miami, Tulsa, Dallas, Tampa, or Los Angeles; whether we are rich or poor, young or old? What is the designed purpose of the Cherokees?

We begin this inquiry on sacred ground, here at our courthouse and capitol. The spirits of our ancestors come here to reminiscence about their days of long ago and reflect upon our behavior.

This is a place of strength, perseverance, pride, compassion, and reflection.

It has also been the focus of controversy, chaos, and pain.

In our acknowledgment, rededication, and assertion of the principles of sovereignty of our Nation, we respectfully remind our Oklahoma neighbors that this courthouse is the most visible symbol of our existence, our endurance, our commitment and desire to survive, and our respect for law. Without question, it is Indian Country. It is within our jurisdiction. It's our territory. We will never give it up.

Designed Purpose

My great grandfather, Redbird Smith, one hundred years ago spoke of a "designed purpose of the Cherokees." He stated:

> I have always believed that the Great Creator had a great design for
> my people, the Cherokees ... Our forces have been dissipated by the

external forces. Perhaps it has been just training, but we must now get together as a race and render our contribution to mankind ... We are endowed with intelligence, we are industrious, we are loyal, and we are spiritual, but we are overlooking the particular Cherokee mission on earth, for no man nor race is endowed with these qualifications without a designed purpose.

Bobbie Gail Smith, my wife, has captured for me the spirit of the designed purpose. She said we are "survivors not victims." We are not only survivors, but we adapt, prosper, and excel.

In 1881, Senator Dawes stated, "The head chief told us that there was not a family in that whole nation that had not a home of its own. There was not a pauper in that nation, and the nation did not owe a dollar. It built its own capitol ... and built its schools and hospitals."

However, Senator Dawes concluded with an absurdly ironic statement: "Yet the defect of the system was apparent. There is no selfishness, which is at the bottom of civilization. Till these people will consent to give up their lands and divide them among their citizens so that each can own the land he cultivates, they will not make more progress."

The Cherokees are a hard-working, spiritual, and intelligent people. We have continued to survive and prosper in every circumstance.

We must not be afraid to prosper and excel. As Redbird Smith said, "Work and right training is the solution of my following ... A kindly man cannot help his neighbor in need unless he has a surplus, and he cannot have a surplus unless he works."

The end of our journey and the success to be celebrated will come when we no longer have the needy among us, when we each are so self-reliant that we may contribute not only financially but also spiritually back to our family, clan, neighbors, and Nation. I believe this is our designed purpose.

Journey

It is here and today that we mark a continuation of our journey to fulfill our designed purpose.

The task on our journey is preserving our rich culture, reestablishing our strong tribal government, and achieving economic self-reliance of our people.

On this journey, we must help the elderly and frail. We must lead and teach our children. To complete this journey, we must be strong, wise, and joyful.

It is no longer a journey toward doom and extinction. It is a journey to fulfillment as people and as a people.

Strength

Along this journey, we must pray—not for an easier path or for a lighter load. Instead, we must ask for strength to face challenges, wisdom to make the right decisions, and perseverance to never give up. We ask the Creator for compassion to help our hearts become loving, warm, and vibrant so that the journey is praise to He who set us on this way.

We must turn to the Creator when we grow tired, we must turn to our elders when we become confused, and we must look to ourselves for responsibility. We must hold to our family when our hearts are saddened. We must turn to our culture when our spirits are challenged. We must find our strength as Cherokee people.

Our Guidance

We are a matrilineal society. From our mothers we get our clans and identity, just as we get life. Women have been given a special place in our culture. "Grandmother" is one of the most sacred words in the Cherokee language.

We ask our women to step forward and guide us. The leadership of our Nation has been entrusted to our women since the earliest times. Our laws in the 1820s first memorialize the ancient and honored leadership status of women.

Perhaps the greatest honor noted to our women is that in our language, there is no gender difference. We are one people. But over the last 200 years of influence by an external culture, we may have forgotten that it is the women of our Nation who carry our indomitable spirit. We humbly ask that our women—our grandmothers, mothers, daughters, aunts, and nieces—step forward and lead us as they have so many other times in our history. We ask them to hold us responsible for our actions, to discipline us, and to praise us when warranted.

We ask our grandmothers to speak our language to our children, to teach the old ways, to instruct us with wisdom, compassion, and patience. We ask our grandmothers to speak the language to our children from the time of the womb until the time of passing, to nurture and guide our children in the strengths and values of our culture. We ask our daughters, aunts, nieces, and all the women of our tribe to join in the cultural leadership. Without the leadership of our women, we will lose our most sacred values and die as a people.

In this most crucial time, it is the strength, guidance, and nurturing of our women that will help us through our present difficulties. It is important for the voices of both women and men to be heard in every aspect of our lives, from raising our children and keeping our homes to leading our nation.

Lay Aside Differences

It is proper that here, we lay aside our differences, both political and personal, that we declare our dedication to the service of our people, that we focus on the same horizon and future, and that we continue our journey "holding hands."

We must listen to the admonition of John Ross from his annual meeting on October 9, 1861, in which he stated: "The Cherokee People stand upon new ground. Let us hope that the clouds which overspread the Land will be dispersed and that we shall prosper as we have never done before. New avenues to usefulness and distinction will be opened to the ingenious youth of Country. Our right of self-government will be more fully recognized ..."

He continued, "No just cause exists for domestic difficulties. Let them be buried with the past and only mutual friendship and harmony be cherished."

Hasting, Loretta, Bobbie, and I listened to respected elder Agnes Cowen several nights ago at her hospital bed. Despite the weakness of her illness, I heard the strength of wisdom when she said, "We must teach our children to work together. After all, we are but one large family." The Cherokee Nation is a family of families.

In this spirit and with the example of our ancestors, let us declare that we are one people, working together for the common good of the Cherokee Nation.

Renaissance

Here in the presence of our loved ones, including those who have passed on before us, and with their blessing and encouragement, we commit ourselves to renaissance, reawakening, and renewal.

Redbird Smith said one hundred years ago, "Our mixed bloods should not be overlooked in this program of racial awakening. Our pride in our ancestral heritage is our great incentive for handing something worthwhile to our posterity; it is this pride in ancestry that makes men strong and loyal for their principle in life. It is this same pride that makes men give up their all for their Government."

These principles ring true today. Unfortunately, efforts to dissolve the Cherokee Nation continue. We, the Cherokee Nation, believe as Redbird Smith believed one hundred years ago that we have something unique and sacred to share with the world. We will do our best to preserve, protect, and express that unique spirit that is the Cherokee Nation so that we may fulfill our responsibility to the Creator, our ancestors, our children, and their children.

Closing

How do we close this ceremony on this glorious morning, where we have the warmth of the sun and the fellowship of the Cherokees among us; where we are protected by the shade of the trees and the shadow of our capitol buildings as we gather in community; and where we sit in hope and anticipation of the coming days and years? The answer is, we don't.

Let us move forward to our final destination and fulfill our designed purpose. Let us, armed with our indomitable Cherokee spirit and ancestral pride, proceed on our journey relying upon the strength and wisdom of our Cherokee women and guided by our Creator.

Wado.

Your humble servant,

Chad "Corntassel" Smith
Principal Chief

2000 State of the Nation "Sga du gi," the Community Focus

INTRODUCTION

The Cherokee Nation Constitution requires an annual state of the nation report by the principal chief. By custom, this report is presented on the Saturday during the Cherokee National Holiday, which is held on Labor Day weekend. The holiday commemorates the signing of the Cherokee Nation Constitution on September 3, 1839, after the Trail of Tears. There was a large gathering at our national capitol building on the town square in Tahlequah, Oklahoma. I had been in office one year. I had not fired any Cherokee Nation staff that supported my predecessor because I believed in their constitutional rights of freedom of speech and association. There was still a lot of animosity and division resulting from the Constitutional Crisis. The fundamental systems of accounting, procurement, human resources, finance, and cash management had to be rebuilt. Under the previous administration, there had been no plan or vision. I engaged several consultants to review our systems and provide recommendations and training. I was anxious to build the Nation and improve the lives of our citizens. There were also external challenges, such as a splinter group of Cherokees that the Bureau of Indian Affairs was propping up as a separate Indian tribe within the boundaries of the Cherokee Nation, the United Keetoowah Band of Cherokee Indian in Oklahoma. There was anti-Indian sentiment from local and state government officials and leaders. But it was clear the greatest challenge was a lack of internal leadership and the overarching sense of entitlement and victimhood to which some tribal council and community leaders pandered. My 2000 state of the nation address focused on our most important cultural value, sgadugi, which means "to come together and work for the good of the community."

STATE OF THE NATION: "SGA DU GI," THE COMMUNITY FOCUS

September 2, 2000

Greetings Cherokees, friends, and people of goodwill. A warm welcome to everyone, especially those who have traveled thousands of miles to join us in this annual reunion of the Cherokee family. It is my hope that you enjoy a weekend of warmth and a renewal of relationships with family and friends.

It is a great honor to stand before you today. You have given me the opportunity to serve you this last year, and I wish to report on our progress and plans for the future.

At my inauguration, Benny Smith admonished me to be a student of our people. I took that challenge to heart. I have studied, observed, thought, analyzed, sought counsel, and learned much this last year. He also instructed us on "sga du gi," the Cherokee way to come together and help each other.

I have been inspired and disheartened. I have been invigorated and exhausted. I have been encouraged and disappointed. I have seen our people excel with the ever growing and progressing Cherokee spirit, and I have seen our people trapped by their poor decisions resulting in family dysfunction and despair. I sincerely wish that each of you had the opportunity to share some of the great inspirational experiences I have enjoyed.

Introduction

One year ago I stood in front of you and delivered a message of healing, working together, and planning for the future. Today I will share with you where we have been and where we intend to go. This first year we had to get the house of the Cherokee Nation in order to provide services to our people. We had to first fix the problems with the administration of the Cherokee Nation, before we could help our communities. We have done that.

In this next year, we will focus our efforts on communities. We will help the communities renew themselves. I will advise you of the accomplishments of this last year, which include our service improvement project, the Free Press, financial responsibility, and cultural education. I will share with you some of our challenges, which include tribal survival and the need for vision and leadership. I will outline solutions, which include "sga du gi," the Cherokee spirit, principles of the Cherokee Nation, volunteerism, and our focus on communities this coming year.

Reminder of the Past

Before I talk about our accomplishments and vision for the future, let me briefly remind you of our recent past. When I took office one year ago, we were coming out of tremendous turmoil, and there had been great conflict within our Nation. There was a constitutional crisis. The executive branch defied the court and our laws. Our finances were a mess, with no audits for three years and no budget. The morale of our employees was at an all-time low. Many people were dismayed and embarrassed by the Cherokee Nation government. You may also recall that in 1997, this courthouse had been seized. Our courthouse had been taken away from the courts and the Cherokee people. Further, during the Cherokee Nation Holiday, there was a SWAT team on the rooftops just across the street.

This also marks the end of my first year of service as your principal chief, an awesome responsibility. A year ago I had the pleasure and honor of standing in this historic place to speak to you about the future of our government, the Cherokee Nation. At that time I made several commitments to you. I would like to briefly revisit some of those commitments and report our progress.

Accomplishments

It believe it is a precious gift to serve as your principal chief and that my job is to represent your interests at all times. As such, I try to take a measured, steady approach to everything I do.

The turmoil and chaos have ceased. The council and I may have differences from time to time, but we have not aired those differences in a divisive way. We have embraced difference of opinion as an opportunity to make our Nation stronger. I thank the Cherokee people for giving me this year to return to good government.

A year ago when we gathered here with so much faith, hope, and optimism, most people simply wanted the government to be unified, for the constitution to be respected, and for their elected officials to work together in a respectful way. For the most part, that has been accomplished. However, fair-minded people can often have differences of opinion about important issues within the Cherokee Nation. In a few cases, some members of the council and the administration have had very different interpretations of the constitution and the laws governing the Cherokee Nation. Ideally, these differences could be settled by debate and discussion. However, when consensus cannot be reached, these differences may be settled in the courts, as they are in many democratic nations, including the United States. Hopefully this type of situation will not often present itself in the future, because it causes all of your elected officials to expend unnecessary energy and resources on issues that could be resolved by forthright, open debate and discussion.

Refocusing the Cherokee Nation

This year, we worked tirelessly to align our organization to better serve you, the Cherokee people. Like you, I wanted the changes to occur quickly. However, I learned that healing had to take place first, and with a budget of $160 million and 1,800 employees, it takes time and training to get everyone headed in the same direction. Thank you for being patient. We've made the turn. You will see positive changes this year.

Our main focus was to put our Cherokee people first in everything that we do.

One application of this principle, was the opening of an Information and Customer Service Center, which is located at the front of the Tribal Complex.

Cherokee FIRST is the mandate that our employees become advocates for our Cherokee clients and make them feel at home.

Hastings Shade and I had the reserved parking places for principal chief and deputy principal chief painted over for handicap parking.

Hastings Shade and I executed our open door policy by literally tearing down the walls that prevented Cherokees from walking into our offices.

These changes are good, but we know that this is not good enough. We have much work to do.

Our second focus was to reorganize our work so that we could better serve you.

Our government should be efficient, effective, and culturally compatible. We have begun the work to implement serious changes to our service delivery. This year, you will see change.

The Health Department found ways to increase the value of our health services by billing insurance companies, Medicare and Medicaid more effectively. They want to spend the estimated $2 million of additional revenue on increased contract health care. This means that we can get more people the surgeries they need so that they can get back to work and provide for themselves and their families.

The Education Department has reduced the 26 step college scholarship application process to four steps. We should be helping our Cherokee people to get a higher education, not hindering them.

The Social Services Department is reducing a total of 42 applications for various programs to one base application. The Cherokee Nation is getting out of the business of confusing forms and applications. We can do better, and with the leadership of our employees, we will do better.

The Housing Authority and Community Development departments are going to build more houses faster. These organizations will work cooperatively to build and rehabilitate houses for you.

With these changes, our focus will change from thinking that the Tribal Complex is the center of the universe to thinking that the Cherokee community is the center of the universe. We will build our foundation on the communities. You will no longer have to come to us. We will come to you.

Challenges

We have unquestionably made great strides, but we have serious challenges before us. The Holocaust took place within one decade, just 10 years. So did the Cherokee Trail of Tears and allotment. During those 10-year time periods, the world turned upside down for our people. We must be ever diligent.

Survival

The greatest challenge I have faced this last year, which I believe is a concern for each of you, is our survival as a tribe and nation. And I speak of surviving as a government and as a people. American Indian tribes and nations are under constant attack by certain congressmen. Many of our local congressmen and law enforcement agencies have declined to assist us with surviving as a tribe.

There is a congressional race for this district. Today we have the Republican and Democratic candidates with us: Brad Carson, Bill Settle, and Andy Ewing. Please visit with them and confirm their commitment to being our advocate in Washington.

And even some who claim to be Cherokee have for their own political and selfish gain attempted to undermine the Cherokee Nation and the legacy that our ancestors paid so dearly for. There are over 218 groups who in some form or fashion claim to be a Cherokee tribe or organization. In the last few months, two such groups claimed the legal history and assets of the Cherokee Nation. Let us be ever diligent to expose these charlatans and frauds.

But greater still is our survival as people. This concern has faced our people for hundreds of years.

One hundred and forty years ago, a number of traditionalists came together and formed the Keetoowah Society. The organization still exists, and is known as the Nighthawk Keetoowahs. They meet at Stokes Stomp Grounds near Vian. Do not confuse these traditionalists with the political organization of the United Keetoowah Band that was created by the federal government in 1946. On the eve of the American Civil War, the Nighthawk Keetoowahs came together and eloquently reflected in their bylaws the issue that continually faces us. In 1860, the Keetoowah Society wrote:

> We must not surrender under any circumstances until we shall "fall to the ground united." We must lead one another by the hand with all our strength. Our government is being destroyed. We must resort to our bravery to stop it. Few members of men of the society met secretly and discussed the condition of the country where they lived. The name Cherokee was in danger. The Cherokee Nation was about to disintegrate. It seemed intended to drown our Cherokee Nation and destroy it. For that reason we resolved to stop from scattering or forever lose the name of Cherokee. We must love each other and abide by treaties made with the federal government. We must cherish them in our hearts. Second, we must also abide by the treaties made with other races of people. Third, we must abide by our constitution and laws and uphold the name of the Cherokee Nation."

In 1861 the Keetoowah Society enacted a provision that stated:

> If any urgent and important message from the chief of the Cherokee Nation should be received by head captains to be looked into, it shall be the duty of the head captains to send up the message to all parts of the Cherokee Nation. If anyone or any one of us Keetoowah is called upon or chosen to take a message for them, he shall willingly without hesitancy respond to the responsibility.

This state of the nation is the message I want to send to all people of the Cherokee Nation. I hope my concern is misplaced, but it appears that we face similar challenges today.

Need for Leadership

Since I have been in office, one thing has become clearer; there is a weakness in many who define their successes or failures by comparison to others. In other words, do we compare ourselves to our neighbor, or do we judge ourselves on our own accomplishments? Some leaders define their successes by how well they establish roadblocks or barriers for others. Some leaders find reward in running others down rather than building them up. Some of our people have given up their Cherokee pride and initiative by resigning themselves to expecting the government to provide for them.

People often have a very narrow view of themselves and others. They can't see the big picture. Their perception is limited. Their vision and world are limited. These are people who define their own identity by how they can hurt others. These are people to be pitied because they live such a hollow existence that invites mischief.

I have found there is a strength when each of us, including our leaders, takes a broader view of ourselves, our people, and especially our future. When that happens, when we look around to each corner of the Cherokee Nation, to our people and communities and to the future, then we learn to define and judge our successes or failures based on what we have envisioned and accomplished rather than on how we stack up against someone else or how we have kept others from accomplishing their goals.

Sga du gi

Today we have many Cherokees who desperately need help but have no family to help them. Then there are Cherokees who need help, but their own families believe it is the government's duty to take care of their mother, not theirs. One answer is the Cherokee concept of "sga du gi."

The Cherokee Spirit

It is a solid Cherokee value to take care of one's family and neighbors. Why have so many of our people drifted away from that? We need all of our leaders in the communities, in the office, in churches, and at the stomp grounds to remind our people of this great Cherokee value.

Without question the Cherokee Nation should help those who need it, but the tribe has very limited resources. We have set about the mission to design our programs to help people help themselves, their families, and neighbors.

But in any event, the duty and honor of a person's family is so much greater than the government. We can never be a strong people if we don't take the loving responsibility and accept the honor of taking care of our own families.

The most important thing I can say to you today is to refresh our knowledge about "sga du gi." It is the Cherokee concept from our language that means "come together and help one another." As Benny Smith a year ago affirmed these teachings, let us take them to heart and use them this year.

Sometimes it is so simple, like "not seeing the forest for the trees." But "sga du gi" is not only the key for tribal survival; it is the key for personal fulfillment. We must learn the joy of giving and doing for others. Those who receive these gifts are best served when we help them help themselves rather than do for them.

This last year, I have attended the funerals of several great Cherokee statesmen, including Lowell Townsend, Mike Shotpouch, and Goodlow Proctor. At each of those services, there was but one theme. Each exemplified the Cherokee spirit of not asking what others could do for them but what they could do for others. They would not ask, "What can I get from the Cherokee Nation?" but instead would ask "What can I give to the Cherokee Nation?" The Cherokee spirit is being generous, kind, and patient.

We are doomed to extinction unless we as a people abandon and condemn jealousy and adopt and embrace our historic value of "sga du gi," which is to come together and work. It means that each and every one of us must grow up and set aside small behaviors to understand we are but one people with a common mission and a shared reward.

This is a burden that we carry, a concern that challenges our best intentions and our greatest minds. How do we survive another 100 years and regain the valuable strengths that carried us this far? As your elected leaders, Hastings Shade, the council, and I are mandated and charged to find ways to insure we are not destroyed by outsiders or by our own weaknesses.

The Cherokee spirit is seen in the churches, where the teenage girl has her arm around her grandmother as they sit on a pew during services; underneath the shade trees, where men enjoy the music and laughter of the Cherokee language as they discuss old stories and modern issues; and around the cook fires, where the women visit while making beans, ka nu che, and cornbread.

This Cherokee spirit is expressed if the council, the administration, and the public are fully informed and participate in vigorous debate of policy issues. That is good government. Unfortunately in this regard, we have a long way to go.

If we don't come together as a people now, we will become nothing more than a footnote in a book that will say, "Once there was a great Cherokee Nation, but it is no more." In the future, our descendants may find a generation of dark haired and brown-skinned people, with Cherokee names, but the Cherokee spirit will be gone, and these people of the future will know nothing about the Cherokee legacy, history, art, heritage, music, religion, culture, or wisdom.

We have the resources, intelligence, and ability to rebuild this nation, our people, and ourselves. The only reason or perhaps excuse not to is the absence of will, the absence of Cherokee spirit.

Volunteerism

One of the ways we can preserve the Cherokee spirit is volunteerism, where we help our families, communities, and Cherokee people. We should enjoy the spirit of giving and sharing. We are making an effort to coordinate volunteers with activities. We need volunteers to read stories at our daycares, to maintain the homes of the elderly and disabled, to help in office work and customer advocacy, and to design community buildings and projects. We are passing out volunteer cards that request information from each of you about your talents and ways that you could volunteer in our communities and at the tribal level. Although volunteerism does not offer financial reward, it provides the spiritual reward of enriching your life by helping others. Please complete this card and drop it off with me or our staff, or place it in the marked boxes at the information booths.

Community Revitalization

To continue our accomplishments and to bring our mission and principles to life, this next year we will be focusing on investment and revitalization of core Cherokee communities. We need each of you to help us accomplish this mission. The task is the Cherokee Nation helping families and communities to help themselves.

Conclusion

The legacy given by our forefathers is not only to face adversity, to survive, and to adapt as we have but also to prosper and excel. Only if we live by the principles of "sga du gi" will we carry on this legacy. We have made progress this year. We will focus next year on community investment. We, each and every one of us, must help to fulfill the mission of the Cherokee Nation and enjoy our precious and valuable lives.

Wado.

Your Humble Servant,

Chadwick "Corntassel" Smith
Principal Chief

2001 State of the Nation
Embrace and Carry Forward
the Great Cherokee Legacy

INTRODUCTION

Two years had passed since I was inaugurated, and I was hearing a repeated criticism: "All Chad does is plan." We engaged consultants, read our history, studied, asked many questions, and tried to determine the best course for the Cherokee Nation. It was Redbird Smith's speech about people endowed with such attributes having a "designed purpose" that inspired me to title our strategy and philosophical document "Declaration of Designed Purpose." At the state of the nation, we outlined that declaration and shared five Cs, our desired outcomes: country, community, competency, capacity, and culture. Those concepts later morphed into jobs, language, community, capacity, and sovereignty.

Many adored Wilma Mankiller, the principal chief of the Cherokee Nation between 1985 and 1995. I remember at a small office birthday party for her, someone asked her to speak to the 15 people in attendance. She politely said it was her birthday, and she would prefer not to give a talk. It dawned on me that people, even her friends and office staff, wanted to be reassured and inspired. Prior to my tenure, the state

We have a stronger *country*, a stronger Cherokee Nation, than we did two years ago.

Our marshal service enforces the law on Cherokee land, not the U.S. government.

Our tribal courts are fully staffed and operational.

This courthouse, the historic Cherokee capitol building, is open to the public, as are all financial records and documents of the Cherokee Nation.

The budget of our first year was the first on-time budget in five years. We've completed and received clean financial audits for each year of this administration.

We have a Free Press Act and a Freedom of Information Act that ensure those policies will outlast any administration or council.

Our leadership as a strong nation took center stage at a recent business conference in Minneapolis attended by 400 Indian business leaders. As I addressed the audience, an Indian journalist asked to comment. She then proceeded to compliment the Cherokee Nation for passing the Free Press Act. We now have a Cherokee newspaper that is charged with printing the news and the truth whether it's good, bad, or ugly.

By Cherokee Nation law, our tax commission must issue automobile tags before October 29. Cherokee Nation license tags are on order, and the tax commission plans to have at least one tag office selling the plates as soon as possible. In short, tags will go on sale sometime between now and October 29. Once all arrangements are final, we will formally announce the date for tag sales.

Secondly, we are helping our *communities* to be stronger than they were two years ago.

This year the Cherokee Nation is providing materials for 10 communities so they can build their own community buildings.

Communities that have taken leadership in that project include: Bell, Greasy, Rocky Ford, Chewey, South Coffeyville, Chelsea, and Dry Creek, among others. Other communities that are providing leadership include Proctor, Kenwood, Evening Shade, and Gore.

People like Bill Davis of South Coffeyville, Johnson Soap of Honey Hill, Thomas Muskrat of Bell, Johnny Backwater of Kenwood, Don

Greenfeather of Jay, and Geo Cummings of Piney provide critical community leadership as do the volunteers at the Rainbow House in Marble City and Locust Grove, whose motto is "Cherokees helping Cherokees," as well as so many other people who lead and build Cherokee communities.

Another community building program involves a partnership with the Internal Revenue Service. We are placing 300 computers in Cherokee communities. The goal of this program is to help individual families claim the Earned Income Tax Credit, which can mean more than a thousand dollars to working Cherokees. The communities can use the computers for other purposes throughout the year, and during tax season, we can use them to keep more money in the pockets of the Cherokee people.

Our survival as a nation depends on the health and progress of our communities, and we are executing that strategy.

Third, our employees have the *capacity* to serve the Cherokee people better than they did two years ago.

Serving the Cherokee people is an honor for us as elected officials. But it is also an honor for our staff of nearly 1,800 employees. Cherokee Nation staff are now evaluated not only on performance but also on how friendly, knowledgeable, and helpful they are to the citizens we serve.

I'd like to share part of a letter to the editor that appeared in the *Tulsa World* on October 16 last year. It reads: "After all I had heard, I thought a bunch of lawyers and politicians run the Nation. Not so. I saw ladies that have worked there for 20-plus years, and their children and sometimes even *their* children. I saw them all embrace my children like family, and it made me cry all the way home because of the wonderful reception we received there from everyone."

We applaud Cherokee Nation employees for striving to make our offices a friendly, caring place. I invite everyone here today to come to our open house at the complex this afternoon for a little Cherokee hospitality.

In 1998, the employee turnover rate was 30 percent; this year it is 12 percent.

Fourth, our programs are more *competent* than they were two years ago.

Hastings has a saying about serving the Cherokee people: "We just make our work hard."

We are finding ways to serve Cherokee people better. For instance, our human services group two years ago required 45 different program applications. Forty-five! No wonder people got discouraged and thought we were unfriendly. Today we operate the same programs using just three different applications.

We have achieved similar results in several other programs such as housing and education.

Cherokee Nation Enterprises has increased its profits for each of the last two years. Cherokee Nation Industries is profitable and recently signed a $6.5 million defense industry contract.

Fifth, Cherokee *culture* is revitalizing.

Almost 1,000 employees and other Cherokees completed the 40-hour Cherokee history course. Several hundred Cherokees have completed basic Cherokee language courses. Attendance at youth/elder camps and other cultural camps continues to increase. We have begun a Head Start class for three-year-olds in which Cherokee is the only language spoken.

Our award-winning Cherokee Nation website now translates more than 7,000 English words into Cherokee and has the Cherokee font available.

We have released our second children's choir CD with recording star Rita Coolidge. It is outstanding.

I commend Hastings Shade for his cultural wisdom and dedication in leading the effort to retain our language and culture.

Lesson from Our Ancestors

We as a people often forget the valuable lessons learned and taught by our ancestors. These lessons guide our future. This capitol building is the living symbol of our great Cherokee legacy. Whenever Cherokees gather, I must share with you the great Cherokee legacy.

Cherokee Legacy

Our history shows in episode after episode that we are a people who face adversity, survive, adapt, prosper, and excel. From the smallpox epi-

demics of the 1730s, which killed one-half of our people; to the genocidal wars of the 1760s; to the land cession treaties in the 1770s; to the
Trail of Tears in 1838; to the Cherokee Civil War; to the American Civil
War; to the allotment of the 1890s; to the effort to dissolve our government in 1900; to the Depression, which was an economic Trail of Tears
in which one-half of our people left Oklahoma; to relocation in 1950s;
to what one federal judge in 1975 called "bureaucratic imperialism," we
have demonstrated this legacy.

Now in the year 2001, we have the choice to carry on this legacy or
allow it to lapse by default.

The Cherokee legacy was paid for with thousands of lives and millions
of acres. But it comes with a duty, responsibility, and obligation to carry it
on. Although that might seem to be a burden, ask yourself, what greater
honor can there be? Every decision we make today must be a wise one so
that 100 years from now, our grandchildren and great-grandchildren may
come to this spot in front of our capitol building and have a strong tribal
government, enjoy economic self-reliance, and share an enriching culture.

And to fulfill this legacy, we must ask the questions:

Where will we be as a people 5, 10, 50, or 100 years from now?

Do we talk only of ancestors, or do we plan for our descendants?

Do we brag about our full-blood ancestor, or do we brag about our
Indian grandchildren?

Do we live in the past, or do we focus on the future?

Is being Cherokee a novelty or a way of life?

Is being Cherokee a heritage or a future?

Our ancestors who walked the grounds of this capitol building resoundingly cry: Don't forget the legacy we have passed on. Don't
let it lapse. Pass it on, stronger and stronger, to your children. Let the
Cherokee language laugh, speak, and sing again. Let our history be
known and discussed. Live by our wisdom. Don't let us die as a people.
If you do, then all of our sacrifice will be for nothing, and you will lose
those things that fulfill your life.

Strategy for Survival

Those lessons from our ancestors have given us a strategy for survival. Our history tells us that the federal government changes policy toward Indians every 20 to 40 years. That means in the next hundred years, we can expect the United States to try to destroy us two or three more times.

Are we prepared? Do we have strong communities and families? Are we driven by our culture of "ga du gi," or are we becoming weaker by consumerism and entitlement mentalities?

I share with you our plan to pass on our great Cherokee legacy.

The plan is based on *community investment* and *self-help*. It is very simple. First, we coordinate the investment of our resources so that Cherokee communities can exercise their own leadership and develop into strong, healthy, enduring, cultural communities.

Second, we institute self-help components into every program we have so that our people can develop skills and talents that will take them forward when those programs end.

As a result of our planning, the housing authority of the Cherokee Nation is decentralizing. Instead of one main office in Tahlequah, we now have seven area offices and a total of 19 field offices, so that wherever you live within the Cherokee Nation, the housing authority will be able to serve you near your home.

We have six rural clinics to assist our two IHS hospitals.

Lessons from Children

I observed that the lessons we learn from children are often the most meaningful ones.

Hastings said that is how it is supposed to be. Children are here to teach us. They teach us how to feed them and how to take care of them when they cry and talk to us. They teach us to laugh, care, share, provide, and love. We taught our parents, and our children teach us. Children teach us all that they can, and then they begin learning from their children. Sometimes, children teach us all they can, and then the Creator calls them home.

On the walls of my office, I have pictures of my family, my wife, my parents, and a framed picture of a young man named Shane Foreman. He was a 12-year-old from Oaks who had cancer. For the last two years his family and the Oaks community held a powwow to honor Shane. Bobbie and I had the opportunity to attend. It was family and community at its best. He served as an inspiration. We danced in the grand entry together although it was all he could do to go around the arena once with his walker. His family and community rallied around him and shared in the mysteries and magic of this life.

On my youngest daughter's birthday several months ago, Shane passed on. First it brought the sobering reality of the precious nature of our children. His display of that indomitable Cherokee spirit to fight and endure the pains and agony of cancer for eight years and then rise above that battle to live his life as a typical little boy put things in perspective.

I look about and see shining through on more and more occasions that indomitable Cherokee spirit and pride. When I see Shane's picture on the wall in my office, he teaches me to focus on things that are important and not to get caught up in the clutter of personalities, politics, and pettiness. Shane taught us all he could and then was called on to be with the Creator.

Just as in Hastings's story, many of us learned a lesson about keeping our perspective in a painful way four weeks ago. Four 16-year-old high school students died in a car wreck. From visiting the families and attending the funerals of Smokey Mankiller, Kyle Hutchinson, Chad Craig, and Erica Christie, we learned again to set priorities and give the important things energy and attention.

Passing on the great Cherokee legacy is one of those important things we can do. We can count a number of Cherokee patriots and elders who did their part but who have gone to be with the Creator. From Ed Grass, Jan Morgan, Agnes Cowen, Sam Stool, Kelly Craig, and Sanders McLemore, we have learned.

We've learned to focus only on the things that count.

Rather than focus on putting ourselves first, we should focus on others.

Rather than involve ourselves with petty politics, we should focus on statesmanship.

Rather than consuming ourselves with continually buying, we should be focusing on sharing.

If the future ever looks gloomy, study our past and look to our children and elders. It is becoming more clear to me daily. We must look to the long haul and prepare.

Personal

I come from humble beginnings. My dad grew up in a house with a dirt floor. When he was a teenager, he plowed the family allotment and built a house with a real floor for his family of 10 brothers and sisters. One of my most valuable possessions is a painting of him cutting railroad ties with a broad axe. My wife, Bobbie, grew up in a two-room cabin.

I was the first in my family to graduate from college because of the encouragement of my dad. When he retired, my three brothers and I gave him and my mom a certificate reflecting our eight college degrees. He earned each one through this encouragement and support. We should encourage our children as he encouraged me.

I would never have thought, coming from those humble beginnings, that the son of a tie cutter would be elected principal chief of the great Cherokee Nation.

That is why I must thank you for the honor of serving as your principal chief. It was two years ago that you elected me and allowed me to serve. I have worked hard, diligently, and with passion 50 to 70 hours a week. It has been good work. It has been the work of our people. In two more years, I will ask you for the opportunity to continue to serve you. We must build on our successes and remember the failures of the not-too-distant past.

Closing

The years prior to my administration were difficult and contentious, divisive and disruptive. This is not the first, nor is it likely the last time, that our survival will be tested. It would be fatal for the Nation to overlook the urgency of the moment and to underestimate the determination of those who have continuously sought to terminate our government, our language, our traditions, and sovereignty in the name of greed, power, selfishness, ignorance, or even self-professed goodwill. There are those, both internal and external, who want us to fail. Let us never lend or grant them the power to make us do so through our own lack of resolve. We must not be guilty of thinking wrong and doing wrong. Let us not seek to divide and conquer ourselves by allowing bitterness, jealousy, and hatred to direct our decisions and actions.

The most offensive thought I can have standing here, as principal chief, is that the government and way of life for which our ancestors fought so hard, sacrificed so much, and defended so vigorously would be destroyed. It could be destroyed by outside forces or, worse yet, by our own apathy and neglect.

In closing, I invite your attention again to the picture of the 1899 Cherokee girl on the cover of our annual report. It is our duty to make wise decisions so we have these precious little Cherokee children happy and healthy 100 years from now.

For the next two years, Hastings and I will be focused on economic development for the Cherokee Nation.

Now is the time to develop an economy of self-reliance that supports our culture.

Now is the time to challenge ourselves to exert all our ability, our industry, our intelligence, our will, our ambition, and our love for our Nation in the service of our people and the survival of our Nation.

Now is the time to open the doors of opportunity for our Cherokee children, families, and elders.

Now is the time for renewal, a rekindling of those things it means to be Cherokee.

Let us individually, and as a people, resolve to treat each other with human dignity, show respect for one another, and enjoy the most genuine blessings bestowed by our Creator, each other.

Together, we must work toward the day when we regain our enriching cultural identity, economic self-reliance, and strong government.

Let us resolve to embrace and carry forward the great Cherokee legacy.

Wado.

Your Humble Servant,

Chadwick "Corntassel" Smith
Principal Chief

2002 State of the Nation
Building One Fire

INTRODUCTION

I gave the 2002 state of the nation address during the third year of my first term. We were able to build the essential management and operational systems to have reliable data and information in order to make sound decisions. Finance, accounting, procurement, legal, and human resources had been built with solid staff and strong leadership.

Each year, the Cherokee National Holiday has a theme. In many organizations, event themes are some combination of words that sound good at the moment but do not have much significance. Themes are branding and educational opportunities. We had the opportunity to look back at what was happening in the Cherokee Nation a century before during one of the most challenging and debilitating periods of our history. By 1902, the United States was executing a "forcible assimilation" policy, in effect killing the Cherokee Nation, marshaling its assets, determining heirs, and distributing the property. It was like a probate in which the murderer is also the administrator of the estate. In this state of the nation speech, I reflected on the Cherokee Supplemental Agreement of 1902 in which Cherokees accepted the allotment plan after having rejected it the year before. It is arguably the worst moment in Cherokee history; Cherokee people succumbed to the assimilation pressures of mainstream society and the federal government's coercion. It was a surrender of tribal lands and the Cherokee national government as a republic. That period of time, with the outside influences and the issues swirling in the Cherokee public, provides a great case study of hostile public sentiment, erosion of traditional values, and the dynamics of greed and a lust for power by both Cherokees and whites. The Cherokee Nation was up for grabs, and how did the very diverse Cherokee public respond? Many embraced and advocated for Oklahoma statehood and private property; some resisted, arguing that the white man's economic system had failed every other place and time in American history; and a large number sat back and watched.

In this state of the nation, I reflected on the Cherokee Supplemental Agreement of 1902, surveyed moments in the last 100 years, focused on achievements during the last year, and acknowledged Cherokee community and professional leaders. We used the metaphor of a traditional fire with four logs at the center: government, enterprise, community, and culture. Our message was being refined each year.

STATE OF THE NATION: BUILDING ONE FIRE

August 31, 2002

Greetings, fellow citizens of the great Cherokee Nation, friends of this nation, members of the Cherokee community, families, and guests. It is my honor to be here with you on this 163rd anniversary of the signing of our Act of Union and Constitution of 1839. This is the fiftieth celebration of this patriotic event. Fifty years ago, W.W. Keeler initiated this celebration as part of the vision of revitalizing the Cherokee Nation.

Upon my inauguration as your principal chief, Benny Smith admonished me to be a student of the Cherokee people and Nation. He also instructed us to "build one fire," to come together as a people, put our differences aside, and work for our common good. That has become the theme of our administration, and it is the theme of this National Holiday. It is a pleasure to present to you the state of the Cherokee Nation address.

The symbol of building one fire is especially fitting when we come and stand together to build one fire; we get and share more heat, greater light, and more comfort. One hundred years ago, the federal government set out to extinguish our national fire. It failed. The flame of this awesome and powerful Cherokee Nation burned low for the first 75 years of the last century as the coals beneath the surface burned intensely. It took the tending of many, including J.B. Milam, W.W. Keeler, Ross Swimmer, and Wilma Mankiller, to enable that fire to once again grow and burn with the brilliance and determination that we see today.

If you examine the brochure from the first Cherokee National Holiday in 1953, you will find on the cover a picture of Indians watching a great fire. It is more than fitting that this symbol should be carried through today and provide us understanding for the future.

Our traditional fire burns with four logs, one each facing north, west, south, and east. Symbolically, four logs are necessary for the burning of the one fire of the Cherokee Nation. Those four logs, for the purpose of this message about the future and challenges of the Cherokee Nation, symbolize government, enterprise, community, and culture.

Government

As the Cherokee Nation builds one fire, the first log is government. Beginning in 1898, through the Curtis Act, the United States in violation of treaty after treaty condemned the Cherokee Nation to a national death with a pronouncement that the government of the Cherokee Nation would be terminated in 1906. A reprieve was granted, and the Cherokee Nation continued in "full force and effect" pursuant to Section 28 of the 1906 Five Tribes Act. We should never forget that provision.

In 1902, the United States, through its Department of Interior and Bureau of Indian Affairs, began a regime that a federal judge in 1976 characterized as "bureaucratic imperialism." It was a regime designed to "frustrate, debilitate, and generally prevent from operating" the constitutional government of the Cherokee Nation expressly preserved and perpetrated by the 1906 act. It was 100 years ago, pursuant to the Cherokee

Supplement Act, that the federal government began this most vicious assault on the Cherokee Nation.

W.A. Duncan wrote a stirring letter in the *Cherokee Advocate* on July 19, 1898, titled "Treaties Ignored" in response to the federal government's passing of the Curtis Act, which mandated the allotment scheme. He wrote, "[The federal government] had not the courage to repudiate in terms all treaties with the Cherokee; it simply proceeded just as if they had never existed." He continued, "The affair in this case was simply a struggle between right and wrong, a little legislative tragedy in which the amount of men, money, and ammunition was too small to make the play entertaining."

In the 1902 Act, we find the following:

Sec. 11: Allotment of Cherokee lands for the average of 110 acres per individual.

Sec. 22: Exclusive jurisdiction by the federal Dawes Commission to determine all matters relative to appraisement and allotment of lands.

Sec. 25: The Dawes Commission shall enroll the Cherokees, not the Cherokee government.

Sec. 32: The U.S. Secretary of Interior took control of our schools.

Sec. 40: The U.S. Secretary of Interior created town sites and gave preferential rights to squatters.

Sec. 53: Provided that the *Cherokee Advocate* be sold prior to allotment.

Sec. 58: The U.S. Secretary of Interior furnished the principal chief with blank allotment deeds for conveyance of tribal land to individual allotees.

Sec. 63: Death warrant of Cherokee Nation. The Cherokee Nation shall not exist longer than 1906. (We must note again the termination of the Cherokee Nation did not occur.)

Sec. 74: Ratified by a majority vote of the Cherokee Nation voters.

Our public buildings were reserved to be sold and the money distributed per capita. In this oppressive environment, similar to that imposed by Georgia in 1828, the Cherokees affirmed the agreement by a vote of 2–1.

It is now 100 years later, 100 years after one of the darkest days of our history, in which the effort to dissolve and terminate our Nation clearly failed. This effort was to dissipate our assets and accomplishments to the wind of American manifest destiny. But it took almost 75 years to see the rebuilding.

Fifty years ago, W.W. Keeler and thousands of other Cherokees sought to find ways to rebuild the Cherokee Nation. Here, 50 years ago, Benny Smith's father, Stokes Smith, spoke at the first Cherokee National Holiday. The Cherokee Nation lived under a regime of "bureaucratic imperialism" best shown by the BIA solicitor's opinion in 1953, which stated that the Cherokee Nation existed in name only for the purpose of executing allotment deeds. We know that opinion was fundamentally wrong, but it was only in 1975 that the federal courts removed the oppression of the BIA by acknowledging our constitutional government.

Fifty years ago, our people hungered to take our own government back in order to control our own destiny. It was only 32 years ago that we were allowed to elect our own principal chief again. In 1967, with proceeds of the Cherokee Outlet Settlement, the Cherokee Nation hired its first employees. Those were Flossie Girty, Cora Harder, Crosslin Smith, and Ralph Keen. The Cherokee Nation had a budget of $10,000 and worked out of a storefront on South Muskogee Avenue.

It has been only 14 years since we have regained the function of all of our branches of government with federal court decisions such as *Harjo v. Kleepe* in 1976 and *Muskogee v. Hodel* in 1988.

In those early years, Principal Chief Keeler formed the Cherokee Community Representatives, which served as an advisory council. They began the restructuring our government. They met in a time of oppression, indifference, and frustration. I would like to recognize them today: Robert Swimmer, Lucille Maish, T.V. Thorne, Jim Chuwalooky, Will Rider, Glen Henson, Bob McSpadden, Rachel Lawrence, Don Mabrey, Mary Sellers, Moses Frye, W.W. Keeler, and Kenneth Wright.

Today, we are once again considered a leader among Indian tribes and non-Indian communities. We have formed strong partnerships with our neighboring governments to benefit others and ourselves.

We must be ever mindful that our lives can turn upside down within a decade, just as in the decade before the Trail of Tears in 1838 and before the allotment of our lands in 1902. Just five years ago, our government was on the threshold of the collapse. The Cherokee Nation had a constitutional crisis so severe that armed snipers perched on the building across the street during the holiday parade. We must be ever diligent so that no internal or external forces can take away our government and damage our lives.

A greater case for resilience, perseverance, and patience of a people cannot be found. Since electing our own principal chief in 1971, the Cherokee Nation has begun exponential growth and resurgence.

Today, with our instrumentalities, we have 3,000 employees, a budget of more than $250 million, and we are the largest employer in eastern Oklahoma. We have provided thousands of scholarships and homes and scores of jobs and community infrastructure projects. We stand and assemble again in front of our national capitol building. We assert the sovereignty of taxation, we operate our judicial system, and we protect our people with our marshal service.

On August 5 of this year, we announced an innovative $50 million loan program to build housing. It was "gadugi," coming together to work for the good of others.

One hundred years ago, Redbird Smith stated, "Our pride in our ancestral heritage is our great incentive for handing something worthwhile to our posterity. It is this pride in ancestry that makes men strong and loyal for their principle in life. It is this same pride that makes men give up their all for their government."

Fifty years ago, John Ketcher—our esteemed statesman, former deputy chief, and current council member—was fresh off a navy warship and had come home to the Cherokee Nation. The prospect of opportunity was bleak; times were tough. He and many others like him who persisted in believing in the Cherokee Nation and the Cherokee people have brought us to this day.

I want to recognize several of those who in the service of our Cherokee Nation and the United States sacrificed their lives. Brian Moss was on duty as a navy communications officer when he died at the Pentagon on September 11. Shelby Blackfox, a marshal of the Cherokee Nation, died in a motorcycle accident on November 6, 2001. Jack Montgomery, who was awarded the Congressional Medal of Honor during World War II, passed away in June. We should never forget these sacrifices.

Two years ago, I asked our staff to implement a veterans advocacy office at the Cherokee Nation. I am proud that we are the first tribe to do so, using our own money. It has been a great success in helping veterans. One project is a veterans memorial so that we never forget their contributions. On display is the artist's conception. It will be funded with tribal and private resources. You may purchase a brick with the name of your beloved veteran to help fund this memorial. Our government is good, but before us are challenges to survive in changing times.

Enterprise

As the Cherokee Nation builds one fire, the second log is enterprise.

The lesson of history is clear. Redbird Smith said 100 years ago, "A kindly man cannot help his neighbor unless he has a surplus, and he cannot have a surplus unless he works."

My dad, Nelson Smith, was a tie cutter in his youth. A tie cutter used a broad axe to hew logs into railroad ties. It was hard work. He, like many Cherokees, had to leave the Cherokee Nation to get a job in the 1930s. In the 1930s there were 40,000 Cherokees in Oklahoma according to the U.S. Census. A decade later there were 20,000 Cherokees. What happened to one-half of our population? They left Oklahoma as the family in *The Grapes of Wrath* did on U.S. Highway 66. It was a second Trail of Tears, an economic trail.

We must lead a vibrant economy that is diverse, provides career path jobs, and supports our government. One hundred years ago we were self-sufficient. Fifty years ago we were in dire poverty. W.W. Keeler established the Cherokee Foundation to provide shoes and coats for our

Cherokee children. We must build an economy so our people must never again leave their homeland to sustain themselves. In the last year, through partnerships with the city of Tahlequah, we have brought in two businesses that will bring 700 jobs to the Cherokee Nation. Under outstanding corporate leadership, a proactive board of directors, and the hard work of staff and hundreds of employees, our gaming operations have doubled their profits in the past year. We have awarded 1,500 scholarships and created a career services department. Sixty percent of my time is devoted to business and community development. Of course, we must do more to see the day that every Cherokee who wants a sustaining job will have the opportunity for it here in the Cherokee Nation.

Community

As the Cherokee Nation builds one fire, the third log is community.

Gadugi means "to come together and work." It is the cultural concept that has allowed us to survive. History tells us that the federal government will abandon us two or three more times in the next 100 years. We can be prepared only if we have 100 strong Cherokee communities. A community is a union of families who help each other. Historically, we had towns or clans. In the last century, our communities have become the unit of survival.

The famous Indian advocate and author Angie Debo wrote about gadugi in the 1930s. She recounted the story of Lyons Switch. The members of that community decided that they would build a community building. At that time they were barely surviving. The community was split into two factions, and acts of crime and vandalism were common. But the community members began organizing themselves to plan a place where they could meet, a building. Someone donated a piece of land near a spring. A group of men decided to furnish logs. Women and children brought stones and clay from the hillside and built a lime kiln. Pretty soon the work on the building had superseded all recreation, and the people all worked together. When the building was complete, the entire community held a big celebration. The building was used for many years. It was never locked, and there was never an instance of vandalism.

The spirit is still alive in Cherokee communities today.

Many in Evening Shade, a Sequoyah County community, took the leadership to acquire and build their own community building. Through pie suppers and turkey shoots, they raised the money and built the structure relying only on themselves. Today they host a series of programs and come together regularly to enjoy each other's fellowship. Jim McCoy, a respected elder, has been a consistent and steady facilitator for the community.

In the next few months, seven communities will begin construction on community buildings that they designed on land they developed using construction labor that they organized. These communities are South Coffeyville, Rocky Ford, Greasy, Dry Creek, Bell, Marble City, and Chewey. The Cherokee Nation provides the materials, and the communities provide the leadership and labor. Charlie Soap, Don Greenfeather, and Willard Mounce assist this project.

In Bell, a committee of community members with the assistance of Cherokee Nation's community services department is designing and building 20 homes themselves on sites they developed with plans they designed. It is called Our Generation Housing Project. The Cherokee Nation will lend them the money, which they will repay in full.

Only with 100 strong Cherokee communities can we survive the next 100 years. These communities can be any place that Cherokees find themselves, from Lyon Switch to Kansas City.

Culture

As the Cherokee Nation builds one fire, the fourth log is culture.

The attributes that have allowed us to enjoy our Cherokee legacy include our history, culture, and language. Our culture is not the simple artifacts of games, utility, and dress. Our culture is the values that have given us strength in times of weakness, hope in times of despair, and happiness in times of little. Most critically, our culture is communicated, protected, and embedded in our language. When we lose our language, we are no longer a Cherokee people; we are merely people whose ancestors were Cherokee.

Preserving and protecting our language is our greatest and most important challenge.

How fortunate we are to still hear the Cherokee language spoken in our homes, court, communities, churches, traditional grounds, and in the halls of the Cherokee Nation. We offer financial incentives for employees speaking the language; we released tens of thousands of CDs sung in Cherokee; we have immersion classes for three- and four-year-old children; we offer more language classes; and we print more literature in the Cherokee language than ever before. We even have a 30-minute radio show all in Cherokee that has aired 38 different programs thanks to talented employees and volunteers. But we must do much more, or we will lose the battle to maintain our precious language. We must dramatically increase programs and budgets to deal with this crisis. As leaders, parents, and grandparents, we must not let this be the last generation in which our joyous and instructive language is written, spoken, heard, and understood.

There is hope. Everywhere I go, I hear children singing along with our children's choir CD. Some children are in daycare about to take their naps; others are wearing their CD headphones; and others stand in the church choir in places like Pine Tree Baptist Church—all singing the beautiful Cherokee language. Thanks to the children's choir directors, staff, the parents, and many others who contributed to making our youth choir possible.

Our 40-hour history course has been a great success thanks to dedicated staff and employees who over the last two years made it possible to teach over 1,800 students. The Cherokee History Course received an Award of Honor from Harvard University. The course is so popular, there is usually a waiting list to enroll. It has changed the lives of hundreds to see the historic spectrum of the Cherokee legacy.

We must identify our cultural values and teach them, from the youngest child to the oldest student—Cherokee values like honesty, hard work, integrity, and sharing. The principal of Sequoyah High School found it remarkable how honest our Indian students are. He said when you get on them for something, 80 percent tell the truth and take responsibility. He says it is the opposite in the public schools; 80 percent will try to get out of trouble by telling stories.

Several weeks ago at a leadership award banquet, Rena Hammer Wells, who received recognition for raising many of her extended family members and other children in Westville, said, "After I lost my niece and mother, I was about to give up, and then I remembered that my grandmother said, 'Never shut the door on anyone.'" That is Cherokee caring.

Our artists and craftspeople are at the forefront of teaching our culture. People like Lena Blackbird, Anna Mitchell, Knokovtee Scott, Bill Glass, Talmadge Davis, Mary Adair, and many others memorialize and teach our culture and traditional arts. But as each of them knows and would tell you, their Cherokee projects must be historically accurate and culturally true; otherwise, they have compromised the value of their work.

Our culture is taught at youth/elders camps organized by Hastings Shade. To date, more than 600 people have attended these camps. For the past two years we have held summer culture camps for children that lasted six weeks and served 278 students. Principal Chief Keeler in his 1963 state of the nation address said, "Let us remember the lessons of the past and live our lives so that all men will hold us in high regard. Let us live the kind of life that brought love and respect to the Cherokees. Cherokees must have a high degree of honesty, be humble, and believe in a Great Spirit. We have the common denominator of Cherokee blood. Let's not turn our back on our heritage."

We have a great Cherokee legacy that we must carry on. It is a legacy paid for with thousands of lives, 81 million acres in the old country, 15 million acres in Indian Territory, and countless individual family stories of heartbreak and tragedy. We are a people who face adversity, survive, adapt, prosper, and excel. Today it is our responsibility, duty, and honor to pass this legacy on to our children, grandchildren, and great-grandchildren. I believe in the Cherokee Nation and the people.

We are not a people of the past; we are a people of the present and future. We are a special people because of our culture. In fact, the Creator has given us the name of the "real people," aniyvwiya.

Closing

In summary, I must thank you for the honor of serving as your principal chief. It was three years ago that you elected me and allowed me to serve. I have worked hard, diligently, and with passion for 60 to 70 hours a week. I have worked hard because I enjoy it, and it has been good work. It has been the work of our people. I cannot rest because I see our people's needs. I witness our successes, I feel our frustrations, and I share our aspirations.

I sincerely express my appreciation to the dedicated and caring employees at the Cherokee Nation, the housing authority, the Indian hospitals, Cherokee Nation Industries, and Cherokee Nation Enterprises. They work very hard and are determined to make the Cherokee Nation better.

In closing, we are here to celebrate our government, our people, and our future. We have many hard decisions to make in order to survive and prosper. Next year, we will have elections for the executive and legislative branches of our government. I ask you to consider during this coming election focusing on those candidates who are statesmen, who care sincerely for the Cherokee people, and who will consider facts, deliberate issues, and prepare for the future of the Nation. Too often elected officials function on self-interest, shortsightedness, and arrogance. You can make good decisions only if you are involved with the government, so please observe committee and council meetings and ask your representatives meaningful questions.

Who would have thought 50 years ago, when our leaders were courageously trying to revitalize our government, that the Cherokee Nation would become a model in Indian county, that we would be exercising our sovereignty by entering into mutual compacts with local, state, and federal governments for taxes, law enforcement, environmental protection, and social services programs? Who would have thought that we would have sold 18,000 automobile tags, demonstrating our sovereignty? Our ancestors of 150 and even 20 years ago would be amazed and proud of what we have recaptured as of today.

Principal Chief Keeler suggested in 1973 that the Cherokee nation should reacquire this capitol building, and it actually occurred in 1979, just six years later. Likewise, we should look to the future and effect a 100-year plan to reacquire our assets and confirm our treaty rights, such as a delegate to the U.S. Congress, our hunting and fishing rights, our water rights, and other attributes of sovereignty. Our vision is clear; we must have a strong tribal government, economic self-reliance, and an enriching cultural identity.

Now is the time to challenge ourselves to exert all of our ability, all of our industry, all of our intelligence, our will, our ambition, and our love for our Nation in the service of our people and the survival of our Nation. Now is the time to open the doors of opportunity for our Cherokee children, families, and elders. Now is the time for renewal, a rekindling of those things it means to be Cherokee. Let us individually and as a people resolve to treat each other with human dignity, show respect for one another, and be a model for the world that is looking on.

As Redbird Smith said 100 years ago, let us resolve to do right and think right. Let us build one fire that will never go out.

Wado.

Your humble servant,

Chadwick "Corntassel" Smith
Principal Chief

2003 State of the Nation
Critical Crossroads

INTRODUCTION

I was elected for a second term as principal chief, and the state of the nation speech came six weeks after the inauguration, expanding on the basic principles and themes of my inauguration speech. The council sued me over my challenge to their "slush fund." The idea of making decisions based on principles was becoming stronger within my administration, but the council still was driven by political decisions of self-ingratiation. One example was the building of a new gymnasium at Sequoyah School. The school had tremendous success in basketball, and the team had to go to other schools in the area because the gym was so small and the fans were so many. There was a great sense of community and support for the students and the school. Rather than rationally analyze the school's needs, the council arbitrarily allocated a sum of money to build a gymnasium. It was a political decision, not a strategic one. In any event, we proceeded to build a gym, and the cost was twice what was budgeted by the council, which created more political chaos. The gym was under-budgeted to begin with, and the political expectations were unrealistic.

There is a fluid division among Cherokees along blood quantum lines and community affiliations. In broad terms, "full blood" or "Indian" refers to racially identifiable and cultural and community orientated Cherokees.

"White" Cherokees, or Cherokee citizens with a "blue card," generally referred to those Cherokees with a small blood quantum who were not racially identifiable as Indian and not associated with Cherokee culture or community. A blue card was a Cherokee citizenship card. One example of the difference: generally a full blood would say he was from a particular community; a white Cherokee would say he was from a particular county. Regardless of your racial appearance, if you were from a known Cherokee community and family and held yourself out as an Indian, not just a "card carrier," then you were generally accepted as Indian. That said, one of the comments about the gym was, "Those white Cherokees have everything else, but the new gym is for Indians." Of course, no one was excluded from the new gym, but Sequoyah High School became a symbol of Indian pride; family and community members vicariously enjoyed the youthful competition and success of the students and community. The gym in English translation was named the "place where they play." As the Baptist preacher would say, "I say all that to say this." People need monuments to remember and affirm their identity.

The Cherokee immersion school began with kindergarten students. It was an experiment based on the fact that out of 8,000 fluent Cherokee speakers, only a handful were younger than 55 years old. Some unexplained cultural phenomena occurred after World War II to discourage Cherokee parents from teaching their children the Cherokee language.

There were also external challenges. A group of white businesses and business associations organized under the name One Nation to lobby against Indian tribes and nations. Generally, the constituencies of One Nation were those convenience stores, gas stations, and oil and gas companies that were opposed to tribes avoiding state taxes and regulations and imposing their own. Their mantra was to "level the playing field." History clearly reflects that the playing field was skewed dramatically to the advantage of the white interests at Oklahoma statehood a hundred years ago, and now One Nation wanted to further erode the sovereignty interests of Indian tribes and nations.

The other external challenge came from descendants of Freedmen who were slaves of Cherokees or freed Negroes in the Cherokee Nation before the American Civil War. If they had Cherokee blood, they were allowed to enroll during the allotment process between 1898 and 1906 as "Cherokee by blood." If they did not demonstrate Cherokee ancestry, they were placed on a Freedmen role. Both Cherokees and Freedmen received land and per capita distribution payments upon the liquidation of the Cherokee Nation assets in the 1910s. Their status as citizens of the Cherokee Nation did not matter until 1975, when the citizens of the Cherokee Nation passed a superseding constitution that excluded them from citizenship, and the growth of the Cherokee Nation began to provide some individual benefits. Between 1906 and 1971, the Cherokee Nation as a government was basically dormant.

The issues of self-help versus entitlement, principled decision making versus political expediency, development of internal leadership, and external challenges from white business interests, Freedmen, and federal paternalism would continue. The theme of the 2003 state of the nation address was being at a critical crossroads. Unfortunately, it seemed in Cherokee history, such was the case every day.

STATE OF THE NATION: CRITICAL CROSSROADS

August 30, 2003

Greetings. Today, I believe that we are at a critical crossroads as a Nation, as communities, and as individual citizens. We must come face-to-face with a serious weakness that has become epidemic. We see symptoms of the trouble in the growth of diabetes, the clamor for free housing and social services, and the devastating effects of methamphetamine production and use.

This epidemic has blinded many of us to our own abilities, responsibilities, and opportunities. Our vision is cloudy, and we often stumble and grasp for things to help us stand. But the things that we take hold of are not things that build us up. They are props that hold us up, barely keeping us from falling.

Over the past four years I have observed many things. Too many of my observations didn't reflect what I've always held to be true characteristics of the Cherokee people.

Instead of seeing strength, I often see weakness.

Instead of responsibility, I often see people blaming each other.

Instead of self-reliance by planning to improve, diligently working, and doing a good job, I often see a sense of dependency on subsidized housing, free health care, scholarships, and donated foods.

Instead of leadership, I often see confusion.

Instead of tribal patriotism, I often see efforts to destroy the Cherokee Nation's sovereignty.

Instead of gadugi, I often see destructive selfishness.

Immediately after getting their Cherokee citizenship card, I have heard people ask for the list of free things to which they are entitled as tribal members. This is not the Cherokee way. It will lead to the demise of the Cherokee Nation.

Within the last year, I met with a 22-year-old college student and mother of one. She expressed to me how she wanted an Indian house while she was going to school and how disappointed she was that I could not give her one. She began to cry. I explained that usually students go to school to get an education so they can get a better job to earn enough money to buy a home. She did not understand. She thought she was entitled to a free home—right now.

That's a common story that some here in Tahlequah encounter daily. Thankfully, not everyone who comes to the Cherokee Nation feels or acts this way. But stories like this show that some of us have an odd perspective. That perspective is, "I am entitled to free things simply because it is my right as a Cherokee citizen." This perspective becomes an attitude that has devastating effects on our Nation. If we continue enabling a dependency mind-set, we will become weaker and weaker as a people.

But let me also say, there are Cherokees who need our help. We as a Nation, as a people, and as their Cherokee kin should help them. But those who can help themselves should help themselves. We need to be in the business of helping people help themselves. Nothing real or worthwhile is gained by doing for those who can do for themselves.

I've heard our Cherokee people say, "No one owes us a living," and that is true. Not the federal, state, or tribal government. Not the business world or society in general. Not our parents, children, or relatives. How many of us have forgotten that a living is earned? Jobs, houses, scholarships, and quality lifestyles are not given to us; they are earned by us.

While the picture of the Cherokee Nation that I see contains warnings, it also abounds with promise. The greater picture begins with images of the past; it is freshly painted with the present and is unfinished for the future. It is full of people, places, and acts. Gadugi is working together for the benefit of the community. And gadugi is the critical tool and skill we must practice today to reach the tomorrow we all want.

So too with our government. The Cherokee Nation is a family of families, community of communities, and a nation of people. The Cherokee Nation must choose to be economically self-reliant, to have an enriching cultural identity, and to have a healthy tribal government. History and the well-being of our children provide only one answer. I submit to you: we must proceed with the vision of rebuilding our nation.

My 10-year-old daughter, Anaweg, loves to climb the magnolia tree on Capitol Square. What a great experience. She and her siblings and friends will climb high into the tree, giggle, and enjoy themselves in their adventure. It makes my heart light to see our children full of life, energy, and anticipation—enjoying themselves on the sacred ground of our historic capitol. It is the history and future of this ground that makes it sacred. And 25 years from now, my daughter and her generation of Cherokees will judge us on what we did to pass on our great legacy.

In order to fulfill our legacy, I commit to you and every one of this council, I will keep an open mind on all issues, apply our cultural principles, endeavor to use sound judgment, respect our differences, and make an honest and sincere effort to work with each of our officials for the benefit of our people. None of our officials, including myself, are entitled to hold political grudges. I am pleased to say there is a refreshing new spirit of cooperation with our new tribal council.

Gadugi. We must live by it. Not because it is the right thing to do— even though it is. Not because it is the best strategy to save the Cherokee Nation—even though it is. But because it is the principle, the perspective, the opportunity for us to pause and enjoy ourselves, our lives, and our kin by doing something worthwhile. By sharing, we receive. By coaching, we build. By working, we become stronger. By listening, we understand. By respecting each other, we endure.

Wado.

Your humble servant,

Chadwick "Corntassel" Smith
Principal Chief

2004 State of the Nation
Where There Is No Vision, the People Perish

INTRODUCTION

The 2004 state of the nation speech refined our vision and the strategy to achieve it. After several attempts, the formula boiled down to "jobs keep people home in their communities and allow them to retain the culture and language, all of which improves the quality of life." Chief Martin of the Mississippi Choctaws used a similar expression over his 30-year tenure when he led his tribe from poverty to prosperity. We used the litany of "jobs, language, and community" to convey to the general public our strategy. This state of the nation speech had substantial details, going into each part of our strategy and why it was important. In the previous year, there were events that reinforced our work and strategy and taught us lessons. The council lost its lawsuit against me for its "slush fund." We were building self-help community buildings using volunteer labor; we completed tobacco and gaming compacts with the state of Oklahoma; and our Cherokee National Youth Choir, which sang exclusively in Cherokee, won Best Gospel album from the Native American Music Association.

I want to address an issue for each of these areas of focus. For language, I will address why it is important to save our language; how it increases our quality of life; and how it directs our government. For jobs, I will address why self-help or community contributions by program participants is important. And for community, I will address why it is important to understand that the Cherokee Nation is a government and not just a social service agency.

Quality of Life

But first we must understand what quality of life means. Central to the idea of quality of life are the ideas of fulfillment of life and Cherokee thought. Quality of life spans a range of life's requirements and desires from the basics of food, clothing, and shelter to spiritual fulfillment. The highest aspect of quality of life is being able to choose our own destiny and to contribute to that destiny with meaningful work. It's having the means to be happy and healthy for ourselves and our families, our communities, and our nation. Quality of life really comes down to whether we are happier and healthier people. We sometimes get confused about what quality of life really means.

Quality of life is fishing on the creek bank. Quality of life is not expensive fishing trips to Alaska.

Quality of life is watching our children and grandchildren at tee-ball games. Quality of life is not being able to sit in the owner's box at a professional baseball game.

Quality of life is the security of knowing that we have job skills in the market, knowing that we have talents and skills and that we can perform meaningful work. Quality of life is not winning the Powerball lottery.

Quality of life is appreciating the moments that we have on this earth and enjoying them and sharing them with others. Quality of life is not getting caught in the insecure trap of complaining and moaning about others.

Quality of life is having richness and an abundance of love among family and friends. Quality of life is not having a host of cars and money or fancy houses.

Quality of life is understanding the world around us with such clarity that we each are poets and artists, amazed by the simplest things such as dew on the morning grass, the haze on the eastern horizon in the mornings, the majesty of geese and mockingbirds singing their respective tunes. Quality of life is not dulling our senses with alcohol and drugs and jealousy and pettiness.

Quality of life is knowing our own history so we can make decisions better. It is knowing our own language so we can more clearly understand the world around us and the values that drive us. Quality of life is not blaming others for our shortcomings and misfortunes and playing the victim.

Quality of life is being and doing, not having.

That is what we talk about when we talk about quality of life. Many times due to the advertising bombardment we get every day, we lose sight of what really brings value to our quality of life—language, jobs, and community.

Language: The Importance of Its Survival

Each year I am amazed when I see how far we've come as a Nation and people and where we can go. On the way to a future that we choose, we must understand where we've been in the past. Thanks to the instruction and leadership of Julia Coates, 3,000 people have completed the 40-hour Cherokee history course, which teaches us lessons of the past that we can apply to the present and the future. We are now better prepared to face our adversaries, resolve conflict, and develop a better quality of life.

What do we see in the future? What we define as the future is our choice. What can our quality of life be 20, 50, or 100 years from now? These are our decisions, no one else's. We must be driven not only by our understanding of the lessons of history but also by our cultural attributes and values, which have allowed us to survive hundreds of years under horrific circumstances. Those values and attributes, including a sense of community, perseverance, and humility before the Creator, are all imbedded in our language. We will not survive as a people when the language is lost. And with the passing of each Cherokee-speaking elder, we are at risk of losing our language.

But our language is not yet lost. One of our employees told me a story just this week that brought tears to her eyes at one of our language immersion classes. She saw two adults from behind carrying on a conversation in Cherokee and looking down occasionally. After she moved to see what the adults were looking at, she saw a precious little four-year-old who was speaking Cherokee right along with them.

That little girl is just one of the new generation of Cherokee speakers. Our language immersion classes in Lost City public schools have produced high academic achievers. You have heard our Cherokee young people today singing in Cherokee, and this is just the start. We must have more Cherokee language immersion classes, more children speaking Cherokee to each other and to their parents and grandparents. If we do that, our language and our culture have a bright future, but we must devote our time, energy, and resources to make our vision a reality.

Equally important is how our Cherokee language improves our quality of life. The best way I can show that is by example. When we speak English, this is what we see and think: "This is a picture of a rose; it's in black and white." When we understand Cherokee words like *gadugi*, we acquire a quality of life we did not know before. It is an understanding of creativity and inspiration that we could never imagine if we only knew English. I'll show you another picture, the same rose, this time in color. This is *utsilvsgi*, a rose. Like many Cherokee words, *utsilvsgi* means more than just "flower"; it means "something blooming." When you are color blind, seeing only black and white, you can neither appreciate nor imagine what it is like to see in color. Do we want ourselves and our children to be blind to the richness that Cherokee language brings to us? Quality of life is seeing and understanding the radiance, vibrancy, and clarity of Cherokee thought. We must hold on to that language. We must teach our children. They will learn, they want to learn, and it is the job of each and every one of us, speakers and nonspeakers, to find the resources to teach them, to ensure a bright future for our language, culture, and identity. I am asking every Cherokee speaker to be a teacher, to use the language as often as possible in everyday life, and to share your knowledge with those around you.

The Ability to Earn Meaningful Work

It is very clear that the work of the Cherokee Nation is to build individuals, families, communities, and our Nation. The work we do should not enable weakness; it should not provide handouts that increase entitlement expectations among our citizens. We should not be in the business of doing for people but helping people help themselves. With that comes a responsibility, the responsibility of the Cherokee Nation as a government to make strong long-term decisions. Part of that responsibility is for each of our people to understand that the Cherokee Nation is not a social services agency; the Cherokee Nation is a government. Often, people get their tribal citizenship card and then immediately ask for a list of things to which they are entitled.

The Cherokee Nation as a family of families and a community of communities has the responsibility to encourage each and every one of us to build ourselves, build our communities, build our families, and build our Nation. That is why we have launched an effort that every one of our programs shall have a self-help or community contribution requirement. In other words, all of our social service and assistance programs should be partnerships between our government, our staff, and our people to help participants help themselves so they can gain skills to make wise decisions and to support themselves, their families, their communities, and their Nation.

Several years ago, I submitted a proposal to the tribal council and I encouraged them to pass it as law. That proposal requires a self-help component or community contribution for each of our social service programs. This requirement would not apply to those physically or mentally incapable of doing self-help. What this would do is bring value to those programs by helping people to help themselves. In our discussions with program participants and community people, this idea has received overwhelming support. It goes back to the idea of gadugi, coming together and working for the benefit of the community. It will allow us to build our own destiny.

Last year I reported to you the success of eight communities that built their own community buildings with the Cherokee Nation supplying the material. This year we will also acknowledge and honor the Our Generation project, a community of younger people who took the opportunity to build their own homes.

Several years ago I was in the Bell community with the late Johnson Soap, and he reflected upon the success of the Bell waterline, where the community pulled together and actually built the waterline themselves. A number of the younger people in the community knew and understood that story. I made a commitment to them that if they would build the houses, I would find funds for materials.

Since that demonstration project began, they have experimented with different construction techniques. As of today, six houses are built or under construction. Participating in a self-help project is quite an experience. When you go and work on these houses, as I have done, it actually becomes a celebration. People get off work when their shift ends and volunteer until ten at night. It is a true sense of gadugi, the sense of community, the sense of just enjoying doing something with and for other people.

In that spirit, I am proud to report that council passed the self-help proposal at their rules committee meeting, and the full council will vote on the law on September 13. Passing that self-help law will mean more and more self-help community projects like the Our Generation project.

Working together highlights the benefits of work, the core foundation for strong Cherokee communities. If people have jobs, they can stay here in the Cherokee Nation and keep our language and culture alive in our communities.

That is why I am so proud of the Cherokee Nation's business successes. Cherokee Nation Enterprises has created more than 700 new jobs this year alone while still showing record profits. Cherokee Nation Industries had its best performance in years.

The reason our business success is important becomes clear when we look at financial research. It shows that every dollar we spend on job development or training helps 10 times the number of families than if we spent the same amount on social services.

It is easy to understand why. If the breadwinner has a good job, he or she can pay the family's mortgage, health insurance, food bills, and other social service needs instead of the Cherokee Nation picking up the tab. So we can help one family by providing them with a subsidized house, free healthcare, social services, and donated food, or we can help 10 families with the same amount of investment by creating jobs and the ability to get jobs so they can provide for themselves.

Community: The Cherokee Nation as a Government

At times we can't see the forest for the trees. We must step back and get a panoramic view not only of where we are today but where we are at this moment in history. In that context, we must ask the question, "Why have a Cherokee Nation government?" When we do that, we see the value of the Cherokee Nation as a government and how it protects and promotes quality of life, especially for Cherokee communities.

Think back to Oklahoma statehood, back before the Bureau of Indian Affairs assumed a position of bureaucratic imperialism. Think back before the time when we lost control of our destiny and our communal title to our land was stripped away by the Curtis Act of 1898. At that point in time, you recall U.S. Senator Dawes held an examination of the Cherokee Nation. He found there was not a pauper in the whole Nation, everyone owned his own home, and the tribe owed not a dollar.

He went on to say that fallacy of our system was that there was no selfishness, which he saw at the foundation of civilization. Dawes said that until we agreed to give up our communal lands to be held individually, we would make no more progress because there was no incentive for any of us to make our homes any better than those of our neighbors. So we look back to that remarkable era. We had 150 day schools, nine courthouses, a supreme court building, an asylum for orphans, a national capitol, and a national prison that provided vo-tech training. We had 90 percent literacy in our language and countless college graduates. We had a domain of wealth that sustained us and a government of our own design that protected our quality of life.

Our success was challenged due to the jealousy and greed of outside interests. When the lands were allotted and the efforts to destroy our government took place, we went into a dark age, and during that dark age, without the protection of the Cherokee Nation government, what happened to the Cherokee people?

By 1920 we had lost 90 percent of our lands. Forced into a cash economy, half of our population left Oklahoma on a second Trail of Tears, an economic Trail of Tears on Route 66 to California and Texas during the Great Depression. In the 1930s people were dying, literally, of starvation; poverty was at it worst; and discord and misery had found us.

W.A. Duncan, a Cherokee writer, saw this coming in 1898 when the U.S. Senate passed the Curtis Act. He wrote of a time "when the Indian problem is solved, that is to say when the Cherokees as a distinctive community have been long forgotten, and the poor people who once wore the name have long been on the duty assigned them in the walks of poverty and contempt by the merciless decrees of civilization."

And that nearly became our fate. By 1975, when I worked for Cherokee Nation as a planner, Adair County was the second poorest county in the whole country. That is what happened to us, our people, when there wasn't a healthy and strong Cherokee Nation government to protect us.

Now I ask you to look at how our quality of life has improved since 1970, when those dark ages began to pass and the Cherokee Nation began its revival. Since 1991, the United States has been forced to recognize each branch of our constitutional government and our territory as Indian country.

In 1968 we had three employees and a $10,000 budget. Now we have 4,000 employees and a $270 million budget. But that is not what's important; what is important is that today we have less poverty.

Even though we each know that our people and our government can do better, look at the last 100 years of our history. It's very, very clear what happens when our government functions and we are allowed to design and effect our own government. We can very easily see how harsh conditions can become when we don't have a Cherokee Nation government to protect us.

How is the Cherokee Nation doing today? In the spectrum of time, we're getting back on our feet. Our government never died. As one federal judge recalled, we lived in a state of "bureaucratic imperialism" beginning in 1898. We must be ever vigilant; we must never accept those times again.

The Cherokee Nation has built 6,000 housing units in the last 30 years. We have eight clinics and two IHS hospitals, a high school, a marshal service, health services, social services, and programs that provide services for our people, all with outstanding reputations. Our healthcare funding is at its highest level ever. Employment and profits at our businesses are at all-time highs. Our children are learning our language. The financial structure of the Cherokee Nation is rock solid, and we have the national accounting awards to prove it.

But the greatest measure of the state of our nation is the state of our people, the state of our communities, which can't be motivated by government or money or power but rather by each one of us having an understanding and a passion to give our children a Cherokee quality of life. Then they can think and act and see in all the color and vibrancy of cultural intelligence, language enhancement, and spiritual thoughtfulness. Each of our families must draw closer together and build those strong bonds so we can be there for each other in times of trial and peril. We as communities must put aside territorial differences and help each other.

Closing

Last year these council members joined Joe Grayson and me in taking our oath of office right here on Capitol Square. At that time each of us also took another oath, and to make sure we remembered it, we had it carved in stone.

About 100 yards in that direction, embedded in the sidewalk is a stone that reads, "In 2003 Cherokee Nation leaders gathered at this capitol building and made a decision to pass on the great Cherokee legacy and not to let it die knowing that coming generations would judge them on whether the legacy was truly passed forward."

That is a decision we all must make, and we must make it daily. Our great Cherokee legacy is that we are a people who face adversity, survive, adapt, prosper, and excel. Do we pass on the great Cherokee legacy? We must pass it on or allow it to lapse. If we allow it to lapse, history books 20 years from now will report, "Once there was a great Cherokee Nation, but it is no more."

I can say this with the strongest conviction: this great legacy even today is still being granted by citizens of our Cherokee Nation with the ultimate sacrifice, their lives.

We have lost four of our Cherokee citizens in the conflict that has arisen since September 11, 2001, when our country was attacked. Petty Officer Second Class Brian Moss of Sperry was killed at the Pentagon that day. Fern Holland of Tulsa, Sergeant Kyle Adam Brinlee of Pryor, and Lance Corporal Caleb John Powers of Washington State were all killed in Iraq, and we will honor each of these patriots in just a few minutes. But we must remember that each died not only for the United States but also in the service of the Cherokee Nation so that we may strive for quality of life and pass on the Cherokee legacy.

We have with us on leave from Iraq two Cherokee Nation employees, Shawnna Eubanks and Barry Boomer. We are pleased to have them home and out of harm's way, if only for a short while, and we hope they are able to return home to stay soon. By their service they are standing up for our Cherokee legacy.

The strength and magnitude of this legacy grows and is appreciated more each day. To carry forward this legacy, we have strong leaders emerging. But adversity awaits them.

There is a powerful painting of the Trail of Tears by Charles Vann that hangs in the lobby of our tribal complex. It shows the impending doom of the West with dark clouds of thunder and lightning,

History does have a way of repeating itself, and we are once again at a point in history where impending doom lurks on the horizon.

Prior to the Trail of Tears, Georgians argued in the U.S. Supreme Court that the Cherokee Nation could not be a "sovereign within a sovereign." We prevailed in court, but we still suffered the Trail of Tears. Before Oklahoma statehood, with the efforts to allot our lands and dissolve our government, our opponents in Congress argued that the Cherokee Nation could not be a "sovereign within a sovereign." We retained our rights to government, but we lost our land.

Today, we are faced with anti-Indian hate groups and political candidates repeating the same outdated slogan that the Cherokee Nation cannot be a "sovereign within a sovereign." I am not an alarmist, but history's lessons are undeniable. Every 20 to 40 years, public sentiment and federal policy turns against the Cherokee Nation and other tribes. Now, instead of historical policies of genocide, removal, ethnocide, assimilation, extortion, allotment, dissolution, and relocation, the federal policy could shift toward abandonment. These groups and their candidates do not believe in federal programs, tribal sovereignty, and gaming.

If it has not sunk in yet, let me put it this way: if these people get their way, there will not be gaming or tribal programs that employ more than 4,000 people here at the Cherokee Nation. There will not be money for our government, our healthcare, and our education programs. The Indian hospitals and clinics will shut down for lack of funding. Housing and other social services for our most vulnerable citizens will become nonexistent. Our employees will lose their jobs.

These groups and their candidates are not only against our self-sufficiency and our government. They seek to nullify the rights guaranteed in our 23 treaties with Great Britain and the United States.

So what are we going to do? Do we stand firm and get involved in the political process of resisting these hostile efforts? Or do we roll over and see our rights eroded and terminated? We cannot blame anyone but ourselves if these people and their anti-Indian policies are put into office.

We are at a defining moment in history. But there is a clear choice for us to make as Oklahomans and as Cherokees.

Joining us today is a man who we will honor in just a few minutes with the Cherokee Statesmanship Award, Congressman Brad Carson.

In the tradition of the great Cherokee statesmanship of Sequoyah, John Ross, and Will Rogers, Brad Carson, a Cherokee from Claremore with a long family history of service to the Cherokee Nation, will be honored for his leadership.

It is time for another Cherokee to provide leadership in the U.S. Senate and help us carry forward this great Cherokee legacy.

In the November election there are two votes that will change the future of the Cherokee Nation. One is the vote for U.S. Senate. Our future will be brighter with fellow Cherokee Brad Carson in the U.S. Senate.

The other is State Question 712, which deals with gaming and horse racing legislation. If passed, this provision will allow the Cherokee Nation horse industry and Oklahoma education to grow and prosper. I personally ask each and every one of you to go to the polls and vote yes on State Question 712.

What is the state of the Cherokee Nation? We are on solid ground. The future is within our control. We each must come to understand that the Cherokee Nation is not about receiving but giving, not about taking but about sharing, not about harboring petty jealousies but about simply and strongly holding on to family and neighbors so we can face challenges and succeed. There will be challenges, tribulations, and difficulties. But if we do not pass on this great Cherokee legacy, we will be nothing more than a footnote in a history book. Our task is to make our vision a reality. Language, jobs, and community are the keys to our future and our gift from the past. We must keep our culture alive. We must keep our people from leaving home, and to keep them from leaving home, they must have jobs. When we stay home, here in the Cherokee Nation, our communities can thrive, and our great Cherokee Nation will once again prosper and excel.

Wado.

Your humble servant,

Chadwick "Corntassel" Smith
Principal Chief

2006 State of the Nation
Full Force and Effect

INTRODUCTION

The 2006 Cherokee National Holiday theme was "Full Force and Effect." Even though the federal government had legislated a plan from 1898 to 1906 to liquidate the Cherokee Nation's assets, terminate federal recognition of the Cherokee Nation, allot our lands, and forcibly assimilate the Cherokee people, it could not complete the process, so it enacted a provision in 1906 that the Five Civilized Tribes would continue "in full force and effect." This provision was the equivalent of the federal government dragging the Cherokee Nation up the gallows to be hung and at the eleventh hour issuing a reprieve. This reprieve is so important in our legal history that it became custom during our history class to stop, have all the students stand, and recite the "full force and effect" provision. The status of the Cherokee Nation as a federally recognized Indian nation has not changed since then.

The Cherokee Nation continued to grow, adding jobs, increasing enrollment at the immersion school, and building self-help community buildings. We strove to reduce our dependency on federal funding. In 1999, 8 percent of our budget was tribal revenues; by 2006, it was 23 percent. The goal was to reduce our dependency on the federal government by 1 percent a year until we did not need the federal government any more. I hope to see the day when we can send back to the federal government grant funds because we do not need them anymore.

STATE OF THE NATION: FULL FORCE AND EFFECT

September 3, 2006

Greetings. I thank you for coming this morning. It is my pleasure to be here with you today as we celebrate the fifty-fourth Cherokee National Holiday in celebration of our Act of Union of 1839, which brought all factions of the Cherokee Nation together under one body politic—the Cherokee Nation—and the passage of our constitution of 1839.

This holiday also commemorates the 100th anniversary of Section 28 of the 1906 Act, which provided for the continued recognition of the Cherokee Nation by the U.S. government. It is so important we acknowledge that the legal continuum of the Cherokee Nation has never been broken, and the government of the Cherokee Nation, as a constitutional government since 1839, has never been terminated. In fact, during one of our darkest hours, the eve of Oklahoma statehood, our constitutional government was continued "in full force and effect" by the United States.

The Act of 1906 inspired the theme of this Cherokee National Holiday, "In Full Force and Effect." The Cherokee Nation government continued in full force and effect, surviving attacks from the federal government and others that tried to divide and eradicate our people and Indian Country. Many of the attacks were made by people who wanted tribes out of the way in order to create the state of Oklahoma. This Cherokee Nation, as a government, was continued in full force and effect, surviving the attacks of the Dawes Commission and hundreds of special interests striving to consume and devour our assets and to create the state of Oklahoma.

But we must remember the heartaches and tribulations that followed the legal pronouncement that our government continue in full force and effect, by what a federal judge, in *Harjo v. Kleppe*, called "bureaucratic imperialism" by the Bureau of Indian Affairs "designed to frustrate, debilitate, and generally prevent from functioning" the constitutional governments of the five tribes.

In the aftermath of Oklahoma statehood, we began to lose the lands of the Cherokee Nation as exclusive territory. Do we remember how meaningful this love of our Nation was to our ancestors? Let me share with you a story. I quote:

> [Edward Everett] Dale, the dean of Oklahoma's white historians, writes with some surprise of the sadness an Indian woman still felt when she remembered the 1907 festivities to celebrate Oklahoma statehood. The Cherokee woman, married to a white man, refused to attend the statehood ceremonies with her husband. He returned and said to her, "Well, Mary, we no longer live in the Cherokee Nation. All of us are now citizens of the state of Oklahoma." Tears came to her eyes thirty years later as she recalled that day. "It broke my heart. I went to bed and cried all night long. It seemed more than I could bear that the Cherokee Nation, my country, and my people's country, was no more." (Dale 1948–49:382.)

After 30 years, there was still pain in Mary's heart. She still had strong feelings of patriotism for the Cherokee Nation. One hundred years later, we now know that Oklahoma statehood did not end the Cherokee Nation. Actually, it took 70 years to begin rebuilding the Cherokee Nation. That process continues today. Today, we strive to achieve what we had 100 years ago: an enriching cultural identity, economic self-reliance, and a strong tribal government.

So today, what is the state of the Cherokee Nation? We have come a long way in rebuilding our government. Since 1970, we have understood ourselves to be citizens of a government that predates the United States. We understand that we have dual citizenship with great pride and patriotism to both the Cherokee Nation and the United States. We have faced adversity, adapted, and survived. We are now on the path to prosper and excel.

In the last few years, our government operations have increased dramatically. In healthcare, our expenditures have gone from $35 million

We see thriving community groups in different stages of cohesion and development. The Cherokee Nation has partnered with 40 community groups to construct 15 buildings as community projects. There are new buildings going up all the time, buildings being constructed through the practice of gadugi, coming together, for the benefit of the community and helping each other.

Yes, the Cherokee Nation is headed in the right direction. It is headed in a direction dictated by our heritage and tradition, in a direction where we can answer the prayer not to lighten the load but to make us stronger. We are headed in a direction to become self-reliant rather than to become dependent or victims. We are headed in a direction where we can increase the quality of our lives for our families and children rather than yielding to the threat of drugs, diabetes, and child abuse. We are headed in a direction away from doom and despair and frustration. We are headed in the direction that we should be—the direction of optimism, of promise, of hope and hard work.

We now know we have a choice to make, and we know what the wise choice is. That choice is to take our great Cherokee legacy that we are gifted with; to face adversity, survive, adapt, prosper, and excel; and to pass that legacy on to our children and grandchildren.

Gadugi means "come together and work for the benefit of the community." Will Rogers said: "I am a Cherokee, and it's the proudest little possession I ever hope to have." Whether we are light skinned or dark skinned, speaker or nonspeaker, rich or poor, educated or not, female or male, young or old, we each can be bound by the spirit of gadugi in addition to our common ancestry. We can each be bound together by the promise and dedication that we will pass on our great Cherokee legacy.

This past year, I was talking with our deputy chief, Joe Grayson, about the success of our self-help initiatives and their popularity in Cherokee communities. Joe told me something that still sticks with me. He said, "Chad, if Cherokee people want to, we can be writing Cherokee words in the dust on the moon. Cherokees can do anything they set their minds to."

The Cherokee Nation, as a government, was condemned to death by the 1898 Curtis Act. We went to the legal gallows and took the 13 steps onto the platform. The noose was tightened around the neck of the

Cherokee Nation. The hangman was ready to pull the trap door. And then, 100 years ago, a reprieve came to the Five Civilized Tribes by Section 28 of the 1906 Act. The noose was loosened and we descended the gallows. And ever since that day, we have resolved to never be extinguished, to never be defeated, to never give up hope, to never give up our on fellow Cherokee people. We celebrate that day now 100 years later that we as a government have been recognized and are continuing in "full force and effect."

My hope for this talk is to touch your heart, to stimulate your thinking, and to reinforce your determination so that we may share together a vision— the vision that we as a nation regain the quality of life that every society struggles to achieve. That can be accomplished by us working for a healthy tribal government, a rich cultural identity, and economic self-reliance.

I submit to you that 100 years ago, before the Cherokee Nation climbed up the steps to the gallows, we had a healthy tribal government, rich cultural identity, and economic self-reliance. And we can have that again. It may take 10, 15, or 20 years. It may take 100 years. But we can have that and more if we work together to create jobs, build our communities, and strengthen our culture.

So I have only one message, and it's this. If we want the best education system for our children, it just means 50 years of hard work. If we want the best healthcare system, the best economic system, the best quality of life, we can have that too. It just means 50 years of hard work. But let me ask you, do we have anything better to do with our next 50 years? Do we have anything better to do with our next 50 years than to succeed, to prosper, and to excel? All it takes is vision, hard work, and dedication. As it says in Proverbs: "Where there is no vision, the people shall perish." Joe Grayson understands vision, and I know the Cherokee people do too. Joe and I will not be here in 50 years, but if we make wise decisions, our children and grandchildren may be the ones writing the Cherokee syllabary in the dust on the moon.

Wado.

Your Humble Servant,

Chadwick "Corntassel" Smith
Principal Chief

2008 State of the Nation
Planting the Seed Corn

INTRODUCTION

I began this speech like most of my other state of nation addresses by reciting Benny Smith's admonition for me to be a student of the Cherokee Nation. It seemed like an overwhelming challenge to influence the mind-set of so many people regarding the value of the Cherokee Nation or government. A sense of entitlement showed up in areas that were surprising. It was not just poor people desperate to make ends meet, but also some Indian businessmen who believed they were entitled to business and contracts from the Nation without regard to their competitiveness, as well as Oklahoma state agencies, politicians, and non-Indians who saw the growing prosperity of the Cherokee Nation and believed they should get their "fair share" of the success.

One success story was Sequoyah High School. In 1999, it was known as a school of last resort, with a 50 percent enrollment. By 2007, there was a waiting list, and it was known as a school of choice. Sequoyah was winning state championships in sports, and Indian students were leaving public schools to go to Sequoyah. It was safe and had a family atmosphere. As a result, public schools complained about Sequoyah recruiting students and about not having the facilities and services that Sequoyah had. A decade before, the public school community had looked down on Sequoyah, and now many envied it.

I heard a female tribal leader from another tribe talk about gaming profits as the "seed corn" for the future of tribes. It was a brilliant metaphor. You have to hold back some corn to plant for the next year; you don't consume all you have; you save and invest in the future. The result is a greater harvest next year, and over time the harvest grows dramatically. I asked Cherokee speakers about the idea, and they shared a concept and phrase in Cherokee that means "people do this so their children can help themselves." We checked and found a particular variety of corn that had its origins at the time of the Trail of Tears in north Georgia. It is called Cherokee White Eagle corn because on the edge of 2 percent of the black kennels, it looks like a white eagle flying. We distributed the corn to the audience at the state of the nation and encouraged them to plant it and bring one ear back the following year to present onstage. The idea was to invest our resources in the future of our Nation and children and not consume it all through distributions and social service entitlements.

The historic lesson was in 1895. The United States forced the sale of several million acres of the Cherokee Outlet at $1.25 an acre from the Cherokee Nation for a total price of $7.8 million. Instead of investing for the future, the Cherokee Nation paid a per capita payment, and without a war chest for lobbying and litigation, the Nation was liquidated by Congress three years later. A hundred years later we had to make similar decisions: to give money out or to invest in the future of the Nation.

During this year, challenges continued. The federal Congressional Black Caucus backed Congresswoman Watson's bill to terminate the Cherokee Nation because Freedmen were excluded from citizenship. On a brighter note, in partnership with the town of Sperry, Oklahoma, we helped build a bridge that opened up their downtown better; the Nation had an expansive road building program that helped the entire region. Cherokee Nation Businesses purchased an aerospace company in Huntsville, Alabama, to expand a jobs creation portfolio. And U.S. Supreme Court Justice, Sandra Day O'Connor, visited the Cherokee Nation for a women's leadership conference and left with a different and positive view of the Cherokee Nation.

STATE OF THE NATION:
PLANTING THE SEED CORN

August 30, 2008

Greetings. Welcome to the state of the Cherokee Nation. It is my greatest honor and obligation under our constitution to report to our Cherokee citizens where the Cherokee Nation government and people are today and where we are going. It is a journey, and we must, pursuant to our God-given and inherent right, choose the path of the journey. On behalf of the legislative branch, our council, our judicial branch, our supreme and district courts, and our executive branch, our group leaders, boards, commissions, and staff, I welcome you all here today. I acknowledge the hard work and dedication of each branch of government, and I ask our group leaders who lead the various disciplines and departments of the executive branch to stand and be recognized.

Introduction

You have heard me say this many times before, that upon my first inauguration, Benny Smith admonished me to be a student of the Cherokee people. Each day, I have done that diligently. I listen, observe, think, and plan how to advance the Cherokee Nation further toward that "designed purpose" that Redbird Smith described more than 100 years ago. I believe that "designed purpose" is for us to become a happy and healthy people, and to attain that "designed purpose," we must have a plan. The root of this plan lies in an observation made in 1898 by Senator Dawes that there was not a pauper in the Nation, that every family owned a home, and that the tribe owed not a dollar. Those observations reflect a milestone and a benchmark that we can once again achieve: an enriching cultural identity, economic self-reliance, and a healthy and strong tribal government. We can create that future by listening to the wisdom of our culture and by using the values Cherokees have used for centuries.

Planting the Seed Corn

A tribal leader once referred to gaming revenue as seed corn. When she spoke, it made tremendous sense. Seed corn, that corn you keep to plant for next year. You keep it even though the harvest may not have been that great. You keep it even though times may be tough and you are hungry. You keep it even though you are tempted to eat it and celebrate. You keep it so you can plant it next year and have something for your children and grandchildren to eat. By planting the seed corn, nurturing and harvesting it, and holding back seed corn for the following year, each year the harvest gets greater and greater. Prosperity grows. Planting the seed corn is caring, critical thought, responsibility, and respect.

I asked Charlie Soap and Fredia Vann, both Cherokee speakers, if there was a similar concept in Cherokee. Charlie replied after some thought with the word *diniyotli unalisdelvdodi*. He said it means "we do this so our children can help themselves." He said if you referred to a person or family with these words, it meant they were held in highest honor and esteem in their community because they were working for their children. That is the same as planting the seed corn. Unfortunately, many of our people don't understand the lesson of the seed corn. Sometimes we hear people say that we need to give away all the gaming revenue to the people. Of course the fallacy of that logic is evident: there would be nothing for next year, and the businesses would close. People would lose their jobs. You would have nothing left and be back where you started. So how do we apply this lesson, this seed corn lesson of saving some this year, planting it next year, nourishing it to grow, and having a harvest of prosperity? We apply that lesson to each of our long-term initiatives: jobs, language, and community.

We must become economically self-reliant so that all of our people can have meaningful jobs that enable them to support themselves, their family, their community, and their nation. Jobs provide us a means to help each of our people make good decisions and support themselves. That is why, by law, we invest 70 percent of business and gaming profits into expansion and into creating new jobs.

We plant the seed corn to create those jobs, jobs with good benefits, located in Cherokee communities. We don't take all the profit from the gaming operations; we reinvest it in jobs and business expansion. We have created thousands of jobs while funding the largest service budgets in Cherokee Nation history.

Language is the highest intelligence we as people have. It is the glue that has held us together and guided us over the last three centuries when we faced adversity from Europeans and Americans. It will be the guidance we desperately need for the next centuries. We must revitalize our language so we think, read, write, and act Cherokee. The language is the vessel that holds the values and attributes of our culture.

We plant the seed corn by teaching and learning our language. Each speaker must learn to become both a student and a teacher of the Cherokee language. I visited with one Cherokee speaker who talked about how his child's participation in the youth choir made him develop a deep appreciation for the Cherokee language. The father began listening to the speakers, learning more, and polishing his own Cherokee. In this case, the child gave back to the father. Each speaker must be a teacher of every student, every child, every grandchild, every niece and nephew; they must teach them, tell them, and support them in learning the language. We should love our language and share it. We love our children and grandchildren, so we should give them the greatest gift, a love of the Cherokee language. The rest of us must make the effort to learn to speak Cherokee.

Cherokee speakers must encourage us. The other day I was trying to get out the word *diniyotli unalisdelvdodi*, and I struggled with it. Later a speaker came up to me and said, "You know, I admire you for trying," laughing that I didn't get it quite right. That's how you plant the seed corn, rather than ridiculing people for not being able to talk.

Communities are the foundation of our government. There are physical communities with long histories that emulate our historic towns. We also have communities of shared interest that form around art, sports, patriotism, politics, or work. We must bind ourselves together cohesively into healthy communities.

We plant the seed corn in the community when we take the initiative and inspire others. Look after the elders in your community, and make sure their grass is cut and their mail is brought in. Help young people who are having a hard time; encourage them to go to school and improve their lives. Pick up the trash along the roadside so that you can take pride in your community. Be a volunteer. It is truly rewarding to work with your neighbors to provide a needed waterline or a community building that you will all enjoy. Every time you see a group of Cherokee people working together, they will be laughing and having a good time. Often they bring food and enjoy a meal together. They make it fun. Working together brings out the best in people.

The plan boils down to three words: jobs, language, and community.

By achieving economic independence, fluency and literacy in our language, and cohesive communities, we will have the strength to survive the ebb and flow of public sentiment and the repeated cycles of hostile federal policy, whether it is ethnocide, removal, abandonment, forced assimilation, relocation, or the current threat, termination. Jobs, language, community—these simple words are not just sound bites. Jobs, language, and community are the vision and strategy for the next 100 years for the Cherokee Nation.

Challenges

We face challenges to our vision from outside the Cherokee Nation. Our history repeats itself. The Trail of Tears occurred in 1838 as a result of Congress passing the Indian Removal Act of 1830 and ratifying a fraudulent Treaty of New Echota in 1835. A special interest caucus of southern Congressional members actively worked to take the land, assets, government, and identity of the Cherokees and to move our ancestors to Indian Territory. This was in violation of U.S. Supreme Court rulings and in breach of scores of treaties. The vast majority of the Cherokee people filed a petition protesting removal. The Cherokee Nation hired the best lawyers to enforce the Supreme Court ruling. They lobbied Congress to follow the rulings of the federal courts. This special interest caucus executed a scorched earth policy against the Cherokees, designed to hurt the weakest and most infirm: the young, old, and ill. The attack came when the Cherokee Nation began to prosper economically. Special interest groups wanted the gold found in Georgia. Members of that Congress demonized the principal chief and made personal attacks on him for defending the will of the Cherokee people. These members of Congress peppered the newspapers with fraudulent accusations against the Cherokees evidencing racism, bigotry, and paternalism. Does any of this sound like a situation the Cherokee Nation faces today?

Earlier this year, members of the Congressional Black Caucus asked the U.S. Senate to punish the Cherokee people because we voted that every citizen must have an Indian ancestor on the Dawes Rolls. They abuse the power of the U.S. government in violation of federal courts and are trying to punish us for attempting to protect our sovereignty and retain our cultural identity. Their repeated legislative attacks ignore the federal court rulings that acknowledge the right of the Cherokees to determine their own citizenship requirements and federal statutes limiting rights of Freedmen. Members of the caucus proclaimed disdain for the rule of law by saying they did not care what the law was and they refused to wait for the courts to decide.

In response, as the Cherokee Nation did in 1830, we hired the best lawyers to enforce the rule of law and have lobbied Congress to follow the rulings of the federal courts. The recent attack came when the Cherokee Nation began to prosper economically. These members of Congress had no interest in the Cherokee Nation previously. Members of this caucus have made clear they are not interested in addressing the United States' serial breaches of Cherokee Nation treaties. Members of today's Congress have made personal attacks against me for defending the will of the Cherokee people, as their predecessors did against Chief John Ross. Just as happened 170 years ago, this special interest caucus has peppered the media with fraudulent accusations against the Cherokees evidencing their racism, bigotry, and paternalism. Members have even complained in the press that we have hired lawyers and media advisors to defend ourselves.

In the 1830s, very few members of Congress stood to defend the Cherokee Nation. Those who defended the Cherokees included men of the highest integrity such as Davy Crockett, Daniel Webster, and Henry Clay. Today, we have several members of Congress of the highest integrity and public service defending the Cherokee Nation, such as Congressmen Tom Cole and Dan Boren. They understand that Cherokees respect the law, and we will follow the ruling of the courts. We only ask the United States Congress to do the same.

Progress Report

I am pleased to tell you that on this fine day, on our historic capitol square, the state of the Cherokee Nation is vibrant. Our nation is strong. As elected leaders, we have done what you have asked of us, and what the constitution has asked of us. We are creating jobs for Cherokee people. The Cherokee Nation and our businesses now employ more than 6,500 people, and when I talk to you next year, I fully expect that number to be more than 8,000. That's more than 5,000 more jobs than the Cherokee Nation provided just eight short years ago. By creating these jobs in our communities, we are planting the seeds of economic independence, not only for individual Cherokees but for the Cherokee Nation as a government as well. Less than 10 years ago, more than 90 percent of the Cherokee Nation's funding came from the federal government. In 2008, only 62 percent of our funds come from federal sources.

We have done our duty in preserving our language. Today you heard just a few of our young people singing in Cherokee. Every day, you can see a language revival happening not far from here at Cherokee Nation's Tsalagi Junadeloquasdi (Cherokee Immersion School). Children from the age of three years to third grade learn the same lessons as in any other classroom, but everyone in the class speaks only Cherokee. One visit to those classrooms makes us realize that if we can repeat that experience in other Cherokee communities, our language will survive for generations.

The very language that was beaten out of some of our ancestors now flows freely from the mouths of future generations of Cherokee leaders.

We have done our duty by helping Cherokee communities help themselves. In the past year, we have opened new or expanded healthcare centers in Muskogee, Sallisaw, and Nowata. We have opened a new center for elders, Cherokee Elder Care, that is designed to enable frail, older adults to continue living at home and in the community for as long as possible. This past year the Cherokee people gave public schools in Oklahoma more than $2.8 million from the sales of Cherokee Nation car tags. We have listened and worked with citizens to help them build their own community buildings in places like Watts, Victory, Muldrow, and Eucha. Citizens have worked with us to build waterlines in their communities and we have given thousands of college scholarships to young Cherokees.

In short, our citizens have done more to help themselves in the past year than in any year in modern Cherokee Nation history. They are able to help themselves because the Cherokee Nation has invested in the future; we have planted the seed corn.

Today's success comes from the vision and hard work of the Cherokees who saw a bright future for the Cherokee Nation when there was nowhere to go but up. Cherokee people have sacrificed and made hard choices to lay the groundwork for a growing Cherokee economy and a strong government. The question—the challenge—for us today is to have the courage to make the hard choices that they made.

The politics of American culture urge us to do otherwise. American politicians have been trained to say yes to every need, to spend every cent trying to meet the overwhelming demands of today, not caring for the future. Cherokee leaders must make tough choices, just as the Cherokees who came before us did.

The Cherokee Nation has made a strong commitment to planting the seed corn. The commitment is so strong, we've made it into a law. We allocate 70 percent of our business profits for creating new jobs. The formula has been very successful, which is how we have increased the funding for services dramatically while creating 5,000 jobs. The challenge now is to continue the growth, to continue to plant the seed corn instead of robbing the future to meet the shortsighted needs of today.

The Cherokee Nation Tribal Council understands and has affirmed this concept. They have seen that it works. It is your job, as Cherokee citizens, to hold us all accountable, to make sure that we don't become shortsighted and forget the example of our ancestors.

Finally, as we close, I ask you to look across the street to the south and east at the Cherokee Nation Supreme Court building. Three weeks ago, we had a groundbreaking ceremony to begin the restoration of this sacred symbol of the Cherokee Nation. It marked the beginning to develop cultural tourism and to allow us the opportunity to tell our story. It also serves as an example of something true and enduring: our ancestors built something to last nearly 130 years ago. We have the privilege today to make sure it is a monument to the Cherokee Nation far, far into the future.

Today, you have received a packet of corn seeds. Those packets contain a rare blue and white corn for making flour that many believe came West on the Trail of Tears. It is often referred to as Cherokee White Eagle corn. It is called that because on the side of some of the kernels, there appears to be a white eagle in flight. In the spring of this year, one-half cup of this seed corn was planted by Pat Gwinn, who works in the Cherokee Nation's natural resources department. From this humble beginning, he grew 15 quarts of Cherokee White Eagle corn. Right now, you hold in your hand the literal and symbolic seed corn of the Cherokee Nation.

Take these seeds home and plant them in a place that is important to you, a place with good soil. Nurture it, harvest it, and share it with your community. And hold some back for next year to plant for our future. Perhaps within our livetimes, this Cherokee White Eagle corn will adorn every part of the Cherokee Nation and every home to remind us that our Cherokee citizenship is not a license to grab and get, but an honor to give.

Wado.

Your Humble Servant,

Chadwick "Corntassel" Smith
Principal Chief

2009 State of the Nation
Going from Point A
to Point B

INTRODUCTION

I began this state of the nation address in my customary way: I recited Benny Smith's admonishment for me to be a student of the Cherokee Nation. In this speech, I talked about the Point A to Point B leadership model and shared several stories about leaders overcoming adversity such as bull rider Ryan Dirteater and football player Sam Bradford. Another story involved a youth leadership exercise in which participants traced the 950-mile Trail of Tears on bicycles. I rode with the youth group. There were twelve riders; most were 16 to 24 years old and in great shape. It was a teamwork exercise to develop leadership and to learn about the Trail of Tears. It was not an academic exercise; the Trail of Tears became very real as we saw the land and places where our ancestors walked and suffered.

I also talked about our progress in the past year using examples of successful entrepreneurs, Cherokee language development, and academic achievement. We took over management of Hastings Hospital over the objections of several council members who still wanted the security of the federal government running our healthcare.

making good decisions. For us, as a collective people, as the Cherokee Nation, our choice as a sovereign nation is that we, and no one else, choose our own future. We choose to build a future in which we are a happy, healthy people. We believe the way to reach that vision is to focus on jobs, language, and community. Jobs, because we must become economically self-reliant; language, because we must use our cultural intelligence in thinking, speaking, and being Cherokee; and community, because we must bind ourselves together in a spirit of gadugi so we can withstand the ebb and flow of hostile public sentiment and destructive federal policies. We need leadership to reach our vision, and we need education to develop leaders.

Leadership: How We Conduct the Journey

The process of mapping, navigating, and completing the journey from Point A to Point B is called leadership. Does leadership mean only elected officials need to have a clear vision for the future and make wise decisions to build that future? Of course not. Leaders are each of us who navigate the journey of going from Point A to Point B, from where we are to where we want to go. Leaders meet and overcome the challenges that always crop up in any journey. Take, for example, the 22-year-old Cherokee professional bull rider from Hulbert, Ryan Dirteater. Ryan overcame a broken leg and returned to the pro circuit two full months before the doctors predicted. He got up after being dealt a blow, dusted himself off, and got back on the bull. In only 18 months, Sam Bradford, a Cherokee citizen, went from the disappointment and frustration of being the third-string, red-shirted quarterback at the University of Oklahoma, to being the first American Indian winner of the Heisman Trophy. Sam attributes his ability to deal with tough times to his dad, Kent, who came into his room every night when he was growing up and told him ten things; one of them was that he could be anything he wanted to be.

Just this past weekend, Jon Michael McGrath, 17, from Tulsa won the International Skeet World Championship. He set a new world record by hitting 199 out of 200 targets. Jon hopes his journey leads to the Olympics. These are great examples of leadership from Cherokee citizens mapping their journeys and having the vision and commitment to work toward their goals, or their personal Point B.

This principle does not apply only to sports. Many years ago when Wilma Mankiller was principal chief and I was the tribal prosecutor, I took a group of interns with me when I prosecuted a child support enforcement case. One of those interns was a young Cherokee woman named Catina Drywater. Catina said that she was impressed by the way I challenged a delinquent father on his frivolous spending when he failed to send money to ensure his children were fed and clothed.

This experience inspired Catina to become a lawyer. For many years she worked for Legal Aid Services helping people who could not afford an attorney. Along the way, Catina realized that there were some very basic legal filings that people could do for themselves if they had a little guidance and understanding of the law. With that thought in mind, Catina developed a set of self-help materials to assist people with representing themselves in legal matters. The results of her efforts are twofold. Using her materials, low-income clients can advance their cases faster, instead of being forced to wait for state help from DHS offices that are often overloaded and understaffed. The materials also give people confidence and a sense of empowerment, assisting them to make intelligent decisions for themselves to protect their rights.

Catina said she just wanted to do something she loves and to make a difference in people's lives and her hard work and dedication to helping others have not gone unnoticed. This October, Catina will travel to the U.S. Supreme Court in Washington, DC. While there, Justice Samuel Alito will present her with the Sandra Day O'Connor Award for Professional Service. Catina has lived her life demonstrating what I believe to be two innate Cherokee qualities: caring for those around her and using her abilities to join the ranks of a whole new generation of leaders who lead their lives, lead their families, and lead their communities.

Learn from All I Observe: How We Learn Leadership

Benny Smith passed on the knowledge of how generations before us have learned leadership and insight. He instructs us to recite a traditional

Cherokee saying each morning as the sun rises, washing our faces with moving water and acknowledging the sun as it illuminates the world. He says we have the opportunity to learn from both the images created by the sun's light and from the shadows it casts. If we do this, at the end of the day, we will be wiser. The English translation of part of this saying is that we will "learn from all we observe." This applies to our entire lives. In the morning we are children, and as the sun transverses the sky, we age. If we learn from all we observe as we age, we become wiser. Unfortunately, if we lack humility, we let our arrogance blind us, and we think we already know everything; then we cannot learn from all we observe and suffer in our ignorance.

As leaders of our own lives, we each have the choice to learn from all we observe. We can also choose what to focus on as we observe the world around us. We can choose to see challenges as either obstacles or opportunities, as excuses for failure or reasons to work even harder to succeed. We learn to be foolish or wise.

Let me tell you a story about a Cherokee named Jess Ussrey. When he was 16 years old, Jess went to Cherokee Nation's Talking Leaves Job Corps. You know what he says he learned there? He says he learned to get out of bed, show up on time for classes, and pay attention to what was going on. He was learning every day, not just in the classroom, but from those around him who were successful. Today, he's a PhD rocket scientist, working for the federal government, and he did it by being a lifelong learner. He did it by taking personal leadership in his life and turning challenges into opportunities. He did it by learning from all he observed.

There will always be positives and negatives in life, those things that uplift us and those that wear us down or tear us apart. On our journey, there will be potholes, detours, and curves. What we learn from these situations is a choice that we make as individuals and as a people, as citizens and as a Nation.

Recently my staff and I studied a program called Bridges out of Poverty, to learn the best ways to lift our people out of poverty and to help our people help themselves. One discussion was about the perception that, on some level, Cherokees have come to associate our own culture with a state of poverty. To some being a real Indian is to be poor. It was interesting to analyze all the factors that create that kind of mind-set. After sorting out the influences of the last 100 years, we can see that it is the culture of poverty itself that chills initiative, responsibility, and confidence. It is core Cherokee culture that encourages keeping a positive attitude, working hard, enjoying life, and striving to excel.

Remember the Removal

I share with you a story about learning from all we observe and about leadership.

Earlier this summer, I joined nine students and two other adults who retraced the Trail of Tears on bicycles. It was a 950-mile trek that took 20 days. It was a chore for me to keep up with these fine young people. Coming down the steep mountain outside Dayton, Tennessee, I was traveling 35 miles an hour, which is fast on a bicycle, and a bumble bee struck me in the chest and stung me several times there and then moved over to my side and stung me a half dozen more times before I could stop. Later, when I was last in our column of riders, I hit a huge rock on the shoulder of the road and flipped into the ditch, bending my front rim. I was glad to just have some scrapes, and then realized I had landed in poison ivy. I never thought my casualties of this bicycle trip would be bee stings and a poison ivy rash.

But the trip on the "trail where our ancestors cried" led me to some serious thoughts. A bicycle shoe has a metal cleat to lock in on the pedal in order to fully use the power of your leg. On one part of the trip we had to walk our bikes a half mile on a gravel and dirt road. The shoe's cleat sounded like a horse's shoe in the gravel. The sound of 12 cyclists walking sounded like a team of horses pulling a wagon on the Trail of Tears. As we walked along that dirt road, it was easy to imagine what a hundred horse-drawn wagons sound like, clinking, creaking, clattering, and bouncing over the rough, rutted roads. Then one could hear the noise of the animals, the horses snorting and laboring, cows mooing, and an occasional dog barking. I thought about the other sounds from the trail—the disturbing, muffled sounds of children crying from hunger, cold, or the terrible knowledge that their parents were dead; the sound of the sick moaning in pain, gasping for the air and the energy to take another step; the sound of women suffering; the sound of elders shuffling along, carrying every possession they owned. Then I heard the quick footsteps of strong young men who did everything in their power to assist, lifting, leading, carrying food and water up and down the trail to others. Next was the terrible shriek of grief when another family member died, when the realization hit you that your mother, father, child, grandparent, or lover lay in a shallow grave miles past. And when all those sounds were combined, it had the undeniable sound of despair. They did not know where they were going; they did not know if this place in the West where they were condemned to move actually existed; they did not know if and when they would get there; and they did not know where they were at any given time. They knew only that they'd left their homes months ago, left the fond memories of their youth, the birthplace of their children, and the graves of their loved ones.

Then my other senses began to kick in, penetrating the tunnel of sounds. First, it was the smell of manure and urine of horses and cows on the road. It was the odor of dirty, worn clothes and the undeniable stench of sickness that filled their nostrils. I could imagine the pain of cold, the exhaustion of every muscle as they walked or resisted the bounce and jolt of wagons on empty stomachs. Then I could see their eyes opened with clarity to the sight of misery in the face of every child, desperation in the faces of elders, and despair in the faces of adults unable to protect their loved ones. Even the last sense of taste was bitter from the moldy flour, salty pork, and alien water.

When all these senses were to the point of exploding, a sense unnamed and greater than the five we know took over. This sense feels and knows the presence of life and living and of death and dying. This sense was overwhelmed by the shallow graves of relatives dug and passed each day, the lifeless bodies laid aside on wagons awaiting the brief farewell of families and a return to the earth.

Our people begged for an answer to the question, "What did we do to deserve so much pain?" This burden of heartache was coupled with the unimaginable knowledge that we had been betrayed by the U.S. government and Americans and this was our punishment for the simple crime of being Indian.

As we rode our bikes through our homelands of northern Georgia, I noticed the homes were big and less than 30 years old. We did some research and found that for the hundred years after Georgians took our homeland, the population did not significantly increase. Many of those who won tracts in our homelands in a lottery did not move to the tracts when they found there was no gold or water.

The reason for the Trail of Tears became obvious and undeniable. Georgia did not need our homes. There was enough land for both the Cherokee Nation and Georgia. Georgia simply wanted it, and we had it. Governor Gilmer and Senator Lumpkin of Georgia and President Andrew Jackson had enough political might to get the U.S. House of Representatives to pass the Indian Removal Act by a vote of 102 to 97. If the Congress had had three more men with integrity and a sense of fairness, 4,000 of our people would not have died, and we could have held onto our homes.

It was a Trail of Tears. For each step taken there was a tear of sorrow, pain, desperation, or grief. It was a march of horror driven by the U.S. government. There is no nice or diplomatic way to say it: the acts of the U.S. Congress and president were a crime against the Cherokee people, the Cherokee Nation, the people of the United States, and humanity. Those who voted for the Indian Removal Act and ratification of the Treaty of New Echota were uncaring and unworthy of the human race, and history should list them on the roll of evil.

Now, after having caught a glimpse of what our ancestors went through, the sacredness of our Supreme Court building here in the background is even more important, and there can be no symbol that better captures the Cherokee spirit. Because just five years after the Trail of Tears, the Supreme Court building was our first government building, constructed to house our judicial institution dedicated to justice and fairness for all, in sharp contrast to federal and state governments that sentenced our ancestors to death on the Trail of Tears.

The Benchmark: Where the Journey Began

A benchmark is the surveyor's corner pin or post that never changes position and is the reference point for determining all direction. It is where journeys begin and the point from which they are measured. There are certain principles that are benchmarks for the future of the Cherokee Nation.

I invite you to turn your attention to the restored Cherokee National Supreme Court building. It stands as a tribute to a number of these benchmark principles of our Nation. Completed in 1844, it is the oldest public building in Indian Territory and the state of Oklahoma. It was built to house our court, which brought order and justice to our society in the wake of our greatest civil unrest. It later housed our newspaper, the *Cherokee Phoenix*. It is a solemn symbol of our great legacy handed down from generations: to face adversity, survive, adapt, prosper, and excel. It is a benchmark of our sovereignty and a reminder that we decide our laws and determine our future, not anyone else. And our historic Supreme Court building should serve as a reminder to our judges and justices that the quality of law and justice is not found in the prestige of a physical space but in the clarity of our courts' intelligence, articulation, and principles in decisions, judgments, and orders.

In the next few years we will plan to renovate this capitol building, the historic place of the administration of our government by the principal and deputy principal chief, the site where our legislature met and passed laws for decades. Every member of every branch of our government should remember that our work is not measured by the office we inhabit but by the foresight and soundness of the decisions we make, decisions guided by principle, not by political expediency or personal gain.

Each of our branches of government should strive to become a model of public service, intelligence, and statesmanship. And as Cherokee citizens, these are the benchmarks that should guide your decisions at the polls. I urge you to select leaders who are statesmen and lifelong learners who learn from all they observe.

Progress: How Far We Have Come

I invite you to look at a copy of the *2009 Report to the Cherokee People*. It contains valuable information on the progress we made in the previous year, including facts and figures on the numbers of jobs that have been created, revenues that have increased, and community self-help projects that have been completed, as well as the success of our initiatives like green energy and recycling. These statistics are important ways to measure our progress, but I especially enjoy the stories of Cherokee people who have been helped by our services or have used our services to help themselves.

Education is important to success, and we are very proud that, once again this year, five graduates from Sequoyah Schools were awarded the prestigious Gates Millennium Scholarship for outstanding academic achievement and leadership ability. Two of those five are Cherokee Nation citizens, but one, Shayne Boyd, declined to accept the scholarship so he could accept an appointment to the Air Force Academy, where he is today. Corey Still, a long-time member of the National Youth Choir and Cherokee Nation Youth Council, accepted his Gates scholarship and will start at OU this Thursday.

Last year at this time we were completing plans to assume the operation of Hastings Hospital. It's hard to believe now, but back then there were naysayers and doubters. A year later, those critics are silenced as the employees at Hastings, as well as the outstanding leadership within our Cherokee Nation Health Group, have transformed the hospital, adding essential services like mammography, bringing in new hospital beds, reducing wait times, and making additional drugs available at the pharmacy. Since the Cherokee Nation began operating Hastings Hospital, nearly 1,000 Indian babies have been born at the hospital, including young Isaiah Gage White, who's here today with his parents Robert and Shawna.

This past year the Cherokee Nation and the Eastern Band of Cherokees held the twenty-fifth anniversary of the Joint Council meeting at Red Clay, Tennessee. Red Clay was the seat of our government between 1834 and 1838 because the oppressive laws of Georgia prohibited us from meeting in our own capitol at New Echota. It was a good reunion. One moment in particular touched me deeply. As moving as the physical site was, and as historic as the joint meeting was, with the weight of centuries behind it, what struck me most was a glimpse of our future. Little Lauren Hummingbird, a fourth-grader in our immersion school, was there, using her laptop computer to instant message her teacher and classmates back home; she was using the Cherokee syllabary.

Think about that. In 1838, when our people left Red Clay, Sequoyah's syllabary was barely a generation old, but now, nearly 200 years later, our children are not only speaking Cherokee, they are reading, writing, and even kidding each other in Cherokee via the Internet.

Lauren and her classmates are not just learning their language in school; they are learning leadership. They are learning from all they observe. And parents, aunts, uncles, grandparents: they are learning from us, every minute. Let us model the leadership we hope to see in them someday.

All the programs we've talked about—and the scores of additional programs we don't have time to mention—revolve around one goal and one strategy to get there. Our goal is to be a happy, healthy Cherokee people. To get there, we need to create jobs for our citizens, jobs in Cherokee communities where they can keep our language and culture strong. That's why we say the best service that the Cherokee Nation can provide our citizens is a job, and that's why we have created nearly 5,000 jobs in the past 10 years. These jobs allow our citizens to stay here instead of moving out of state for work. These jobs allow our communities and culture to thrive and allow our personal leadership to flourish.

Challenges: The Opportunities Along This Journey

Along with the accomplishments of the past year, we continue to face challenges in Washington, D.C., regarding our right to determine our own identity, both as citizens and as a Nation. Our right to exist as a "distinct people" and to define what that means through our citizenship laws are rights guaranteed to us by Cherokee, federal, and international law. We have had to defend the Cherokee Nation's inherent sovereignty in the halls of Congress against people who misunderstand federal law. We have been forced to bring our sovereignty to the attention of the bureaucrats in Washington, D.C., who overlooked the laws, treaties, and federal court rulings that affirm that the Cherokee Nation today is the same Cherokee Nation that discovered the explorer DeSoto wandering aimlessly around the southeastern area of this continent nearly 500 years ago. We have seen historically that when Cherokees succeed, when we prosper and excel, external forces will try to crush us, divide us, terminate us as a government, and even ethnically cleanse us.

These efforts to divide the Cherokee Nation have not worked in the past, and they will not work today. I will continue to defend the rights of the Cherokee Nation, not only because I have sworn an oath to do so, but also because it is my firm belief that it is the right thing to do. As Chief John Ross said in his annual message in 1857:

> If our rights of soil and self-government, of . . . self-chosen institutions, are worth the toils and struggles of the past, they are worth present defense and continuation upon the most permanent footing.
>
> Years of trial and anxiety, of danger and struggle have alone maintained the existence of the Cherokee people as a distinct community; and such must continue to be the case, if we . . . would discharge the debt we owe to posterity.

Conclusion

In concluding, I acknowledge our tribal council members, led by Speaker Meredith Frailey, for their efforts and role as our constitutional lawmakers. I acknowledge our justices and judges, led by Chief Justice Darell Matlock, Jr., for providing guidance in interpreting our laws and resolving disputes. I acknowledge the many members of our boards, commissions, and corporations who ensure the success of our many endeavors. I acknowledge our cabinet, Treasurer Callie Catcher, Marshal Sharon Wright, Attorney General Diane Hammons, and Secretary of State Melanie Knight, for their decision making and sound management. I acknowledge our employees for working diligently to accomplish our vision.

Working together, we have accomplished a lot.

We have created partnerships with counties, cities, other tribes, civic groups, federal agencies, and others who will work with us to create jobs in our local communities and to provide an atmosphere for our culture and language to thrive. We are changing that mind-set of dependency and victimhood held by some of our people to an understanding that the work of our government is helping our people help themselves. We know we must always stand against those who wish to divide, destroy, or weaken the Cherokee Nation. It is our constitutional duty and benchmark principle that we should not allow outside forces to determine our future. We are appreciating more that we should focus on our goals for the future and not allow decisions to be made by what is politically expedient and gratifying in the short run. We are passing on our legacy. We are getting a clearer glimpse of our vision of being a happy and healthy people.

I have been a lifelong student of the Cherokee Nation and of the Cherokee people. I have done my best to learn from all I observe. I have come to your homes to listen to the concerns of your families and communities and to be inspired by your accomplishments. I have worked beside you on the waterlines in communities from Park Hill to Spring Creek, and helped raise community buildings from South Coffeyville to Bell. I helped put the last and highest beam in place on the nineteenth floor of our new hotel in Catoosa. I have taken air conditioners and generators to our elders in times of need. I have heard our youth choir charm audiences all over the country with their mastery of Cherokee songs. I have tried to understand our trials and tribulations and our heartaches and frustrations and to find ways for us to help ourselves. I have seen us face adversity, survive, adapt, prosper, and excel.

I have accepted criticism and have tried to respond with logic and reason. I have worked long and hard as your principal chief. I have enjoyed that work. I have been challenged with difficult decisions and have turned to some of our best Cherokee minds to advise me. I thank you for these experiences and opportunities.

I have done all of this because I care about my family, our people, and our Nation. I have done this to honor my deceased father, Nelson Smith, and to make life better for my children and for all our children. Diniyotli unalisdelvdodi. I find satisfaction at the end of each day from seeing our people, our families, and our communities help themselves and make progress.

Yes, we have come a long way, but now, more than ever, I am convinced that when we think, feel, and act in accordance with our Cherokee principles, our lives are happier, fuller, and healthier.

We are on a journey. It is a continuation of the journey traveled by our ancestors who lived through difficult periods of history like the Trail of Tears, the American Civil War, the allotment, the Depression, post–World War II relocations, and the rebuilding of the Cherokee Nation. So we are not alone on this journey. Our Supreme Court building reminds us that we are joined in spirit by those who traveled before us, and we must always be mindful of the generations yet to come. We can successfully carry out our part of this journey and make a better future for our children if we learn from all we observe today as a people and as a Nation.

Wado.

Your humble servant,

Chadwick "Corntassel" Smith
Principal Chief

2010 State of the Nation
Happiness and Healthiness
Are Found in Maturity

INTRODUCTION

As always, I opened my state of the nation address with Benny Smith's admonition for me to be a student of the Cherokee people. This year, I focused initially on what it meant to be happy and healthy. With the greater prosperity of the Cherokee Nation came greater expectations and a sense of entitlement. I searched for a concept that would express success for individuals, families, communities, and our nation. I asked 15 Cherokee people to describe, in Cherokee language using one word, a 28-year-old Cherokee person who was responsible for his or her actions, had a meaningful job, took loving care of his or her young family, and was contributing to his or her community. After several weeks, two different groups came back with the same Cherokee word—*mature*. It seemed so simple. Individuals and nations must mature.

Maturity is happiness and healthiness. Maturity is contributing, not "grabbing all you can."

I recognized that immaturity by leaders and public officials was our greatest internal threat. It leads them to be petty, to pander, self-aggrandize, and deceive. And by example, they lead others to behave the same way. How do you get someone to grow up? I don't know and did not have an answer in my speech. Political will is an expression of strong cultural values. Unfortunately, traditional Cherokee values had been eroded by decades, if not centuries, of strong arm tactics, patronage, and paternalism by the American public and federal government. I questioned the political will of the Cherokee people to pass on the great Cherokee legacy to face adversity, survive, adapt, prosper, and excel. Did we as a Nation have the will to mature?

Why should we do all the responsible things to mature? Perhaps the most effective argument is, "Why not?"

In the previous year, we started a "day training" program. We reached out to hundreds of Cherokees who were unemployed or underemployed due to divorces, layoffs, dead-end minimum wage jobs, or minor criminal history. The linchpin for these people was that money was so tight, they needed to be paid daily. Subject to budget limitations, if they showed up and wanted to work, we tried to assign them for a limited time, to some trade for which they had skills or to some constructive work such as cleaning or painting. We did an assessment of their occupational skills and placed them in training programs or counseling. If there was a delay for training programs or counseling, we assigned them to work. At the end of an eight-hour day, they received a $50 stipend on a debit card. I thought we would have only 20 people show up to work for that little pay, but at times in the program, we served over 200 workers a day. These people were glad to have something constructive to do. It was inspirational to watch people who wanted to help themselves.

Our businesses grew with a gaming expansion in Ramona, Oklahoma, and the acquisition of a security company.

A tangent to the Freedmen issue involved clubs of people calling themselves Cherokee tribes and seeking state recognition or legitimacy. Many of these clubs mimicked Hollywood stereotypes and made outrageous claims. In essence, they try to appropriate the Cherokee Nation's legal and cultural identity. The search for personal identity drives many of these groups; others are driven by financial motives. In Tennessee, the state legislature was considering acknowledging six of these clubs as state-recognized tribes, four of which claimed to be Cherokee. State legislators thought there was no harm in giving them a certificate, but for the Cherokee Nation and other legitimate Indian nations, these groups create mischief that harms our reputation. We hired a lobbying firm in Tennessee to defeat the bill for state recognition.

The sad news of the year was the passing of former Principal Chief Wilma Mankiller. She was the principal chief of the Cherokee Nation between 1985 and 1995. She was devoted to the Cherokee people and was known for being determined, present, and compassionate.

STATE OF THE NATION: HAPPINESS AND HEALTHINESS ARE FOUND IN MATURITY

September 4, 2010

Greetings. It is my honor and privilege to address you and inform you of the state of the Cherokee Nation. When I was inaugurated as principal chief 11 years ago, traditionalist Benny Smith admonished me to be a student of the Cherokee Nation and of the Cherokee people. I have done that each day since then and report to you now on the state of our nation, our progress and our challenges. I remember clearly when Benny Smith gave me that charge over a decade ago because I am concerned daily about our people, our families, our communities, and our Nation. But it is not only my concern; is it not the concern of all Cherokee patriots who want something better for their children, relations, neighbors, and fellow Cherokees? Over 100 years ago, Redbird Smith defined patriotism as being willing to give your all to your government and people. Historian and Indian advocate Angie Debo describes the opposite of a patriot as someone who "grabs all they can for themselves." Our choice is to be patriots like our mothers and fathers before us, to reject the foreign idea of "grabbing all you can for yourself" and instead choose the path of patriotism and building something worthwhile for those who come after us. I submit that when we as individuals and as a Nation mature in exercising Cherokee values and attributes, we become happy and healthy, and we are Cherokee patriots.

Today is a celebration of the signing of our constitution in 1839 and of our government maturing.

Our Designed Purpose:
A Happy and Healthy People

The old saying is true: "If you don't know where you are going, any road will take you there." More sobering is the wisdom from Proverbs: "Where there is no vision, the people shall perish." We can study the history of mankind and of powerful civilizations and societies to see if they achieved greatness. But we need go no further than to look at our own past in order to see ourselves and determine what we want to show for the lives we have and the moments the Creator has given us. Redbird Smith said in 1918,

> "I have always believed that the Great Creator had a great design for my people, the Cherokees. I have been taught that from my childhood up, and now in my mature manhood, I recognize it as a great truth. Our forces have been dissipated by the external forces, perhaps it has been just training, but we must now get together as a race and render our contribution to mankind. We are endowed with intelligence, we are industrious, we are loyal, and we are spiritual but we are overlooking the particular Cherokee mission on earth, for no man or race is endowed with these qualifications without a designed purpose."

So what is this "designed purpose"? What is this calling? I believe it is to enjoy every moment the Creator has given us, to become a happy and healthy people. Is that not the dream of all great civilizations and societies? So what does "happy and healthy" mean in a world of inundating data and information where we can get the latest sports news or scandal at a moment's notice, right in the palm of our hands, on our phones, through Twitter, Facebook, text message, or e-mail? We have a society and economy built on glutton consumerism that does not leave us happier or healthier. We eat fast food that has no flavor, we have more clothes than we could ever really need, and some of us even have more cars than we can drive. As Cherokees we have the right to reject a mainstream society where self-righteous political talking heads tell us what to think and marketing gurus try to convince us we need products that put us on the road to health epidemics like diabetes, obesity, heart disease, and chemical addiction. It sounds a bit trite to say we should take responsibility to become happy and healthy. Some would ask,"Isn't there already a pill for being happy and healthy?"

The Study of Happy and Healthy

Let us take Benny Smith's admonition to heart and study what it is for the Cherokee people to be happy and healthy and how we get there.

The dictionary has its definitions of happy and healthy.

Definition of happy: having, showing, or causing a feeling of great pleasure, contentment, and joy.

Definition of healthy: Indicative of sound, rational thinking or frame of mind; having good health; well; sound.

This Is What We Know

"Happy and healthy" is another way of saying "quality of life." Let me share me with you that portion of my 2004 state of the nation message and substitute "happy and healthy" for "quality of life":

> Central to the idea of happy and healthy are the ideas of fulfillment of life and Cherokee thought. Happy and healthy spans a range of life's requirements and desires from the basics of food, clothing, and shelter to spiritual fulfillment. The highest aspect of being happy and healthy is to choose our own destiny and to contribute to that destiny with meaningful work. It's having the means to be happy and healthy for ourselves and our families, our communities, and our Nation. We sometimes get confused about what happy and healthy really means. (The following regarding happy and health is from the 2004 State of Nation).

Happy and healthy is fishing on the creek bank here at home, not taking expensive fishing trips to Alaska.

Happy and healthy is knowing that we have talents and skills and that we can earn a living with work, rather than counting on winning the Powerball lottery to secure our future.

Happy and healthy is having richness and an abundance of love among family and friends, not having a host of cars and money, or fancy houses.

Happy and healthy is understanding the world around us with such clarity that we each are poets and artists, amazed by the simplest things, such as dew on the morning grass, the haze on the eastern horizon in the mornings, the majesty of geese and mockingbirds singing their respective tunes.

Happy and healthy is not dulling our senses with alcohol and drugs and jealousy and pettiness but having clarity of mind and the satisfaction of confidence.

Happy and healthy is not having; it is being and doing.

Maturity Is Happy and Healthy

Often I assemble a group of Cherokee speakers and ask them to consider how a particular idea would be expressed in the Cherokee language. The process invokes great wisdom. Recently, I asked a group of 15 Cherokee speakers to tell me the word for the kind of young person we all want our children to become, one who has finished high school, gone to college, started a warm and loving family, makes good decisions, and supports his or her family, community, and Nation—someone we are proud of. The Cherokee speakers named many traditional Cherokee attributes to describe such a person.

Respectful/acknowledgment. Hold one another sacred or be "stingy" with another person and yourself.

Determined/persistent. Never give up.

Integrity. Full (to the greatest extent possible). Act in the same manner regardless of the situation. Do what is right and complete, even when no one is watching.

Leader. Lead by example. Show the way by acting the way we want others to treat us. Our actions influence the behavior of others.

Communicative. Be sure to let the others know.

Confident. Have confidence in yourself and do not doubt your abilities, but temper all with humility.

Cooperative. Help one another.

Responsible. Commit yourself to your task or assignment.

Teach. Share your knowledge and wisdom with others to improve that individual, family, or group.

Patient. Be patient, no matter what you are going through.

Humble. Never boast; never think you are better or higher than anyone else.

Strong. Be strong in whatever you do. Take comfort in the strength of the Creator and your ancestors.

But this group of Cherokee speakers came to a consensus that all of these values were part of one concept. The word was *ugvtohvsvi*. A young person who has achieved happiness and healthiness and exhibits these Cherokee attributes would be called *mature*.

Mature means complete, cultivated, cultured, developed, fit, full-blown, full-fledged, full-grown, in full bloom, in one's prime.

Yes, mature. There again the great wisdom of the Bible is apparent: "When I was a child, I spoke as a child, I understood as a child, I thought as a child: but when I became a man, I put away childish things" (1 Corinthians 13:11).

We need to mature as individuals, as families, as communities, and as a Nation. Our adults and leaders need to set the example of maturity. We must, by second nature, understand that each moment is a teaching moment, and every moment is a learning moment to become mature with Cherokee values and attributes. Every teacher, parent, relative, and friend must teach, encourage, and guide our young people toward maturity, preparing them to contribute back to our families, communities, and Nation within a decade of graduating from high school. In Cherokee, that is to "learn from all I observe."

Our designed purpose is to become happy and healthy; we become happy and healthy when we mature with Cherokee values.

Examples of Maturity

Our beloved, fallen Principal Chief Wilma Mankiller left us wisdom on this topic. She said that many people in Bell used to think that life was just something that happened to them. But after they carved out rock hillsides for 18 miles with their own hands to bring a waterline to their community, when outsiders expected them to fail, they knew differently. They learned what all Cherokees should understand: we have the power to shape our own lives and our own communities and to make our own decisions. Each day the Creator gives us a day of living; it is up to us to decide what to do with that day. As Wilma always said, "Every day is a good day."

I had the honor of serving the Cherokee people with Hastings Shade as my deputy chief, and he also left us wisdom on being happy and healthy. Hastings never got caught up with negative thinking and complaining. He always told me, "If you stop to throw a rock at every dog that barks at you, you'll never get to town." He knew that if we decided to take responsibility for our own happiness, we could ignore the distractions that try to keep us from what's really important, like our friends, family, and community.

We can also learn from my friend Dave Blackbird. He led the Rocky Ford community to again become cohesive and finish a community building after it lay dormant for several years. At 77 years old, he came into my office and told me that for three years he had been thinking about what he should give me as principal chief. He ended up carving a beautiful cane. When he presented it to me, he said that with the weight of the Cherokee Nation on my shoulders, sometimes I needed something to lean on, and

I could lean on this cane. I understood I could lean on him and the many other community leaders who make our Nation strong.

Wilma and Hastings passed on this year; Dave is here with us today. They all, like Will Rogers, Redbird Smith, and our ancient ancestors before them, have left us these lessons on choosing to be happy, healthy people. Each was mature in Cherokee values; each was happy and healthy, and each was a patriot.

To Mature Is Our Choice

The most critical question we must ask ourselves, that we must study, that we must understand, and that we each must answer with crystal penetrating clarity is: what does it mean to be happy and healthy? Many people go their entire lives never resolving this fundamental human question. Answers are evident when they are simple. Being happy and healthy is the treasure of our culture and is described in such vibrant terms by our Cherokee language.

I can show you a picture of a rose in black and white. It represents thinking and seeing the world in English. Then I can show you the same rose, this time in color. This is *u-tsi-lv-sgi*, a rose. Like many Cherokee words, *u-tsi-lv-sgi* means more than just "flower"; it means "something blooming." When you are color blind, seeing only black and white, you can neither appreciate nor imagine what it is like to see in color. We need to understand our designed purpose with such vibrancy.

I believe that being happy and healthy is a choice that no one else can make for us. We choose to learn from all we observe, we grow and mature. Individually and as a nation we can work toward becoming happy and healthy, or we can choose to accept the opposite: miserable and diseased.

As principal chief, I hear and see people who have chosen to become happy and healthy. I also hear and see people who avoid their choices in life, view themselves as victims, and blame everyone else for their station in life. They stay children and do not mature.

We must lead by example. There are those who can't help themselves, and we, as family members and neighbors, should help them.

Working Together, We Have Accomplished a Lot in 10 Years

On that path to becoming a happy, healthy people, we should pause and take time to reflect on where we've come from and how we are maturing.

Over a decade ago, a constitutional crisis arose when the principal chief held himself above the law, which led to a black eye for the Cherokee Nation because he and his friends on the council fired the entire marshal service for doing their job, impeached the entire supreme court for issuing orders they disagreed with, and fired the newspaper editor for articulating a dissenting opinion. The former administration and council furloughed 500 employees even though the overall national economy was doing well. Since that time, our administration and council members have created 5,000 jobs without layoffs or furloughs, even though the national economy is doing very poorly.

Back then, there was no auditable financial accounting. During the last 10 years, we have been honored nationally as a model of government finance and have won awards for excellence in financial accounting for eight straight years.

Back then, if you wanted Cherokee Nation assistance to own a home, there was a 50-year waiting list. During the last 10 years, families have been able to help themselves and receive assistance to qualify for a mortgage and earn their own home within months.

Back then, our hospitals and clinics did not have the resources to provide quick, top-level service to our citizens. During the last 10 years, we have built half a dozen new or expanded clinics and have earned national accreditation as a top healthcare provider.

Back then, the administration fired the newspaper editor and controlled the tribal newspaper. We provide a free press that is open to all opinions. And this afternoon on these capitol grounds, we celebrate 10 years of an unfettered press and transparent government.

Back then, the former administration's own lawyers argued that the Cherokee Nation did not have jurisdiction over our own historic capitol. We established that there is no doubt that this land is ours.

Back then, if the Cherokee Nation wanted to do business with someone, it had to pay cash, up front. During the last 10 years, we developed the Cherokee Nation's finances to the point that we became the first tribe in Oklahoma to issue investment grade bonds to expand our health services.

Back then, the principal chief said he, not the courts, would decide what the law was, and his friends on the council impeached the entire supreme court because they didn't like the court's rulings. One council member dismissively called these accomplished attorneys and military veterans "boys" in the process. I'm proud that we obey and enforce the rulings of our court, even on the rare occasions when we might not particularly agree with them.

Back then, Sequoyah High School was known to many as a school of last resort; it is now known as a school of choice. Today we've seen 40 students from Sequoyah High School earn the prestigious Gates Millennium Scholarship.

Back then, during the Cherokee National Holiday, there were armed snipers on the rooftop across the street, filling our community with a dark and foreboding cloud of fear and chaos. During the last 10 years, we have little children speaking and singing Cherokee here on Capitol Square, and we will sit down together in a few minutes and share a meal in the spirit of friendship and community.

By these measures, the state of the Cherokee Nation is good and getting better. We are happier and healthier than we have been in a long time. We are maturing as a Nation and as a people.

We have near record budgets for all our services, even in the midst of a financial crisis that has crippled other governments. In the past year, we have broken ground on new waterlines in Delaware County and a new food distribution site in Nowata County. We finished bridge and road projects in almost every one of our counties. We have given millions to public schools from our car tag revenues, bringing our total to more than $20 million over the years, giving Cherokee children, as well as their neighbors, a chance at a better education.

Jobs, Language, and Community

We continue to focus on a fundamental strategy of jobs, language, and community.

Jobs

I feel that helping people get a job is one of the most important, life-changing things we can do for our citizens. This past year we have created hundreds of new jobs in areas like healthcare and information technology.

This year, when the U.S. economic downturn reached the Cherokee Nation's borders, we decided to try a new approach, a day-work program aimed at providing immediate assistance to nearly 2,000 Cherokee citizens who were unemployed. Our tribal council was extremely supportive and unanimously voted to extend the temporary program with additional funding. I issued an executive order this year strengthening our Cherokee hiring practices at the Cherokee Nation and its business entities to make sure that Cherokees are first in line for jobs. We broke ground on a Cherokee casino located in Ramona, Oklahoma, creating more than 100 jobs in the area. We also broke ground on a dental clinic at Amo Health Center in Salina.

Jobs are important, but only because they help keep our Cherokee communities strong.

Language

We thank Andy Kemp, Jamie Richardson, and Peter Losting from Apple for their amazing contributions in revitalizing our language. We now can read and write in the Cherokee language on Apple laptop computers, iPhones, and iPads.

We opened the doors of the Cherokee National Supreme Court Museum this spring. Originally built in 1844, it is Oklahoma's oldest public building and Cherokee Nation's first wholly owned and operated museum. I hope our citizens will take some of the tours of our historic sites, including our newly designated National Scenic Byway, an 84-mile route that extends from Gore to West Siloam Springs.

Our immersion school expanded into a new space and now offers fourth grade classes. The students there are employing modern technology to communicate in our Native language, including the use of a new high-tech keypad.

We have new programs focusing on preservation of our language, culture, and history. We will start a new initiative to record the oral histories of our elders through interviews with our language immersion students. We also plan to have a new virtual library of Cherokee knowledge that will be online in late spring.

Community

Communities are important because only when we are together can we keep our language, culture, and legacy strong. This is not only my duty as principal chief but the duty of every Cherokee citizen. We also awarded grants for 12 community gardens as part of an effort to use traditional foods for good health and disease prevention in our communities.

We could list more of our accomplishments for the year, but we have lunch waiting. I encourage you to review copies of the Cherokee Nation's annual report and understand what your Nation is doing.

Challenges

As a people, we face challenges. In a number of communities, 60 percent of children are raised by grandparents. Our kids, like kids all over the country, don't exercise enough and face food choices that can lead to diabetes, heart disease, and cancer. But those challenges are nothing compared to what our ancestors faced on the Trail of Tears, or during the allotment and the Depression.

A major challenge is that many of our people, including some elected officials, are immature, such as ones who defend the politics and policies that created the constitutional crisis in the first place. It is even more frustrating when our leaders, especially our elected leaders, look down on our people as being helpless victims. I heard one of our elected officials say in response to a social program requirement for self-help that he "did not want Cherokees doing any more self-help than anyone else." One elected official said she thought it was her job to hand out checks to her constituents. Another one said she was going to fight to get her voters free stuff even though it might not be good for the Cherokee Nation overall. Several of our elected officials refer to our people as "poor full bloods" in a condescending manner. I tend to agree with the author of a letter to the editor of the *Cherokee Phoenix* who wrote that our full bloods are more likely to understand the traditional Cherokee attributes of working together and helping each other. They are the ones who remind us: diniyotli unalisdelvdodi: "We make those decisions every day so that our children can help themselves."

How can our people become happy and healthy if elected officials want the Cherokee Nation to be a welfare organization handing out stuff for free under the self-promoting guise of "helping Cherokees"? How can our people improve themselves if we don't adhere to the traditional Cherokee belief that all Cherokees have a duty to help themselves? Each one of our programs should be a means to help our people help themselves so they in turn can help their families, communities, and Nation.

Conclusion

We are on a journey to becoming a happy, healthy people. To remind us that we are on that path, we have something for everyone who is here today. These red bands simply say, "happy, healthy," and can remind us that we are maturing as individuals and as a Nation. It is a continuation of the journey traveled by our ancestors, who lived through difficult periods of history like the Trail of Tears, the American Civil War, the allotment, the Depression, post-World War II relocations, and the rebuilding of the Cherokee Nation. So we are not alone on this journey. Our supreme court, female seminary, and capitol buildings remind us that we are joined in spirit by those who traveled before us, and we must always be mindful of the generations yet to come. We can successfully carry out our part of this journey and make a better future for our children if we learn from all we observe as a people and as a Nation to become happy and healthy.

We have a decision to make every day. Do we, as Cherokees, want to hand something worthwhile to our children, or do we want them to be empty handed? Do we want them to be strong, happy, and healthy, or do we want them to be weak, helpless, and dependent? Do we want them to remain children, or do we want them to mature into well respected leaders? Rest assured, they will follow our example. And our example will determine the future of the Cherokee Nation and our people.

We as the Cherokee Nation and people have an opportunity that the largest, oldest, and most powerful societies, civilizations, and governments envy. We have the people, the resources, the legacy, and the intelligence to design a plan and achieve the greatest goal a people can obtain: to be happy and healthy. We not only have the chance, but we have the duty, the obligation, and the honor to become a happy and healthy people; that is our designed purpose. We cannot do it by being victims, but we can do it by being leaders. We cannot do it by accepting weakness, but we can do it by exercising strength. We cannot do it if we yield our choices to others, rather than making our own sound decisions. We'll never get there if we only vaguely remember the lessons of our ancestors, but we will get there if we have a tenacious resolve to build a better future for our children. We won't be happy and healthy if we are "grabbing all we can." We will be happy and healthy if we mature to make contributions to our Nation, our culture, and our community as Cherokee patriots. The stakes are high. Will we choose to be a happy and healthy people? Will we mature? Or will we revert to the days of "grabbing all you can?"

It is my greatest charge to remind each of us that we should be patriots of the Cherokee Nation, because it leads us to be happy and healthy people, which in turn makes the Cherokee Nation strong and enduring for posterity. Many of our people have provided undeniable examples of patriotism. Wilma Mankiller led us to personal and community responsibility and showed the world the strength of our Nation, our women. Hastings Shade taught daily the power of our cultural intelligence through our language and arts. Dave Blackbird provided the elderly strength of community leadership.

Citizens of the Cherokee Nation, we gather today in front of this capitol building knowing our historical legacy to face adversity, survive, adapt, prosper, and excel; witnessing the contributions of recently passed patriots; hearing the achievements of our government and people; and sharing the community of our families. We should know we have a chance to fulfill our designed purpose, to mature into a happy and healthy people. I ask you a question: are you not moved and resolved to be a patriot of the Cherokee Nation?

If you don't get it, if you vaguely remember the old days of indifference and chaos, by all means, feel free to retire to the social fog and novelty of having a Cherokee ancestor and blue card. If you do get it, be that patriot of the Cherokee Nation. Give your all to your Nation and people. You will mature to be one of those who make yourself, your family, your community, and your Nation happy and healthy.

Wado.

Your humble servant,

Chadwick "Corntassel" Smith
Principal Chief

Conclusion

History repeats itself, especially the history between the Cherokee Nation and the United States. Hostile public sentiment and adverse federal law swing like a pendulum every 20 to 40 years, with one extreme being punitive to the Cherokee Nation and the other indifferent. It also seems that the Cherokee Nation has been in a protracted retreat for centuries. Between 1721 and 1835, the Cherokee Nation physically retreated from the growing United States expansion along the Eastern Seaboard. During the course of 23 land cession treaties, the Cherokee Nation gave up 81 million acres of land. After the Cherokees were forcibly removed over the Trail of Tears in 1838 to Indian Territory, the protracted retreat no longer involved territory, but the erosion of treaty and political rights by the United States. That retreat ended with the liquidation of the Cherokee Nation's assets during the allotment period beginning in 1898. Now the protracted retreat involves cultural values and identity, the core of who a people are. At some point there can be no further retreat.

The questions are: can the Cherokee Nation reach Point B, its designed purpose of being a happy and healthy people and can we as individuals, families, and communities reach Point B?

Dagny Taggart, one of the main characters in Ayn Rand's book *Atlas Shrugged*, asks another character, "Francisco, what's the most depraved type of human being?" Francisco's answer is, "The man without a purpose." The Cherokee Nation has been blessed with a clear historic and enduring designed purpose: to become a happy and healthy people.

Atlas Shrugged also features a dialogue between two professors that captures the greatest threat to the Cherokee Nation and perhaps to all of us.

> "You see, Dr. Stadler, people don't want to think. And the deeper they get into trouble, the less they want to think. But by some sort of instinct, they feel that they ought to and it makes them feel guilty. So they'll bless and follow anyone who gives them a justification for not thinking."
>
> ... "And you propose to pander to that?"
>
> "That is the road to popularity."
>
> "Why should you seek popularity?"

The protracted retreat of yielding traditional values to popular values of entitlement, victimhood, and excuse-making is the last challenge and perhaps the only major one keeping the Cherokee Nation from achieving its designed purpose. There are looters and panderers seeking to destroy our Nation. I believe we will achieve our designed purpose, because as Redbird Smith said of the Cherokees over 100 years ago, "We are endowed with intelligence, we are industrious, we are loyal, and we are spiritual." Also Will Rogers, a Cherokee, reminds us, "I am a Cherokee, and it's the proudest little possession I ever hope to have." For those challenging times between Point A and Point B, we must proceed undaunted, even if we have to pause and remind ourselves "left, right, breathe."

Many of the lessons I learned and shared as principal chief of the Cherokee Nation are included in this book. Between 1999 and 2011, our team at the Cherokee Nation made exponential strides toward achieving our designed purpose.

The patriots of the Nation—armed with pride in our heritage, legacy of our ancestors, and love of our family and Nation—will overcome the looters and panderers who prey on our people and all of society and will lead us to our designed purpose.

Leadership is the process of going from Point A to Point B. Everyone is a leader. Where are you going to lead us?

Index

About the Author

Chad Smith, the principal chief of the Cherokee Nation from 1999 to 2011, has been a powerful force in building businesses and working toward self-sufficiency for Native American Nations. He has devoted the majority of his adult life to rebuilding the Cherokee Nation and helping Cherokees learn how to help themselves. When he was principal chief, the Cherokee Nation grew its assets from $150 million to $1.2 billion, increased business profits 2,000 percent, improved healthcare services from $18 million to $310 million, created 6,000 jobs, and dramatically advanced its edu-

Photo by Michael Wyke/Tulsa World

cation, language, and cultural preservation programs. The Cherokee Nation's success is a direct result of his principle-based leadership and his "Point A to Point B" leadership model. This model works for businesses, governments, and people in everyday life situations.

His efforts outside of the government and business arenas are diversi-fied. He is a renowned legal scholar and accomplished public speaker; has pub-lished Cherokee art, culture, and history books; produced 10 Cherokee Nation Youth Choir CDs in the Cherokee language; enjoys rebuilding old Studebaker cars; was inducted into the National Wrestling Hall of Fame; rappelled from a 19-story hotel to raise money for Special Olympics; and bicycled the entire 980-mile Trail of Tears as part of a Cherokee youth leadership exercise.

He earned his BS Ed from the University of Georgia, 1973; MPA from University of Wisconsin, 1975; JD from the University of Tulsa, 1980; and MBA from the University of Nevada-Las Vegas, 2008. He has been an iron-worker, tax lawyer, assistant district attorney, public defender, visiting professor at Dartmouth College, and principal chief.

He lives in Tahlequah, Oklahoma, with his wife, Bobbie Gail Smith, a first language Cherokee speaker who translates English into Cherokee. He has a leadership and organization consulting practice, which includes public speak-ing, writing, and development of leadership projects, such as the Vision Center, a hands-on career exploration center. He also practices Indian law.